PENGUIN CANADA

NOTHING FOR GRANTED

Philosopher and critic MARK KINGWELL is the author
of seven previous books, including the national
bestsellers *Better Living* and *The World We Want*; also,
most recently *Catch & Release: Trout Fishing and the
Meaning of Life*. Currently professor of philosophy at
the University of Toronto, he is a contributing editor
of *Harper's Magazine* and a frequent contributor to
Queen's Quarterly, *Toro*, and *The Globe and Mail*,
among others. He has won many awards for his
writing, including the 1996 Spitz Prize for political
theory and the 2002 National Magazine Award for
essays. *Nothing for Granted* is based on his work as
a political columnist for the *National Post* between
2000 and 2003.

Also by Mark Kingwell

Catch & Release: Trout Fishing and the Meaning of Life

Practical Judgments: Essays in Culture, Politics, and Interpretation

The World We Want: Virtue, Vice, and the Good Citizen

Canada: Our Century (with Christopher Moore)

Marginalia: A Cultural Reader

Better Living: In Pursuit of Happiness from Plato to Prozac

Dreams of Millennium: Report from a Culture on the Brink

A Civil Tongue: Justice, Dialogue, and the Politics of Pluralism

nothing for granted

Tales of War, Philosophy, and Why the Right Was Mostly Wrong
Selected Writings

mark kingwell

PENGUIN
CANADA

PENGUIN CANADA

Published by the Penguin Group

Penguin Group (Canada), 10 Alcorn Avenue, Toronto, Ontario, Canada M4V 3B2
(a division of Pearson Penguin Canada Inc.)

Penguin Group (USA) Inc., 375 Hudson Street, New York, New York 10014, U.S.A.
Penguin Books Ltd, 80 Strand, London WC2R 0RL, England
Penguin Ireland, 25 St Stephen's Green, Dublin 2, Ireland (a division of Penguin Books Ltd)
Penguin Group (Australia), 250 Camberwell Road, Camberwell, Victoria 3124, Australia
(a division of Pearson Australia Group Pty Ltd)
Penguin Books India Pvt Ltd, 11 Community Centre, Panchsheel Park, New Delhi – 110 017, India
Penguin Group (NZ), cnr Airborne and Rosedale Roads, Albany, Auckland 1310, New Zealand
(a division of Pearson New Zealand Ltd)
Penguin Books (South Africa) (Pty) Ltd, 24 Sturdee Avenue, Rosebank, Johannesburg 2196,
South Africa

Penguin Books Ltd, Registered Offices: 80 Strand, London WC2R 0RL, England

First published 2005

1 2 3 4 5 6 7 8 9 10   (WEB)

Copyright © Mark Kingwell, 2005

Excerpt from *Far Away* copyright © 2000 by Caryl Churchill Ltd.
by permission of the publishers: www.nickhernbooks.co.uk.

Excerpt from "The Book of My Enemy Has Been Remaindered"
reprinted by permission of PFD on behalf of Clive James © Clive James.

Excerpt on pages 253–254 reprinted with the permission of Scribner, an imprint
of Simon & Schuster Adult Publishing Group, from *Cosmopolis* by Don DeLillo.
Copyright © 2003 by Don DeLillo.

All rights reserved. Without limiting the rights under copyright reserved above,
no part of this publication may be reproduced, stored in or introduced into a retrieval
system, or transmitted in any form or by any means (electronic, mechanical,
photocopying, recording or otherwise), without the prior written permission
of both the copyright owner and the above publisher of this book.

Manufactured in Canada.

LIBRARY AND ARCHIVES CANADA CATALOGUING IN PUBLICATION

Kingwell, Mark, 1963–
Nothing for granted : tales of war, philosophy, and why
the right was mostly wrong : selected writings / Mark Kingwell.

ISBN 0-14-305193-8

I. Title.

AC8.K85 2005   081   C2004-907444-X

Visit the Penguin Group (Canada) website at **www.penguin.ca**

Contents

2001

◆

Preface: War, Philosophy, and Why the Right Was Mostly Wrong

This book is a collection of the 84 columns I wrote for *The National Post* op-ed page during a four-year period from May 2000 to October 2003, first under editor Ken Whyte and then, briefly, Matthew Fraser.

As time went on, it was inevitable that the chosen topics became more polemical, the tone less restrained, and the conclusions more weirdly prescient. While mine was hardly a lone voice, I predicted the second Gulf War, the failure of the WMD searches, and the capitulation of British interests to American power. The Right, meanwhile, was working hard to cover its errors and insist that Osama bin Laden was dead when he was demonstrably still kicking on the eve of the 2004 election.

Unfortunately, one of the key advantages enjoyed by the architects of empire is that they see no need to trade in consistency, truthfulness, or logic. That was surely one reason the Bush Administration managed to win its second term in office, getting middle-class and poor Americans to vote against their own self-interest in a flurry of character assassination and religious bluster. The so-called blue states, with their bicoastal commitment to what one Bush aide derisively labelled "the reality-based community," were no match for prejudice, ill-feeling, and "moral values." Having a basis in reality "is not the way the world really works anymore," the aide told a reporter from *The New York Times Magazine*. "We're an empire now, and when we act, we create our own reality."

It is an enduring irony of this new American empire that it is far more postmodern and spectral than the lurking relativism suppos-edly advocated by those of us on the Left. For the record, I am happy to count myself a card-carrying member of that reality-based community, where reason is judged stronger than force. In the calendar of my university, philosophy is defined as "the discipline where no belief is taken for granted." That is more than just a career path or a lifestyle choice; it is the essence of human reason itself, the basis of all critical reflection, indeed the best and most creative part of ourselves.

I fear the times are not congenial to such ideas. All the more reason to gather these pieces together, then, if only as a minor record of resistance to the current arrangement. I don't really imagine this kind of daily journalism has any massive impact on politics, let alone the course of history, but it is a kind of trace of what we were thinking, and trying to argue, from moment to moment. The pieces are reactive rather than reflective; nevertheless, I hope they convey an attitude, and a position, worth defending at any length.

With the exception of correcting one or two factual errors, I have not altered the columns at all. Though tempted, I have resisted the impulse to remove some of what I can now see is annoying sancti-mony, or to diminish overuse of the words "deranged" and "consider." I thank Molly Montgomery for her patience and excellent eye in designing this book; and Natasha Hassan for being such a wonderful editor even though she disagreed with me most of the time. This work is dedicated to them.

nothing for granted

✦

It's a jungle out there
31 May 2000

The premise strikes many people as bizarre, if not actually evil: strand 12 people on a remote island in the South China Sea, without food or water, and then track their efforts at survival for the next 13 weeks, gradually ejecting or eliminating contenders until just one person is left. Then give the last person standing a million dollars.

The show is called, predictably, "Survivor," and it premieres tonight on CBS and Global. Hundreds of applications vied for the chance to endure the ordeal, which involves a twisted combination of Hobbesian thought experiment, multi-user role-playing game, and lottery-style ostracism. (At the end of each show, the group votes to eject one member from contention. When there are just two left, the previously eliminated contestants pick the winner.) It is the latest in a series of extreme game shows, endurance-based analogues to the low-level IQ testing of "Who Wants to Be a Millionaire?" "Twenty-One," and (a personal favourite, if only for its candour) "Greed." Already early stars are emerging, in particular the 50-something ex-Navy SEAL who is the oldest of the eight male contestants.

There have been other shows in this class, of course, cooked up in Stockholm or London and dressed up, variously, as cinema verité, important social observation, or amusing dissection of human nature. They may be all of these, but what they mostly are is cheap television. MTV's "The Real World," the BBC's "Castaway 2000," and Sweden's "Expedition Robinson" are all in the same family. (An ejected contestant on that show committed suicide, something the producers didn't count on.) Beginning in July, CBS will air another real-life show called "Big Brother," in which 10 strangers living together in a total-surveillance environment will decide every week which two roomies will get the heave. Just like college!

Comparisons to other shows, and standard-issue laments about the current state of television, are really beside the point when it comes to "Survivor," though. Even would-be profound comments about the appeal of bare-bones survival in an age of high-tech gadgetry are wide of the mark. Sure producers and viewers are sick, getting sicker all the time. And yes, most of us couldn't tie a reef knot, let alone start a fire without matches, if our lives depended on it. But the deep lesson of "Survivor" is not that it is a departure from life but rather that it is life by other means.

After all, stranding people on a desert island in quest of a million dollars is child's play compared to dumping them in lower Manhattan, downtown Toronto, or the middle of London without a stock portfolio and a posse of professionals dedicated to your personal care. Notice the camouflage stylings, multi-pocket pants, and Velcro fasteners of today's urban fashion: it's all survival gear out there. The Urban Outfitters chain, which special-izes in youth-directed casual wear, understands this very well. They know that every street is a battle zone, every thoroughfare a firefight.

Out on the concrete of daily life, cell phones and palm pilots and MP3 players, all secured in handy pockets and pouches, are not luxuries, merely necessary equipment. We load up utilities and com-tech accessories like Batman getting ready to take on the Joker. Urban Outfitters even sell caffeinated breath mints, so you can stay alert as you battle through your day. Out there on the civic asphalt, it's *Black Hawk Down* 24 hours a day.

This isn't just a fashion conceit, it's an accurate reflection of the new globalized cityscape. In fact, "Survivor" and its real-world urban analogues don't go nearly far enough in acknowledging the threats and possibilities built in to today's world: they're way too limited in scope. Here's my new idea for a new extreme game show, currently doing the rounds with TV producers here and abroad. I call it "Global Survivor" and it modifies an idea that I stole (naturally) from Julian Bond, the executive director of the NAACP, who pitched it during a recent convocation address.

Here's how it works. Strand 100 people on an island rich in resources but with drastically limited habitable areas. Let's call it Earth, for no particular reason. At the start of the game, six of the people, all of them American, own 59 percent of everything. Just one person in the hundred has a college degree; he or she is also probably American and gets to be designated the referee. Meanwhile, 80 of the rest live in substandard housing, 70 lack basic reading and writing skills, and 50 suffer from malnutrition.

The object of the game is to see whether, week after week, the six Americans can gain control of even more of the island's wealth. The other players, meanwhile, try to eject one of the Americans so that they can become one of the six. This show goes on forever, and nobody gets a million dollars at the end of it.

It's a great game. But here's the best part. The six Americans on "Global Survivor" get to change the rules pretty much as they like, and yet they manage to convince the other 94 people, through the referee, that the rules have been set by someone else—that they are, in fact, unchangeable.

I see good ratings.

✦

Microsoft missed the synergy boat
14 June 2000

New York

The news, all in a span of a few weeks, that the National Rifle Association was opening a Times Square restaurant, Roots was starting an airline, and Microsoft was being split in two as the result of a U.S. federal court order, opened up some new lines of thought in this, the age of the total brand experience.

It was amazing, after all, that such a thing as antitrust legislation should be wielded to curb the predatory business practices of the world's richest man—a man who, according to one famous calculation, made money so fast it wasn't worth the time it would take him to bend over and pick up a dropped $20 bill. Antitrust? In the era of global synergy, the land of the tie-in and the spin-off?

But Gates has always been something of an idiot-savant, not good at seeing the implications of the big picture, and the court's decision reflected his odd lack of judgment. Gates, the vaunted computer visionary, is actually way out of step with the times. His business strategy is downright old-fashioned. Like the robber barons of yesteryear, he cornered a market and then set about eliminating or assimilating his competition bit by dot.com bit. Who could fault him for that?

Well, the United States government, as it turns out. But whatever the merits of the judge's decision, and whatever the chances for a successful appeal—for the record, I think Gates's argument that his megalomania is all in the interests of customers is a load of codswallop—the real point is that Microsoft dropped the ball. Sure, they make pretty good software (even if the idea for Windows was stolen and the early versions more crash-prone than a five-year-old on his first pair of skates). And they have marketed themselves with moderate success (even if their CEO is a charmless weirdo with more arrogance than sense).

What they didn't do, and should have, was sniff the prevailing wind. These days, you don't succeed by getting bigger and better at what you do, crushing your rivals along the way. You succeed by entering sectors of the economy that have absolutely nothing to do with you or your products. This is proof that what you are selling is your brand, and not anything so clunky as actual physical goods or services. From this vantage, a leather jacket and the tailfin of a 767 are different only in the size of logo they can support. So if you make beer or soft drinks, naturally you should start a line of leisurewear. If you already make leisurewear, you need to think about airlines. And if you peddle dangerous political nonsense about the Second Amendment, then of course you should open a restaurant.

In fact, airlines and restaurants and clothing lines are synergy no-brainers. Every company with assets in excess of $500,000 should be getting into those. The really noteworthy brand cross-overs nowadays have to be bigger leaps than that. If you manufacture bath products, for instance, you should probably think about motorcycles. Athletic shoes: surgical implements. Pet supplies: pop records. Courier service: legal advice. I'm a philosophy professor, so obviously I should be considering my big move into cosmetics, video games, and heavy shipping ("Problems moving cargo? Cartesian Industries: we doubt it, so you don't have to!").

Gates didn't get this. So, instead of enjoying a Word Six Burger at Gates-World or leaning back to enjoy the convenient short flight from Seattle to Vancouver on MicroShuttle Air, we have to watch the depressing spectacle of a man trying to justify his own outrageous wealth. Gates is right that we, the consumers, are the big losers in all of this, but only in the sense that we have to listen to more self-serving bleats from him.

Meanwhile, we can look forward to new adventures in the post-material, brand-savvy marketplace. What's so great about things, anyway? They're disappointing. The late graphic designer Tibor Kalman, a self-taught genius who worked on everything from wristwatches and typography to Talking Heads album covers and *Colors* magazine, knew that what really moves us is not the stuff but what the stuff comes in. We crave packaging, not products.

A major retrospective of Kalman's work currently showing at the New Museum of Contemporary Art in New York demonstrates how that awareness led, in his case, to a transcendence of conventional categories. His was the most important, and maybe most unsettling, cross-over: a commercial illustrator and designer who became, almost by the way, an important contemporary artist.

Kalman, who died in May of 1999, has become something of a hero for the commercial design world, but not simply because so many of his designs were so beautiful and so provocative. It's also because he challenged designers to make their practice politically aware and socially responsible. Once you realize how important commercial design is to everyday experience, how could you do otherwise? You can't send fetching images and seductive messages and brand markers out into the world without thinking about their role in the complex economy of human desire.

It's too late for Bill Gates to heed this deep wisdom of the new economy, this awareness of our complicity in a growing collective detachment from reality. But as the cross-overs multiply, as the brands detach from life and become ever more free-floating, synergistic, and pervasive, it's essential mental weaponry for the rest of us.

✦

How to survive the mean streets of Ontario
28 June 2000

Life seems to be getting more dangerous by the week. From deadly contaminated water and overly enthusiastic mounted police to crash-prone highways and rising violent crime rates, life in Canada's most populous province is taking on the cast of a bad apocalyptic science-fiction thriller—not a slick Paul Verhoeven effort, with lots of cool special effects and explosions, but one of those early depressing ones starring Charleton Heston.

It would be easy to blame this deterioration of civility and faith in public institutions on the bland arrogance and divide-and-conquer ideology of the Harris Tories. It would also be right. But that is not the point I want to make right now. Right now, I'm interested in making some extra money over the summer. So I have developed a range of personal-security products suitable for the new air of threat and instability in millennial Ontario, which I propose for the time being to rechristen Perilario.

1. *Personal water filtration machines, all-side airbag cars, and truncheon-proof bicycle helmets*. I figure all of these items will be standard issue for the citizens of Perilario come the fall, and I have my R-and-D guys working feverishly on all of them. The problem is, they're all too obvious. Every other risk-avoidance content

provider in the province is probably developing versions right now, and the market competition is going to be fierce. That, after all, is what Perilario is all about. That's why the Alliance needs us so badly.

We won't give up our share of that market, of course, but in an effort to move laterally, to think outside the box, we have developed some innovative new ways of dealing with stress levels in the public life of Perilario. Avoiding or minimizing risk is always a good idea, but the real action lies in shifting risk onto someone else. As always, here government shows the way and free enterprise looks after the rest.

2. *One hundred percent blame-transferant T-shirts* (BTTs). A province-wide teachers' strike is looming, and there could be more violent protests at Queen's Park any day. That kind of thing can make you late for work; more importantly, why should people get away with all this public complaining?

These shirts, available in a range of colours including fashionable orange and slate grey, sport slogans that fight back. Velcro fasteners make various combinations of denunciation possible— not to mention fun. For example: "Damn _____'s don't work nearly hard enough!" You can fill in the blank with panels reading "teachers," "nurses," "doctors," or simply "workers."

Of course, if customers don't want flexibility, we also plan to market shirts that read "Being poor is your own damn fault" and "Well, why'd you drink the water in the first place?"

3. *Sidewalk urban voiceboxes* (SUVs). We live in a booming economy, things have never been better, and yet there are still people clogging up the sidewalks of downtown Toronto with their pleas for spare change. Skinny kids with tattoos are forever trying to clean the windshield of your car. It's annoying and snarls traffic. The sidewalk urban voicebox deals with them so you don't have to. Compact and simple, the size of a personal pager, it can be carried in the hand or simply clipped to belt or purse.

Most customers will simply set the voicebox to mumble "Sorry" as they move away from the panhandler, head down and shaking in the negative. But why give in to even this much visible discomfort? These people don't have homes: they can't shame you! We program the voicebox to offer a variety of sarcastic questions: "Why don't you sell your dog if you're so poor?" "How'd you pay for those tattoos?" And a perennial favourite: "Why don't you go home to your parents in Bramalea?"

4. *Civil discourse phrasebook* (CDP). Sometimes shifting blame and evading confrontations within the deteriorating public sphere in Perilario will require a little more ingenuity, and for that there is this special new phrasebook, which allows you to forestall debate about the province's downward spiral under the Harris government. Carefully chosen rejoinders from the extensive list, each suitable for almost any occasion, will allow you to go about your business with a greater sense of ease and comfort. (An expanded version is being developed for use by Alliance supporters.)

Here are some samples phrases to use when someone suggests that things could be otherwise in Perilario. "Oh please—as if the Left has any credibility today." "Well, they tried that in Russia and it just didn't work." "Oh yeah? And where do you shop?" "Most of them are mental outpatients anyway." "'Admit it, everybody's a self-promoter." "I'd be happy with a two-month vacation every summer too." "I pay my taxes."

Even more all-purpose examples, which may be followed by any statement at all, however outrageous: "Let's face it," "Come on," and "Bottom line." Or simply use Phrase One of the CDP: "Risk is just a fact of life."

You can say that again! And here in the business, we say the best way to avoid risk is to let somebody else take the heat, preferably someone who lives in a remote part of the province or, better yet, can't defend themselves at all. Long live Perilario, land of profitable insecurity!

✦

Burgled in the world's best country
12 July 2000

To start with, an old joke. Question: what do you call a liberal who's been mugged? Answer: a conservative.

My apartment in Toronto was broken into last week. But the experience, so far from arousing any Giuliani-style, shoot-the-bastards crime policy, has only sharpened my sense that Canada is a weirdly troubled place. Recently we topped the United Nations ranking for an unprecedented seventh year in a row, and yet we still have one of the worst routine poverty problems in the developed world.

I was in the apartment, asleep and alone, when the break-in happened. The would-be burglar didn't know that, because he came in through the window, turned on a light, and was sauntering down the hallway, past my bedroom door, when I woke up. It was the creaking floorboards that did it. He saw me in the bedroom, froze for a second, and then ran out the front door.

I can tell you what you probably already know: being awoken by a stranger walking around your house in the middle of the night is, to say the least, unnerving. I kept thinking of Donald Sutherland and Stockard Channing in *Six Degrees of Separation,* obsessing about the intruder who might steal into their Park Avenue penthouse and murder them in their beds, *throats slashed.*

That came later, of course. At the time I didn't do a lot of thinking, clear or otherwise. I dashed after him, bounding down the front steps and along the deserted sidewalk. You have to picture it, because this is a scene that will not come around too often, in my neighbourhood or elsewhere: a 37-year-old philosophy professor, barefoot and wearing just a pair of tartan boxer shorts, sprinting along the street in pursuit of a burglar at 4:30 in the morning. And let me tell you, I was really moving.

He ran, but I caught him at the corner and discovered that, boosted by adrenaline, my vocabulary of aggression and profanity is more extensive and Tarantino-esque than I had ever imagined. I curse like a well-educated stevedore. It was an encounter full of other weird surprises. First of all, he was not the wiry teenager I expected when I burst intemperately from the door. He was older and shabbier, wearing raggy shorts, a cheap T-shirt, and (what should be an arrestable offence in its own right) a Yankees cap. Not a seasoned burglar, just a guy.

He was also entirely passive, with no repertoire of roundhouse kicks or uppercuts to offer in response to my shaking him by the collar. He said, truthfully, that he hadn't taken anything. Suddenly I realized he had me at an odd disadvantage. For one thing, here I was standing on the dark street, half-naked, angered to the point of derangement. I couldn't see myself tying him up or shouting till I roused the neighbours, who might in any case go all *Who's-Kitty-Genovese?* on me and turn over for more sleep.

More deeply, I realized that my guy was simply after stuff. My stuff, as it happens, in my apartment; but stuff nonetheless. Just like everybody else. So I let him go.

Don't get me wrong. I like my stuff, and I'm not giving it away. I don't condone break-and-enter as a redistributive policy measure. Of course I called the police in case he decided to move on to a neighbour's place. But I did have a twinge of sympathy for some-body who apparently just wanted some of the things that everyone else seems to have. A television. A computer. Some food. (He was barking up the wrong tree there: my fridge contains a carton of milk, a jar of mustard, and some flat tonic water.)

Well, so what? Break-ins happen all the time in just about every part of the country, not to mention everywhere else. But if Canada is such a great place to live, why do they? The authors of the U.N. report noted, quite rightly, that Canada's average income levels are low, and declining, compared to the rest of the developed world. As in years past, however, they played down that indicator. They argued that, contrary to American myopia about what success means, wealth isn't everything.

Agreed. Focusing on income levels while ignoring other factors can only lead to a skewed assessment of citizen well-being. But perhaps the time has come for those of us on the Left to acknowledge that plunging average income is no longer something we can simply shrug off. Sure money isn't everything, but declines in income, set against a cultural background of relentless wealth-celebration, can't help but generate relative poverty. Poverty creates envy. And envy, felt consis-tently and acutely enough, leads to many other social ills we cannot so easily ignore, like crime and riots and beggars on the street.

So here's my new version of the old joke. What do you call a social democrat whose apartment has been broken into? A wiser social democrat.

Not very catchy, I realize. By the way, I figure there's some danger that writing about this experience will encourage future burglary attempts. But I'm not really worried. The day *Post* readers start contemplating crime—or at least crime on such a small scale—is probably the end of the world as we know it.

✦

A visit to bobo ground zero
26 July 2000

One of the most talked-about books of this rather news-poor summer is a piece of popular sociology called *Bobos in Paradise: The New Upper Class and How They Got There,* by American journalist David Brooks. Brooks's thesis—and hence his unfortunate title—is that there is an emergent class of powerful upper-middle-class Americans who combine the goals of bourgeois success with the trappings, and sometimes the values, of their bohemian pasts.

The bobos are not identical with yuppies or Boomers, being in many cases younger, hipper, and more interesting. But the category certainly includes most of the people I met while living earlier this year in Berkeley, California. Berkeley is a kind of bobo ground zero, where post-hippie social consciousness combines with a degree of conspicuous wealth and high living unknown to most of the world. Nowhere else, I suspect, is it possible to see so many Free Tibet flags on four-bedroom Mission-style houses with three-bridge views of the Bay. Nowhere else can you find four dozen kinds of extra virgin olive oil, not to mention a whole aisle devoted just to merlot, in run-of-the-mill supermarkets.

If I sound a little envious, I am. After all, who wouldn't want to live in Berkeley, where the smell of blooming eucalyptus mingles with the fragrance of burning rubber as the denizens ride the clutches of their vintage convertible sportscars up and down the beautiful hilly streets? Bobos may be taking over places like Cambridge and Madison and Providence and Boulder, but Berkeley is where, if they're lucky, they go to collect their final reward in the form of split-level real estate and organic baby arugula. Then they can watch Greil Marcus eating duck enchiladas at Chez Panisse and discuss the terrible scandal of that bitter Brit Christopher Hitchens calling the Dalai Lama a stooge for Hindu nationalism.

Bobos in Paradise is perhaps the best book of popular class analysis since Paul Fussell's biting and accurate 1983 book, *Class: A Guide to the American Status System*. In particular, Brooks fingers something essential about American culture circa 2000, the way privilege immunizes itself against self-awareness in ever more inventive ways. Draping themselves in counter-cultural accoutrements, surrounded by reminders of their lack of conformity in the form of angry music and downtown fashions, this is an establishment that has effaced any sign of its rock-solid, blue-chip, gilt-edged success.

No mean feat. In fact, you could call it the logical terminus of capitalism—capitalism without the guilt, almost without a brain.

This is something subtle social critics have seen coming for a while, of course. The Frankfurt School, that loose coterie of second- and third-generation Marxists, perceived clearly how capitalism's success is not, contrary to Marxist dogma, the subjugation of workers. It is, rather, the subjugation of resistance through annexation. Nothing sells better than social rebellion, and the now-familiar spectacle of shoe or clothing companies acquiring the symbols of dissent and selling them back to us at an outrageously inflated price is, in effect, nothing but the latest stage in a complete viral takeover of the body politic.

True, the bobo category may prove too narrow to catch more than a few hundred thousand people, yet too broad to be illuminating about the real nature of power. The name sucks: with its echoes of monkeys and clowns, "bobo" is not going to catch on like a fun-sounding label like "yuppie." More deeply, as so often with labels, the book is largely an exercise in what anthropologists call avoidance ritual. By naming a problem, creating an analytical category, we think we have tamed a beast, when all we have really done is grant it a bizarre necromantic power. (Hence, for example, the persistent but idiotic influence of demographic labels like "Generation X.")

An even more serious difficulty is that nowadays critical analysis seems forever subject to the very same forces it purports to analyze. Brooks's ideas, like Malcolm Gladwell's equally clever discussions of cool-hunting and trend-creation in the recent book *The Tipping Point,* are swiftly neutered by an enthusiastic reception. (Gladwell now travels the world speaking to marketing executives.) What starts out as social dissection declines into an upscale direct-order catalogue; critique becomes celebration. Skewered bobos merely chuckle over Brooks's description of their granite kitchen counters and water-hogging full-body showers, wondering where they can pick up another Shaker table on which to display his book.

This process of second-order co-optation is hardly new, but it now happens faster and more inevitably than ever. Most people think of Adam Smith as a conservative hero, for example, partly because a generation of influential but neuron-challenged right-wing columnists made him their figurehead. But Smith was first and foremost a Scottish moral philosopher, a fierce critic of conspicuous consumption and the injustices of so-called free markets. He was as tart as Thorstein Veblen a century after him, but with a lot more straightforward social improvement in mind. (Veblen grumbled: the more accurate his assessment, the more pessimistic his mood.)

"With the great part of rich people," Smith wrote in *The Wealth of Nations,* "the chief enjoyment of riches consists in the parade of riches, which in their eyes is never so complete as when they appear to possess those decisive marks of opulence which nobody can possess but themselves." Smith lived in a more hopeful age. He thought criticism of the social order would lead, necessarily, to its improvement. He didn't count on the reduction of such criticism, especially his own, to support the status quo. If you hear about bobos, laugh, and say "Oh, aren't we awful!"—then nothing at all has changed, least of all you.

✦

On being civil: it's not enough to say you are
9 August 2000

New York

It's hard to get over the ability of Republicans to run against Washington. For instance, who would have thought it possible for a tax-and-spend politician to get re-elected on a governs-least-governs-best, throw-the-bastards-out platform? And yet that's exactly what Ronald Reagan did in 1984. Now George Bush's son, a man who gives new meaning to the phrase "to the manor born," is going to make his run for the White House by ... distancing himself from his own party's culture.

"I don't have enemies to fight," George W. Bush said at the Republican convention in Philadelphia last week, putting inventive spin on his ridiculous lack of political experience. "And I have no stake in the bitter arguments of the last few years. I want to change the tone of Washington to one of respect and civility."

You could spend some time pondering the mind of a man who, at one and the same time, is in the running for this job only because of his family name and connections, *and* is trying his damnedest to deny those connections by renouncing the party's attack-dog habits. The Republicans, after all, wouldn't be feeling so jaunty if they hadn't slammed President Bill Clinton silly over Monica Lewinsky. Bush's own father was reigning master of the nasty campaign slur during the 1980s, a snarling scarecrow of spite with an Ivy League pedigree. Just last week he practically called President Clinton out, warning Democrats not to tempt him to reveal what he thought of Clinton "as a leader and as a man."

For those not versed in the delicate semantics of Yalie argot, at least now that Bush Senior is playing the Wise Old Patriarch, that's roughly equivalent to Roberto Alomar spitting in umpire John Hirschbeck's face in 1997. From the other side, it's also a bit like a prep-school weenie having his dad come onto the football field to confront his tormentors. (On second thought, it's not like that. It is that.)

But never mind. Take Bush's claim at face value. Civility is one of those new watchwords of politics, a virtue that has received more and more play in public debate over the last decade even as it's lost any definitive meaning. Political theorists and newspaper columnists alike have weighed in on its importance to a healthy polity. (I know, because I've done it myself.) Civility, the pundits say, is indispensable in a society of differences. It guides debate without eliminating conflict; it gives us a means of dealing with the diversity that is liberalism's hallmark.

On a more mundane level, voters are sick of partisan bickering and negative campaigning. They don't want any more Willie Horton ads or routine character assassination. They don't care about the minor difference between Democrats and Republicans, they just want good government.

Well, actually what they really want is to be left alone while the good times continue to roll. They want lower capital gains taxes and more consumer durables, and they don't much care who coughs them up. By the same token, George W. doesn't want civility so much as he wants to speak his mind without anyone on the other side getting to speak theirs. That's what those high-toned East Coast schools are so good at teaching, after all: when I talk tough, it's me being forthright; when you do it, it's you being churlish. Thus have ruthless gentlemen always managed to rule the world.

But the point of genuine civility is not to stifle debate, or to paper over disputes with a slick display of concern. It is, rather, to make debate more honest and productive, to challenge the status quo, not preserve it. So here are some new rules of civility for what is likely to be, to the untutored eye, a confusing American election campaign.

Rule One: It's rude to pretend you believe things you don't. If you were one of the half dozen people who actually watched the convention last week, you might have been fooled into thinking the Republicans are inclusive, multicultural, and tolerant. This effect was achieved through camera placement, speaker choice, and the herding of all the black delegates, especially hysterical fat women, into a pen right in front of the press-corps photographers.

Rule Two: It's just as rude to pretend you don't believe the things you do. Things like abortion is evil, people on welfare are lazy, and hunting builds character. (This rule applies equally to Stockwell Day and the Alliance.)

Rule Three: It's rude to steal platform planks from the party to the left of you even as you continue to bad-mouth them as laughably unfit to govern. (This rule also applies to Jean Chrétien and the Liberals.)

Rule Four: It's just as rude to confuse voters by claiming that your opponent's running-mate is really one of you. It's not rude, only dumb, for the opponent to pick the guy in the first place, especially if he thinks a Jewish vice-president is going to impress anybody in 2000. Note to Al Gore: the film *Gentlemen's Agreement* was hard-hitting when it was released in 1947. Those days are long gone, and good riddance.

Rule Five: It's rude to pretend the election is about something when it's really just a battle to see which legacy, association, or bloodline gets to take credit for the triumph of global capitalism.

Rule Six: It's even ruder to call it a mandate when voter turnout will be lower than the Nielsen share for a summer re-run of "The West Wing."

Rule Seven: Civility, if it means anything, means every citizen feeling a duty to make society more just and equitable. It's not rude to suggest that George W. is more likely to spontaneously combust than to bring that message to Washington.

✦

"Randland" shows the limits of ambition
23 August 2000

New York

One of the lesser-known tourist attractions of summer in New York is a series of midtown walking tours that view the city through the eyes of Ayn Rand. The controversial author of *The Fountainhead* and *Atlas Shrugged* lived in Manhattan for many years, and its magnificent skyscrapers and railway terminals inspired her to pen huge swathes of her rambling, breathless prose. Along the way she mistook a cramped sense of personal grievance for a coherent philosophy: a common error. But the buildings and tracks remain, a testament to human ambition and folly, if not divinity.

On a recent rainy Sunday, 15 assorted visitors and residents gathered at the corner of Park Avenue and 50th Street, near the entrance of the Waldorf-Astoria Hotel, to walk through what the ads excitedly labelled "Randland!" Rand or no Rand, this is a great corner in a great city. The Waldorf is a superb example of Art Deco, now joined by the wonderful but often overlooked gothic-inspired weirdness of the GE Building, and the Philip Johnson / Ludwig Mies van der Rohe Seagram Building, a trademark matte-black peg like one-third of Toronto's Toronto-Dominion Centre. William Van Alen's beautiful Chrysler Building, the superlative Manhattan skyscraper, is just a few blocks downtown.

Our little group huddled on the northwest corner of the intersection, trying to avoid the shin-kicking pedestrians while simultaneously listening to Fred, the lumpy Rand disciple from Jersey City who was our Virgil. We all gazed up at the battery of towers, their different styles and densities structuring the grey sky. It's a wonderful thing, to be able to gawk unabashedly in New York, because most of the time the thronging commuters demand constant eyes-front vigilance, and anyway you don't want to look like a tourist geek.

It started to rain harder, and suddenly all the tourist geeks, in their windbreakers, baseball hats, and running shoes, produced colourful anoraks and portable umbrellas from their fanny packs, deftly unfolding them like Batman drawing matériel from his utility belt. Their Japanese camera equipment snapped and whirred.

The native New Yorkers huddled deeper into their T-shirts and got wetter.

Rand had a deep appreciation for architecture, especially the organic style pioneered by Frank Lloyd Wright, model for her own architect-hero, Howard Roark. *The Fountainhead,* her novel about Roark, is Rand's best work—which is not to say it is good. Made into a 1949 film starring Gary Cooper and Patricia Neal, the book has drawn generations of rebellious youngsters, including unlikely ones like Art Garfunkel, to the profession. That's not surprising: Roark's decision to dynamite his own building rather than suffer compromise is, after all, pretty compelling to the adolescent mind, rock-and-roll before the fact.

Not that Rand would favour the comparison. Her architects are less rock stars than otherworldly beings, who possess a vision and genius denied mere mortals—a viewpoint that has only gained credence in the current age of the celebrity architect. Jet-set stars like Canadian-born Frank Gehry, the man who made architecture a global obsession with his Guggenheim Museum in Bilbao, Spain, or Peter Eisenman, who views clients and inhabitants alike as vermin infesting his designs, suffer from a form of narcissistic personality disorder that will be familiar to readers of Rand's novel.

In *Atlas Shrugged,* a fourth-rate PhD dissertation in search of a discernible plot, she went even further in linking the fact of urban infrastructure to extreme libertarian ideology. John Galt, the mysterious stranger who so impresses headstrong young railway heiress Dagny Taggart, is another one of Rand's impossibly Olympian industrialist-champions. He rules the complexity of Grand Central Terminal's tracks with shadowy energy, and meets Dagny in the cafeteria of the subterranean Oyster Bar to discuss his conspiracy to disrupt the world's flow.

Park Avenue is the channel beneath which the tracks run north out of the terminal, and the street itself is actually a platform set atop the massive wide tunnel. You can see the metal joins of the street's slabs at 50th Street, and you must walk up one floor in the Waldorf before boarding an elevator because the machinery cannot be housed below ground. In the newly restored Grand Central, the Oyster Bar is returned to its former glory as part of a new food concourse, and the roof of the main hall repainted in the zodiacal patterns of decades gone by. It's awesome.

Rand's obsessions cannot, any more than guide-guy Fred's bad puns and silly accents, obscure that awe. Ironically, Randland's lesson is not the one she taught. The infrastructure that humans have built for themselves is indeed amazing. New York and other spectacular human creations are evidence of our transcendent desires, our wish to go beyond the given. And so we become capable of daily miracles, unlikely successes: the New York subway system and the global airline schedule, the skyscraper and the airplane.

But these are human creations, not divine inventions. They are ongoing negotiations among millions of human voices, not gifts from above. They are also immensely fragile. It was the Dutch architect Rem Koolhaas, himself the owner of a considerable ego, who noted, in his brilliant book *Delirious New York,* that infrastructural success comes only with a constant threat of failure. Gridlock always looms, breakdown always impends.

Such are the limits of human ambition. Unfettered by justice or true wonder, Rand's position becomes a particularly virulent form of anti-humanism: in praise of excellence, she forgets balance. The basic awe of cities is not that they function well, but that they function at all. And for this we must thank not just the daring architects and high-flying railway executives, but each and every citizen who navigates the crowded streets.

✦

What would Hume think?
6 September 2000

New York

I somehow doubt Senator Joseph Lieberman, the Democratic candidate for U.S. vice-president, realized just what he was getting into when he made his now-notorious remarks last week calling for a larger religious presence in public life.

How was he to know, for instance, that everyone from the American Civil Liberties Union to the Anti-Defamation League would come down so hard on him? How was he to know that it would add fuel to the fire of the redoubtable Joe Eszterhas, screenwriter of *Basic Instinct* and *Showgirls,* well-known defender of the public good, who was already urging his Hollywood colleagues not to contribute to the Democratic cause until Lieberman clarified his position on "freedom of creative expression"?

How was he to know, finally, that it would sit so uncomfortably with the announced beatification last week of Pope Pius IX, another believer in religious influence over public life, who often referred to Jews as "dogs" during his tenure as pope between 1846 and 1878? Whatever else may be said about Pius, he illustrates a lesson Lieberman should have remembered. A greater role for religion in public life is all very well—as long as (1) you're religious in the first place, (2) it's your religion that has the role, and (3) it's your public life that is affected.

That's why the Senator's remarks, obviously calculated to curry favour with the Detroit and Chicago Christian leaders he was addressing, were so misjudged. The problem is not really the separation of church and state, or the long history of religious influence on politics. Editorialists and pundits fussed over those issues during the past 10 days, but from a perspective just outside American political culture, they missed the point. The real argument here, the genuine faultline exposed, is about the meaning of life itself.

Lieberman told his mid-western audiences that "there must be a place for faith in America's public life," and he explicitly linked religion with morality and the founding of the American republic. He also suggested that there could be no morality without religious faith—a claim from which he quickly retreated, or anyway mitigated, by admitting under pressure the obvious truth that lots of religious people are immoral and lots of moral ones irreligious.

Lieberman and his supporters saw that as mere good-natured finessing, but it's actually a crucial admission, because if we can (to use the stock phrase) be good without God, then the entire argument for religious influence in public life simply founders. If morals are derivable from sources other than divine fiat or revelation, there is absolutely no place for God in our public institutions. This is not just because, as liberals often argue, people disagree about God. It is, more deeply, because keeping God in the equation keeps us from fully realizing our natures as fragile, anxious, competitive, sometimes compassionate beings.

Justice, the great Scottish philosopher David Hume argued two centuries ago, is an artificial virtue. We create it ourselves, not through singular impulses to do good but through ongoing negotiations with fellow-travellers on the mortal plane. We strive for justice not because God wills it, or because we want this life to resemble as closely as possible some fantasy of contentment described in a religious text, but because the alternative is abhorrent to us.

That means surrendering any illusions we have about what the purpose of human society is. We are not doing God's will, just our own—which means we are answerable to others, imperfect in our efforts, and constantly at risk. There is no eternal reward waiting for us, just the fleeting and uncertain rewards of what we achieve here and now. Life offers no certainty at all, in fact, just the complicated uncertainty of our natural urges in constant (and usually unfair) tension with our capacity to reason.

Hume, no shirker from his own conclusions, concluded from the evidence that reason was the servant of the passions, not the other way around. We are moved by instincts and needs we barely understand, striving without ultimate success to make sense of them, to create something we judge good, to spread the good things as far as we can. And then we die.

That is not drink to everyone's taste. James Boswell, for one, was so deeply shocked by Hume's atheistic equanimity in the face of death that he was thrown into a degenerate round of drinking and whoring—actions that a more Freudian age would have understood perhaps better than poor Boswell did himself. (The encounter is deftly analyzed by Michael Ignatieff in his wonderful 1985 book, *The Needs of Strangers*.)

Not much has changed since Hume's day. The deep irony about the Lieberman fiasco is not the absurd spectacle of an Orthodox Jew of acknowledged personal probity facing off against Joe Eszterhas, with his sleazy Playboy-style necklaces and greying chest hair. Nor is it that the first Jew nominated by a major party for elected office is opposed by the ADL, one of America's most prominent Jewish groups. Nor is it even that the centuries-long hatred between Christians and Jews seems entirely forgotten in this latest round of ecumenical glad-handing on the road to the White House.

It is, rather, that nobody seems bothered by the utter inconceivability of a genuinely atheistic politician making any headway in current American culture. Opinion polls show that Americans are overwhelmingly religious these days, more so now than in recent decades; a majority say they would not elect an atheist as president. Coupled with the unparalleled prosperity now enjoyed by most Americans, the lesson seems clear: God's on our side and don't let anyone tell you different.

Whose God? Well, let's talk about that after the election. Maybe.

✦

Anti-global activists ready for Prague fall
20 September 2000

New York

The anti-globalization protest movement descends on Prague this weekend, in anticipation of the World Bank / International Monetary Fund summit beginning next Tuesday. It's a propitious moment for the protesters, not least because the time has clearly come for this loose aggregation of ecological activists, culture jammers, workers' rights advocates, and anarchists to decide what their lasting impact might be.

Of course they'll be ridiculed once again by the usual assortment of past-it columnists and editorial writers. They'll be called ninnies, tree-huggers, and wackos. Their knowledge of economics will be questioned. Their evident commitment and desire for justice will be presented as a form of delusion. (The irony in play here is instructive: you always know a writer is in the grip of deep bad faith when he resorts to heaping violent abuse on his supposedly powerless, ridiculous enemies.)

But all of that is a sideshow, because the real question now is not whether the protesters are silly, or whether they ought to be getting jobs instead of taking their multinational street-theatre-and-civil-disobedience show on the road. Note to the *New York Times:* that boat has sailed. The real question is what happens when Prague proves to be the most hospitable environment yet for discussion of what the emerging global order could be.

For, despite the likely anarchist presence and the notorious bloodthirstiness of local law enforcement, this is a place where objections and arguments will be taken seriously. Some violence is possible, but I suspect the main tenor of the days to come will be constructive, not least because of the bridge-building efforts of Vaclav Havel. I may be prone to my own form of delusion in saying so, but I have a vested interest: I'm flying to Prague tomorrow to speak at an international "Counter-Summit" organized by activists, politicians, and academics. Havel himself is bringing together politicians, NGO representatives, and IMF functionaries for a special meeting on Saturday.

The dialogue is overdue. Since exploding into mainstream consciousness in Seattle last year, the anti-globalization protests have followed a pattern that is rather depressing even to those, like myself, who are sympathetic to them. Traipsing semi-chaotically from place to place, the movement began to resemble a rag-tag gypsy caravan—or, in the unimprovable image coined by my friend Naomi Klein, the audience of a Grateful Dead concert. Shifting venues as the weeks pass, tagging along after the guys in suits like political Deadheads, arguing the same points over and over again: it's all a little too reminiscent of those passionate but pointless evenings spent under the influence of drugs and 20-minute guitar solos.

After a first flush of success, any reformist movement is liable to stalling. In part, this is simply a matter of theory and practice. The energies and skills of the protesters have so far been concentrated, appropriately enough, on getting bodies onto streets, reclaiming public spaces, articulating cries of dissent when so much of the existing discourse is a chorus of comfortable consensus. This they have done admirably, reinvigorating the art of public protest for a global context and, along the way, giving new life to the idea of participatory democracy. It is no exaggeration to call these protests the first significant acts of transnational citizenship.

But just as theory needs practice to give it life, practice needs theory to sustain it. Politics needs a vision not only of what is wrong but of what might be done about it; ideas and imagination must be sharpened by precision and concreteness. And protest, finally, needs to find its place in a larger project of political decision-making and organization. Like many people, I long for a far more decentralized and varied world than the one we have, a world less dominated by consumerist monoculture and the routine injustices of transnational trade. That's easy to say. What is far harder to see is how we get there from here.

It could take a while, and we will have to feel our way. Hope is sometimes zealous, but it is also, paradoxically, the most patient of virtues. Justice will not surrender to bullet headings and Power Point presentations, and anybody who wants a quick fix here has been reading too many self-help books. More importantly, asking someone to tell you exactly what to do about citizenship is not just impractical but self-defeating. Democracy won't thrive on letting other people do your thinking for you, and (as Socrates, among others, knew very well) someone with all the answers is either a charlatan or a tyrant in waiting.

So there's another issue the protesters must address next week. Thus far the movement has succeeded with its own kind of decentralization, offering no particular leaders or spokespeople as focal points. Its amalgam of disparate interests has been far from perfect, but has nevertheless exhibited a fairly functional form of non-hierarchical action. I suspect this cannot continue much longer. Leaders of democratic movements are often as dangerous as the forces they oppose, especially if possessed of charisma and ambition, but without high-profile, inspiring leaders, even the most righteous movements eventually scatter and dissolve.

Here's my suggestion, offered in the spirit of the times. Mr. Havel should quit his day job and become the first leader of what we might agree to call Global Citizens for Justice. Ralph Nader, when he's done with his U.S. electioneering, can come on board as deputy leader. As for me, I hereby offer my services as staff philosopher. My main qualification? I don't have all the answers. And for the downtimes between bouts of changing the world, I also mix a wicked martini.

✦

You call this a book? Yes
4 October 2000

When a writer publishes a book, as sometimes happens despite everyone's best efforts, certain problems naturally arise.

Case in point: last Saturday's Review section marked the publication of my new book, rather hopefully called *The World We Want,* with a profile of me. Huzzah! Of course, the times being what they are, the piece was devoted in large measure to my physical appearance, knowledge of popular culture, and experience of being on television.

Now, I yield to no one in my interest in my physical appearance. I also enjoyed the article's liberal use of the adjective "hip," and the extensive character assessment based solely on the little sketch of my head that goes with these columns. The accompanying picture was also quite large though miscredited (the photographer's name is actually Christie Johnston) and old (I don't look like that any more).

Along the way, a couple of my learned colleagues took time out of their busy schedules to slight an earlier book of mine called *A Civil Tongue.* Readers might be interested to know that this book was in fact so bad it received quite enthusiastic American and British notices and a major academic prize when it appeared in 1995. Also, perhaps, that the two scholars quoted were responsible for its only negative reviews—both by Canadians in Canadian publications.

Still, these things happen. In the midst of all the fun, however, the new book hardly figured. Since this newspaper has a policy of not reviewing books by its own writers, the profile is the extent of official coverage. Yet it clouds the brow of a responsible columnist like myself to think that a book, good or bad, might escape the proper attention of *Post* readers. That's why I've decided to devote today's column to an interview with the loquacious author of this new work. I have selfish motives, of course; but, then, so does he.

Post: You call your book *The World We Want,* but I looked in vain for the Ten Easy Steps to a Better Civilization that this title seemed to promise me.

Mark: Yes.

Post: How could you do that? Where are the cheap prescriptions and hollow advice? You call this a book?

Mark: Yes.

Post: But for the love of God, man, you've got to tell us what to do!

Mark: No.

Post: You must be joking—we hear you are a famous joker. Are you saying that we have to think for ourselves? That the point of philosophy is to pause and reflect on our duties and desires, before we rush off and barge into yet another thoughtless policy initiative or glib suggestion?

Mark: Yes.

Post: Don't you think that will unsettle people? After all, these days we expect people to tell us what to think. The newspapers, for example, are full of people doing that.

Mark: Yes.

Post: You advocate a 10-percent personal donation to international relief. But what about raising the corporate tax rate, fining people for not voting, lobbying for Canada to leave the World Trade Organization, or demanding debt cancellation for the developing world. Do you believe any of that?

Mark: Yes. Yes. Yes. Yes.

Post: You don't say so in the book.

Mark: No.

Post: Why? Are you implying somehow that this is not the business of philosophy? That, in fact, it would just give critics an opportunity to focus on particular disagreements and ignore the deeper things you want to say about participatory citizenship?

Mark: Yes.

Post: So let me get this straight: when you say "the world we want," you're not offering a blueprint for an ideal society at all, but inviting your fellow citizens to examine their responsibilities—to consider how their lives might be clouded or selfish or dangerous? To ask what they owe to each other, at home and around the world?

Mark: Yes.

Post: And the details of how to deal with the answers are, necessarily, a matter for ongoing democratic deliberation governed by the norms of civility?

Mark: Yes.

Post: Not everyone will be satisfied with that.

Mark: No.

Post: In fact, some would call it a retreat into the ivory tower. Though I notice, often the very same people who say that will accuse you, in the very next breath, of being too much with the world, not retiring or disconnected enough, like academics of old. I suppose you think there's a contradiction in their complaints?

Mark: Yes.

Post: Haven't you also said that there is no ivory tower more impenetrable than the conference room of a newscast or the editorial board of a daily newspaper? You used to write editorials for one of the national papers, so I suppose you think you have a good idea of how they go about their business.

Mark: Yes.

Post: And you decided to pursue political philosophy instead of journalism because it's more connected to reality, not less?

Mark: Yes.

Post: Not everyone will be satisfied with that.

Mark: No.

Post: Okay. So you think philosophy is about thinking things through, reflecting on where we've come from to see where we might be going. Is that why you chose to focus on six historical figures in this book: Socrates and Crito, Montaigne and La Boétie, Benjamin and Adorno?

Mark: Yes.

Post: These people are all dead. None of them offered any policy recommendations or civics lessons for Canada. You still think they're worth listening to?

Mark: Yes.

Post: Not everyone will be satisfied with that.

Mark: No.

Post: Are you saying, finally, that people should read your book and decide for themselves whether it speaks to them?

Mark: Yes.

Post: Will you stop appearing on television just because it seems to annoy some people?

Mark: No.

Post: Thank you.

Mark: You're welcome.

◆

Citizens of America, vote Nader
18 October 2000

Future chroniclers of this year's U.S. presidential election might want to consider "Untrue at Any Volume" as an all-purpose, catchy title for the proceedings, at least as regards the two main candidates. For, adding to the usual haze of false promises and feigned sincerity is the ghostly, blast-from-the-past presence of Ralph Nader, Green Party candidate for the republic's highest office and a tireless proponent of that rarest of political commodities, the truth.

The great thing about Nader is that he just won't go away. Since 1965, when he skewered General Motors in the best-selling book *Unsafe at Any Speed,* Nader has been a fixture on the American political scene, however wavering and spectral. Sometimes (as when his Public Interest Research Groups spearheaded the environmental campaigns of the early 1980s) he comes into sharp relief, sometimes (as during the past decade or so) he fades away to near-invisibility. Always he is the perpetual unwelcome guest, Banquo asking for seconds.

Which makes his current manifestation all the more fascinating. Dismissed by the *New York Times* two short months ago as a nice but dangerous folly, a vote-splitting mistake, Nader's support has remained constant nationwide (somewhere between three and six percent, depending on polls) and climbed in key swing states like Wisconsin. Last week, a celebrity-strewn rally at Madison Square Garden in New York saw 13,500 raucous fans fork over $20 apiece to hear left-leaning Hollywood stars like Tim Robbins and Susan Sarandon weigh in on his side. Michael Moore, the filmmaker who moulded his own criticism of the auto industry into the low-budget satire of *Roger and Me,* told the crowd not to worry about weakening Democrat chances by voting with their hearts. "The lesser of two evils," Moore said, "you still end up with evil."

The Green Party position, radical in these buttoned-up times, is that the Republican and Democrat candidates are indistinguishable at the level where things really matter, namely the extent to which their respective campaigns, and possible administrations, are beholden to corporate and institutional financing. Now jowly, grey-haired, and a little haggard, no longer the energetic college-boy crusader of the sixties, Nader has a wry, inspiring wisdom about the political system. He's the quintessential cynical optimist: hoping for the best, expecting the worst. And his tireless demands for reality, his quiet mastery of the policy issues, put the other candidates to shame—or would, if they'd only let him in on the nationally tele-vised debates.

"You've got to love these people," Nader said recently to *Harper's* editor Lewis Lapham. "They think the American electoral process is a gated community."

None of that quite solves the problem of the split vote, however. The situation that confronts certain American citizens this November is in some ways a classic instance of what strategy theorists calls the "double-bind." In its more familiar guise, it's known as "damned-if-you-do, damned-if-you-don't." Since the days of the great Chinese philosopher of war, Sun Tzu, effective power-seekers have known that the most efficient way to dominate an opponent is to make all of his available choices self-defeating. This works best when you achieve "strategic envelopment": such complete mastery of a situation that you get to determine the very terms of debate or action.

Ideology is a form of strategic envelopment; so is an electoral system ruled by war chests and television access. Tactics, Sun Tzu said, can never defeat strategy. To defeat strategy you must adopt new strategy—invent new rules, not simply continue to play by the exist-ing ones. Hence subversion, infiltration, passive aggression, guerrilla raids. If you can't move laterally, frustration and failure are inevitable.

Thus the problem for third-party supporters. If citizens follow their consciences and choose Nader, they may end up skimming enough Electoral College votes from Al Gore to allow George W. Bush to complete his bloodline buy-out of the White House. If they refrain from voting, or vote for Gore, Nader's essential voice is silenced, and they get a president only marginally better than the right-wing alternative.

Or maybe much worse. Matters of finance and policy aside, Gore, the man who once claimed he invented the Internet, has shown himself oddly unfamiliar with the notion of truth-conditions. As philosophers know, statements are valid only if redeemable in the hard currency of shared sensory experience, otherwise known as the realm of fact. You can't go on saying anything at all and expect to be taken seriously. By the same token, you have to actually say something, not merely stand there and appear to be doing so.

In a recent article called "A New Refutation of the Very Possibility of Al Gore," reprinted in November's *Harper's,* the satirist Crispin Sartwell gives new meaning to the idea of wasting your vote, and incidentally clarifies the split-vote issue with admirable neatness. "Consider, as a thought experiment, a speech by Al Gore," Sartwell writes. "He is not really there, and he is not saying anything; he is nothing and he is saying nothing. Al Gore is a kind of hole or vacuum that expresses the essence of nothingness."

Thus, Sartwell says, "this election poses itself as a question: Will we trip over Al Gore's abysmal foot into the infinite void, falling eternally into dimensionless nonbeing? … Consequently, a vote for Al Gore is a vote not only against the universe in which we happen to find ourselves; it is a vote against the very possibility of any universe, of even a single merely possible lepton."

The implication is clear. In a two-party deadlock, the liberating alternative strategy is not political but existential. Citizens of America, vote Nader. People everywhere—the universe itself—will thank you.

✦

Politicians play Canadian monster mash
1 November 2000

You have to love Hallowe'en, alas gone for another year. Not only is it a form of wealth-redistribution without tax infrastructure, this year it took on the additional role of revitalizing a federal election campaign that left most of us asleep in front of our televisions. As October closed, the tussling main candidates started to lose their cool and display fascinating inner monsters. Detached observers could be forgiven for thinking they'd both gone a little Hallowe'en nuts.

First to court seasonal derangement was Stockwell Day. Last week, the galloping he-man of Canadian politics, a guy who always appears to have jogged in from an off-camera squash game, suggested that Canada under Jean Chrétien was like Russia. He later explained that he was not accusing the Liberals of communistic tendencies, only saying that the Canadian economy is thriving despite the best efforts of the government. That had the added benefit of sounding incoherent as well as nasty.

Then, only the other day, Mr. Chrétien, himself no slouch in the physical-presence department, a guy who doesn't mind brawling with protesters or reporters, countered by tacitly comparing his Alliance opponents with the Nazis. In a speech that warned of the "dark side that exists in human beings," the prime minister argued that a world without Liberals was a world given over to evil. Aides scrambled to deny any direct connection to the Alliance, saying Mr. Chrétien was speaking in world-historical terms. Uh huh.

Right on cue, outraged members of both leading parties complained of "demonization" tactics and the decline in standards of "civilized political discourse." Of course, the outrage and calls for civility are just another part of this great demon dance, the Canadian monster mash. Critics of demonization always seem to miss the point: demonization is popular because it's fun and effective. It means you get to feel superior to the other guy, maybe even call down on his bolt-decorated head a mob of fear-driven reprisal. And in the meantime, demonizing the demonizer is a game that all sides can play.

It's great stuff, really. Spectral Communists and Nazis on every side! Demons to the left and the right! Who knew Canadian politics could be so much fun? I can't be the only one who's reminded of a comically violent video game or low-budget science-fiction feature. The raging candidates, barely in control of themselves or their rhetorical firestorms, stomp through the land like oversized Japanime robots, blasting barely seen enemies and scattering the screaming crowds with their flaming breath. Panicked aides scramble through the wreckage trying to douse the fires, shaking clenched fists at the darkened sky, and shouting inarticulate warnings about the end of the world.

In fact, this is so riveting that we have to hope the passing of Hallowe'en doesn't cause the current level of spectacle to decline into anything as mundane as actual political discourse. We might end up talking about what's happening to this country in the midst of all this economic growth we keep hearing about: why some people are still starving and homeless in our beautiful cities, or why others still think taxes are the devil's work. We might start thinking about ourselves and our responsibilities.

To avoid that dire result, I suggest we take a bold step and extend Hallowe'en until election night. Why not? Just think of it: a month of vacation from reason, 27 days of licensed madness. What could be better for the political process? It's not enough that campaign speeches continue their overheated tone of righteous derangement, though. We also have to demand that the candidates appear in costume for the remainder of the campaign.

Yes, I think so. The outfits will provide the necessary reminder that this is all for show, and allow the candidates to unbutton their emotions even more entertainingly. We all know the freedom from normal responses that comes from putting on a mask. So here are my suggestions:

Mr. Chrétien, already an accomplished street-fighter (his own favourite phrase), should dress as Bruce Campbell in Sam Raimi's monster-horror-action spoof, *Army of Darkness*. Mr. Chrétien is a little older than Mr. Campbell, and lacks his goofy charm, but has the necessary lantern jaw and poor grasp of reality. He rushes into action with the same hilarious arrogance and lack of foresight. All he needs is some basic-black combat gear, a chainsaw, an early-model Chevrolet convertible, and a battery of maces, cross-bows, and flaming catapults. His speechwriters could work on improving the level of comic-book repartee in his stump messages, but even Mr. Chrétien can presumably master something as simple as "Gimme some sugar, baby." Bring on the dark side!

Mr. Day has already made his character choice clear, in fact is dressing up most days already. He is of course the Incredible Hulk as portrayed by Bill Bixby. Today he wears a suit and tie and walks calmly among the humans, rational and composed; tomorrow somebody mentions social programs or abortion and he is filled with uncontrollable rage! He writhes and twists on the floor, muscles bulging through his Tip Top dress shirt. He spits and foams, he tears to bits things other people have spent a long time building. No problem. All he needs is some green body paint. And a little more hair.

I haven't forgotten Joe Clark and Alexa McDonough, even if the voters have. Mr. Clark's pick is obvious: he simply buys a rubber mask and comes as himself. That should be scary enough for anybody. And one of these days Ms. McDonough is going to surprise everybody with her portrayal of Buffy the Vampire Slayer. But she really, really needs to work on that roundhouse kick.

Until then: Candy! Candy for everyone!

✦

Chaperoned to the dentist? That sucks
15 November 2000

I don't know Ione Rockwell of 622 Christie Street in Toronto, an address not far from where I live, but I have a book of hers which, in the unlikely event of her still being with us, I would like to return with my compliments. It's called *Manners,* published in Toronto in 1914 by the firm then known as McClelland, Goodchild and Stewart, and it's a gem.

I have collected old etiquette manuals for more than decade now, a quirky by-product of a theoretical interest in civility as a political virtue. I found this one last Saturday at an antiques stall downtown. After a week that witnessed both the fiasco of the federal election debate and the ill-mannered stand-off south of the border, it was a breath of fresh air. In the first decades of the century, life was simpler: conversation was stately, fun was suspect, and chewing gum signalled licentiousness.

I can't be certain when in her life Miss Rockwell acquired this elegant little volume, but her spidery cursive handwriting on the flyleaf suggests a young woman of perhaps 16 years. If so, she is certainly the book's target audience. For, beneath the sweeping generalizations and stern imperatives characteristic of the genre, it betrays a special interest: it is preoccupied, to the point of morbid obsession, with the sexual horrors that await the innocent girl as she steps into public.

"The custom that makes chaperonage indispensable where young people are gathered together at places of public entertainment obtains in all conventional communities," the editors tell us. "No really fashionable party is made up without a chaperone." That argument was probably as ridiculous then as it is now. *Hey you guys, all the really cool kids are going to the rave with chaperones!* Sure they are, and nobody with a brain smokes drugs, cell phones are for jerks, and those facial piercings make you look silly.

You have to admire the sentence structure, though. "A young woman condemns herself in the eyes of good society who is observed to enter alone with a young man a place of public refreshment, be the restaurant or tea room ever so select. In the same category of offences is ranked that of maidens visiting places of public amusement under the escort of young men alone." Maidens! Places of public amusement! What happened to them?

The editors of *Manners* knew what evil lurks in the hearts of men, and were precise in their counsel. "When it is necessary for a girl to pay long visits to a dentist's office, she should be accompanied by her mother or some woman relative, or a maid." One must feel for the poor thing. Not only does she have to look forward to early twentieth-century dental techniques, she might be importuned at any moment unless her maid is there to beat off the advancing hordes of ill-bred men.

Girls had to watch their step in other ways too. "It is in bad taste, even in quite a large party, for young girls to visit a man at his office." That, frankly, sucks for everybody concerned: I myself look forward with keen anticipation to the quite large parties of young girls that visit my office regularly; and I believe it's fun for them too. "A girl is not supposed to recognize a man who is one of a group standing in a public place, since a modest girl will not look close enough at a group of men to recognize an acquaintance." What's she supposed to do when he shouts "Baby!" across the room, raises his martini glass at her, or jumps on his buddy's shoulders in an excess of masculine exuberance? Feign an interest in her chaperone?

But my favourite injunctions were about bicycling, an activity which in 1914 had associated social risks we have somehow largely forgotten. "As to rules of politeness for bicyclers, one who is truly a lady will show herself to be such as surely when riding a wheel as at any other time, not only by her costume, which will be unobtrusive in colour, cut, and adjustment, but by her manner, which will be even more quiet and self-possessed than usual, as she well knows that by mounting a wheel she makes herself more or less conspicuous."

Mounting a wheel—now there's an expression we should bring back into common use. "It goes without saying that she will not ride fast enough to attract undue attention; that she will not chew gum; and that she will not allow advances from strangers, who may, like herself, be on a wheel, and, to all appearances, gentlemen. In the daytime, when out with a gentleman, she will avoid stopping to rest under the trees and in out of the way places." Put it on a T-shirt: *Not all those who mount the wheel are true gentlemen.*

Things were just as tricky for the young man, naturally. He had to court in the approved manner, with extended campaigns of tightly regulated calls, maximum duration 10 minutes, in which he tried to get at the daughter of the house. What a store of mundane tragedy is contained in this little piece of advice, taken from the "General Hints" chapter of *Manners:* "No young man has any right to spend the entire afternoon and evening every Sunday at one particular house, to the annoyance of an entire family, who do not like to make him conscious of the fact that they consider him a bore." No wonder they started trolling dentists' offices.

We have traversed a long distance since then, not necessarily in the right direction. Loss of romance; or gain of freedom? Edwardian repression banished; or pre-teen puberty and a 50-percent divorce rate? Not for me to say, but there is one last piece of advice from *Manners* that resonates across the decades, and I only hope Miss Rockwell had the chance to witness its truth: "If husbands and wives, generally, would render each other half of the little attentions they lavished upon each other before marriage, their mutual happiness would be more than doubled."

You do the math.

✦

The election's unsung hero
29 November 2000

Every federal election has its unsung heroes, and this time around mine is Ted White, the Canadian Alliance MP who was returned in North Vancouver with a comfortable margin against his Liberal challenger, Bill Bell. Mr. White has done for higher education, especially the fine arts and humanities, what Jim Carrey did for method acting.

Mr. White is not unknown to Canadians, at least those who paid attention to early-campaign controversies about disqualified candidates. In the early days of the race, he hinted darkly of a Liberal conspiracy to stack British Columbia ridings. As it turned out, of course, there was no need, since the Liberals had stacked up most of Ontario in the more traditional sense of whipping everybody's ass. But never mind, it was a noble effort in a noble cause.

Last week, Mr. White rose to view once more when he was quoted in the University of British Columbia student newspaper, *The Ubyssey*, giving his opinion of certain extravagant human pursuits. His comments were in response to a letter from a UBC professor who foolishly attempted to defend the Social Sciences and Humanities Research Council. They are worth repeating at length:

"I cannot conceive of any way in which research in the fields of fine arts, classical studies, philosophy, anthropology, modern languages and literature, or medieval studies, which together accounted for over $5.3 million in grants from SSHRC in the last fiscal year, contributes to any 'understanding of Canadian society or the challenges we face as we enter the 21st century.' Research into such fields, as far as my constituents are concerned, constitutes a personal past-time, and has no benefit to Canadian taxpayers."

I have to admit that, at first, I was too thick to realize that Mr. White had to be kidding—indeed, was playing such an elaborate jape that it ranks up there with the poems of Ossian. Like most people who toil in the bowels of our underfunded universities, paying for my own postage and stationery, watching the concrete walls weep and crumble before my eyes, struggling to guide a generation of confused young people through the challenges of being citizens when the world wants them to be consumers, fending off the dominance of crude economic use-value, I can be a little touchy about the value of higher education. When somebody writes off six central disciplines of human study (more, if you count the modern languages separately), I get annoyed.

This is a shortcoming, and I acknowledge it. For one thing, it momentarily blinded me to the subtle art of Mr. White's humour. He is clearly an impressionist in the league of Dana Carvey or (for Mr. White's generation) Rich Little. Having honed his portrayal of the Cranky Old Duffer to a fine edge, he knows how to take the joke just one tiny hilarious step too far. I almost missed it.

Luckily, a graduate student in my university, who hails from North Vancouver, contacted Mr. White to confirm his original statement. The student journalists at UBC had tried to do the same, but their many calls to his office went unreturned. Mr. White was equally cagey with my young colleague, citing "privacy considerations," but he did respond with a list of specific grants made by the SSHRC. These included the following self-evidently ridiculous projects (in random order): $2,267,350 for "the history of the book in Canada"; $23,740 for a study of "mass media pornography"; $515,000 for "the impact of race and gender on social cohesion, in light of globalization"; $365,000 for "policies and practices for computer use in Canada's schools"; $35,200 for "figure skating and the representation of gender and sexuality in sport"; and $50,900 for "cabarets, nightclubs and burlesque: investigating the subculture of erotic entertainment in postwar Vancouver."

I wondered for a moment if Mr. White's objections stemmed from his own possible participation in the subculture of erotic entertainment in postwar Vancouver, but dismissed the thought as trite. No, Mr. White was issuing a serious public challenge. "Please describe in detail," he wrote, "so that I can publish the information in a display advertisement, in the [local newspaper], for the benefit of my constituents, the ways in which each of the SSHRC grants 'have contributed to the understanding of Canadian society or the challenges we face as we enter the 21st century', exactly why the projects were of value to taxpayers, and in what ways the results of the studies have been applied to make Canada a better place in which to live."

He ended his letter by saying that he looked forward to "a prompt, detailed, and informative response" so he could publish it before Christmas. But really, we don't need any more Christmas presents! Canada is already a better place in which to live, because we have people like Ted White around. I haven't laughed so hard since I first heard that somebody was going to write a history of the book in Canada.

Oh, one final thought: if you don't know who Ossian is, look it up—while you still can.

✦

Seasonal guilt is better than no guilt at all
13 December 2000

Is there an ethical difference between killing someone and letting him die? Does it matter if the person dies close by or at a great distance, perhaps as the result of a complicated chain of actions? We have all heard it said that killing someone in hand-to-hand fighting is infinitely harder than pushing a button which will result in an unseen death. But is there a significant difference in that distinction?

These are rather gruesome questions for a Wednesday morning, but I ask them in the spirit of the season. After all, this is the time of year when our newspapers and television screens are full of appeals to charity. The suffering eyes of children in far-off places are inescapable as you make your holiday-shopping rounds. The argument implied here ("Can you look in her eyes for 10 seconds?") is that it is morally wrong to ignore the plight of others, however distant they may be.

Why is it wrong? Because letting people die, once you know about their condition and can alleviate it, isn't intrinsically different from killing them. In each case, human suffering results from something you freely chose. Your lack of concrete intention does not matter: we are responsible for our inactions as well as our actions. In Catholic school we learned to call them "sins of omission," but you don't need to be a choirboy to see the argument's force.

Charities rarely press the point this far, for the obvious reason that it makes people uncomfortable and therefore less, not more, willing to give. Nobody wants to be told that simply sitting there and doing nothing—or, worse, going out shopping—is morally monstrous. In fact, few of us really accept the equivalency of killing and letting die, even though the argument's logic is inescapable. Typically we fall back on mitigation: we intend no harm; we did not choose our privileged status; we are otherwise ethical.

Those more inclined to sophistry might add that seasonal guilt is an unreliable basis for morality. Ebeneezer Scrooge, for example, hates Christmas not because he is evil; it is, rather, because he despises cant and sentimentality—in a word, humbug. Christmas charity appeals infuriate Scrooge because they suggest the poor are not with us all year round. In his way Scrooge is a moral purist. He's also a kind of Red Tory. When he asks, "Are there no poor-houses," he's really saying taxes exist precisely so that wobbly appeals to fellow-feeling won't be necessary.

Of course, Scrooge might just be dressing up evasion in argument. It's a common manoeuvre. I was struck over the past few months that the passage in my latest book which received the most objection was an enjoinder to donate 10 percent of personal income to international relief. This was repeatedly described by critics as "tithing," presumably because the suggestion of servitude, especially to a religious authority, was usefully unpleasant. People also complained that their money wouldn't get into the hands of the needy. We can't do everything—so we do nothing.

This resistance surprised me, mostly because 10 percent seems a relatively modest commitment given the chasm between the planet's rich and poor. Some philosophers—Princeton University's Peter Singer is a high-profile case in point—demand far more. In a recent *New York Times Magazine* essay, Mr. Singer, a principled utilitarian, argued that people in the developed world had a moral obligation to give away all their wealth beyond what was necessary for basic needs. He calculated that $30,000 (U.S.) would support the average American household, "so a household making $100,000 could cut a yearly check for $70,000."

Predictably, this argument brought down a barrage of *ad hominem* criticism. Mr. Singer owns a Manhattan apartment as well as a house in Princeton, earns a six-figure academic salary, and enjoys a family trust fund—not to mention royalties from more than half a million book sales. He's not restricting himself to anything like $30,000 a year. (A similar attack was launched on his participation in expensive medical care for his mother, who suffers from advanced Alzheimer's disease, after he argued that such a condition rendered its sufferer a non-person.)

Charges of hypocrisy are nothing new in ethical debate, but it's worth remembering that they are based on fallacious reasoning. If Mr. Singer's argument is correct, it is correct whether or not he lives up to it himself. Personal inconsistency might leave a bad taste in our mouths, or make us distrust someone, but it does not actually affect the validity of the position. Anyway, Mr. Singer gives 20 percent of his income to famine relief. If consistency matters so much to his critics, they should keep quiet until they're doing the same.

In a recent interview in *Reason* magazine, Mr. Singer was made to confront another issue of utilitarian principle. "If it resulted in an overall increase in the happiness of morally significant beings, whoever they may be," the interviewer asked, "would you favour the slow, painful torture of professional philosophers, including ethicists?" This was a sly twist on a standard objection to utilitarianism, namely that it violates individual rights in the name of a collective good. The fate of my colleagues everywhere hung unwittingly in the balance.

"I find it fortunately hard to imagine the circumstances in which that would occur," Mr. Singer replied, "but if I were absolutely persuaded that this was the only way to do it, I guess I would have to." Yes, because sometimes individual preferences really are less important than greater well-being. There are always reasons not to give to charity. Fortunately there is one simple reason to do so anyway: because it alleviates vastly more suffering than it causes, at this time of year or any other.

✦

Bad grammar drives me to drink
27 December 2000

We all know that the third millennium of the Common Era begins this weekend. Or rather, some of us do. Others, maybe a majority, did their millennial greeting a year ago when the big cultural odometer rolled its nines into ones. It seemed a finicky point then to insist that 2000 is the last year of the old millennium, not the first year of the new one, but the mathematics are inarguable. With no Year Zero in the calendar, you can't complete a millennium until you rack up the whole thousand years, not just 999 of them.

Still, the calendar's logic was something only a true geek would bring up a year ago. There were some predictable letters to the editor, usually from middle-aged men living on the Prairies, but most of us just shut up and enjoyed the celebrations. We pretty much accepted without further debate that 2000 is the first year of the new century and millennium. The editors of this newspaper even referred to it that way in the big Year in Review package that ran in yesterday's edition, and I didn't see anyone slam down a coffee cup in disgust or rend the pages of Section A apart.

On the upside, that means that we all have another chance for a big party this weekend. But it also means that we lost an opportunity to make a valid distinction and correct a small matter of fact— a rare chance in a culture increasingly intolerant of fine distinctions, not least in how its inhabitants now write and speak. You may wonder how there could be any connection between the year 2000 and bad grammar, but I assure you there is.

This is the time of year professors the continent over face a stack of student papers to read and grade. It's a daunting task. With some notable exceptions, the syntactic garblings and tangled usage of these efforts will combine to make George Bush look like a master of the language. At least you usually know what Bush is trying to say when he uses a word like *resignate* or *dignitude* or *unificator*. In any event, nobody seems too upset about it. Recent election results prove what Marshall McLuhan recognized more than three decades ago, namely that television makes politicians into cool blank slates, ready to be filled in with our desires. A politician making sense is too hot, too much like reading, to be popular.

That's alarming but probably unfixable (a different vote count wouldn't alter the case). The more proximate problem is a generation of Canadians who can't express their thoughts about television, politics, or anything else in well-formed, grammatical sentences. I realize I'm starting to sound like an old fogey, or a middle-aged man from the Prairies, but that's what caring about grammar will do to a guy. I always think of a novel I read once in which a professor, confronted by a student of boundless enthusiasm but no discipline, "felt himself sag inwardly." Every humanities professor knows that the certain route to madness is to dwell for too long on student writing skills.

Which is probably why, when the Christmas season comes around, we consume so much single-malt whisky. The alternative is having a host of hollow-cheeked, dark-eyed professor-zombies stagger through the wintry streets, mumbling the phrases or insuperable confusions that finally broke them down.

The point is, is that ... anyways ... alls I'm saying ... I could of went ... I should of drank ... an agreement between he and I ... don't judge a book by it's cover ... things can not go on like this ...

You may think that none of this matters, and in the higher courts of the universe it probably doesn't. Good grammar doesn't make you a better person any more than good looks make you a more interesting one—though there is lots of evident error on that last count, whisky or not. But in one crucial respect it does matter, because bad grammar makes it less likely you will get your ideas across, and that is after all the main purpose of writing or speaking. (I'm not ruling out other uses for language; but essays, like newspaper columns, should have some kind of point to make.) Paying attention to grammar might even help you see when you don't quite have a point, and need to think some more.

Of course, I know from experience how hard it is to change bad habits, in grammar or anything else. Every year I give my students a little hand-out that warns them against the most common pitfalls of college-level writing. We go over them together. They take these sheets and put them away somewhere, or use the backs to practise graffiti techniques and scribble notes to each other, and then a week later submit papers repeatedly making those very mistakes. I have never been able to decide whether this is just the way of things, something I should get used to, or part of an elaborate plot to wear me down by tiny increments so that one day I will pop and go berserk in the classroom, and then they can tell their friends about it.

Hence the whisky—a bad habit I resolve to change right after the new century begins. In the meantime, alls I'm really saying is that the point is, is that this stuff infers a lack of care about distinctions that matter in small ways but add up to something bigger. It's a little thing with big power, just like the millennium. And some day, when English grammar is all shot to hell and nobody can make themself understood any more, we'll recall this moment, think how it all could of went differently, and sag inwardly.

✦

I watch reality TV, therefore I am
10 January 2001

The new crop of reality TV shows is upon us, with "The Mole" premiering last night on ABC, "Temptation Island" coming up tonight on Fox, and the second round of "Survivor" set to debut right after the Superbowl on January 28, this time with fried dingo a distinct possibility. And that turns our thoughts, naturally, to Descartes.

Oh, I know what you're thinking. Surely this actually turns our thoughts to other reality-TV possibilities. For example:

"Pinochet Ricochet" (Fox). A group of 12 players attempt to bring former Chilean dictator Augusto Pinochet to trial. He counters by evading psychological assessment, feigning ignorance, and just being old. He moves around the world, periodically placed on house arrest, as the 12 try to nail him. Each time they fail, one member is expelled. When it's all over, Pinochet gets a million dollars.

"The High-Risk DVT Lottery" (CBS). Sixty people fly from New York to Sydney in economy class and are not allowed to leave their seats. Those who develop deep vein thrombosis, otherwise known as economy-class syndrome, suffer acute pain and possibly death. The airline gets a million dollars.

"The Bear Pit" (NBC). Ten players, bankrolled by thousands of credulous investors, roll on the NASDAQ. They buy vintage Mustang convertibles and four-bedroom condos in San Francisco. Everybody hates them. Then the market crashes, and people feel smug at their misfortune. Surprise! They all still have a million dollars.

"Hard Landing" (CBC). Thirty million people compete for scarce resources as their overheated neighbours to the south plunge the global economy into recession. Some of them get a million dollars (Canadian).

Of course, everybody knows reality TV is not about reality. The situations are highly artificial, often to the point of cheesiness. The contestants are chosen for their diversity and/or high-percentile good looks. Hours of punishingly boring videotape are then moulded and prodded into a narrative arc that captures viewer interest and creates standard-issue character types: the villain of week three is the eventual winner; the good guy of week four turns out to be a fink. It's all about as realistic as *commedia del arte*.

No, the real mistake is not taking these heavily manipulated fictions for non-fiction, but rather in thinking we ever know what reality is. Hence Descartes, who worried about this way back in the 1640s in his own version of "Survivor."

We all assume the world is real. This means we can move around and get various things done as a result. But Descartes wants to know what rational argument we can offer to vouchsafe the certainty we so blithely assume. After all, we know that we are frequently mistaken about instances of our experience: a straight stick looks bent in a glass of water, a square tower looks round from a distance. How are we to prove that we are not mistaken about all of it? Step by step, Descartes dismantles the common-sense world. What, if anything, remains certain when we start the process of doubting?

Descartes didn't have TV or *The Matrix* and *The Truman Show* at his local Cineplex, so he didn't realize how common this worry would become when technology and perception became so fluid. In his *Meditations on First Philosophy*, he keeps apologizing for how strange his questions must sound, how bizarre his line of thought. Nowadays, with various holodeck-malfunction re-runs of "Star

Trek" available round the clock on cable and *Total Recall* on offer at Blockbuster, most people are instinctive Cartesian doubters.

The crux comes with what is known as the Dreaming Doubt. We might brush aside some forms of skepticism by adverting to other aspects of knowledge—thus are optical illusions defeated, for example—but what about that experience of being inside a dream? With the possible exception of lucid dreaming, we cannot know from within the dream that we are dreaming. Such knowledge only comes when we wake up. Now, what if what we call waking life is itself a kind of dream, but one from which we have not yet awoken? How do we go on? (Descartes's solution: our consciousness at least is certain, and a benevolent God would not deceive us about the rest.)

It happens that I had such a dream last night. Believe me, this is true. In the dream, I got up in the morning to write this column, and quickly discovered that my apartment had been burgled. This appeared to be a cruel comment on a column I wrote last summer about being burgled. Not again! But yes, and this time lots of stuff was gone, including my computer, television, and stereo.

The upside was that I seemed to be living with Sarah Jessica Parker, who was in the kitchen wearing a skimpy cocktail dress and smoking a cigarette. There were empty liquor bottles all over the counter. She looked haggard. I realized without much surprise that it was not actually Sarah Jessica Parker but instead her character, Carrie, from "Sex and the City."

"Carrie," I said, "What happened? My computer's gone. I can't write my column."

"I don't remember," she said, squinting through the smoke. "Those guys looked nice when we met at the bar."

I started to panic. I was on deadline. In the other room there were more dead bottles, bare wires and loose cables, and cigarette burns on the carpet, but the computer was definitely gone. The phone was still there. I swallowed hard and called my editor.

"I can't write my reality-TV column," I told her. "My apartment has been burgled. Again! And this time my computer's gone."

She was, as ever, a pragmatic voice of reason: "You still have your laptop, don't you?"

That's when I woke up.

✦

Just drop the "W" and get on with it
24 January 2001

Karl Marx, criticizing Hegel's idea of progressive historical determinism, said that history always repeats itself, "the first time as tragedy, the second as farce." The world doesn't get ever more rational, attaining new heights of philosophical depth through "the cunning of reason," as Hegel called it. It just gets weirder and weirder as events channel themselves back through our overheated consciousness, these days usually on television.

This past weekend was an object lesson. Not only were we informed that former Chilean dictator Augusto Pinochet, that blast from the past still on the run from his crimes against humanity, was now suffering, according to doctors, from "light to moderate dementia." (Pinochet was finally set to appear in court in Santiago yesterday; there were no forecasts on his precise level of dementia.) Viewers were also afforded the rare privilege of flipping from the inauguration of a new American president with the name George

Bush, damp and chilly in the Washington winter, to lively retrospectives of the decade-old Gulf War, when the last American president with the name George Bush was in office.

The only constant other than the Bush moniker was of course the ongoing presence of Iraqi leader Saddam Hussein, who clearly has dynastic succession figured out even better than the Bush clan. After all, why exert yourself to shove your son into the Oval Office through blandishments, side-deals, and shadowy business connections, when you can just sit tight, let the bombs rain around you, and still be there 10 years on? The United States and Britain have together spent billions of dollars enforcing a United Nations economic embargo on Iraq, but the main effect of its deprivations is that Iraqis are even more dedicated than ever to the 63-year-old leader. And after the late lamented vote dispute in Florida, Saddam Hussein can't be the only one who thinks there's a lot to be said for dictatorship over democracy.

There was something reassuring, almost cozy, about the scenes of the Gulf War airing on CNN the other night. They were like jittery home movies brought out at Christmastime, radiating nostalgia and that welcome snap of familiarity. Old friends like Christiane Ammanpour and Arthur Kent stood once more on their darkened rooftops, ducking spasmodically as the bright rocket lights flashed above them. The phrases came flooding back in a wash of memories. We had almost forgotten the resonance of the words "Scud" and "matériel," the odd anxiety contained in that loose adjective "conventional."

But here's the real point. Bush *fils* now has a sterling opportunity to do the mythological right thing and finish the business his father began. His first step in this fated direction should be to drop the W in his name and just go by plain George Bush. The whole point is to create a sense of continuity, as if nothing has really changed in the declension from tragedy to farce; and anyway, everybody is heartily sick of seeing the word "Dubya" in print. The *Toronto Sun* uttered what we all should hope is the last word on its front page of last Saturday, Inauguration Day, with the bellowing headline "BUBBA TO DUBYA." Enough said. Please.

A new Gulf War, though: now there's a parallel worth pursuing. Even though the vote-count nonsense (and the figure of Al Gore) will fade away eventually, George Bush enters office with a ready-made credibility problem. His mandate is uncertain, his sense of command open to question. Wars, even stupid and self-serving ones, can make a hero of even the least impressive president, and I bet those sky-blue, quasi-military shirts, the ones with the superfluous epaulettes that the other George Bush wore when he lectured the troops in the Gulf, will fit the new George Bush just fine.

There's no time like the present. The infant Bush administration is already embroiled in various controversies surrounding the anti-abortion, possibly racist views of Attorney-General nominee John Ashcroft. Of the possibility that this Christian reactionary and honorary graduate of Bob Jones University may become the top law enforcement agent in the republic, we can only say that he is no Robert Kennedy.

George Bush's most trusted intellectual adviser, meanwhile, is a hitherto obscure University of Texas journalism professor called Marvin Olasky who advocates "compassionate conservatism," which in practice entails shifting social assistance out of government's hands and into those of private companies and church groups. Mr. Olasky, a former Communist who chose his current Christian affiliation by looking for the most conservative denomination in the Austin, Texas, phone book, believes that the traditional separation of church and state in America is based on a misinterpretation of the Constitution. These views have caused a small uproar among constitutional experts and freedom-of-expression groups, though you would not know it from looking at certain newspapers, including this one.

No, there's nothing like a foreign war to damp down the flames of controversy at home. If the new George Bush hasn't seen the political satire *Wag the Dog*, which suggests that an invented war is the best possible domestic policy lever, then one of his associates should rent it for him right away. And while the White House aides are down there deciding between popcorn and Twizzlers, they should also pick up a copy of *Three Kings*, the Gulf War satire starring George Clooney and Mark Wahlberg.

This, the Gulf War update of that classic cynical heist movie of the Second World War, *Kelley's Heroes*, features more freelance soldiers after illicit enemy gold. It contains a memorable, maybe prophetic, opening line. Faced with a surrendering Iraqi soldier, Wahlberg's character wants to know, "Are we shooting today?" Not yet, no. But wait for it.

✦

Stories of a rocket-fuelled Socrates
8 February 2001

Everyone, it seems, has a Christopher Hitchens story to tell, especially now that he is poised between the two parts of his much-discussed public indictment of Henry Kissinger over events in

Indochina, Chile, Bangladesh, Cyprus, and East Timor. (The first part, about 10,000 words worth, was published in the February issue of *Harper's Magazine;* the second part will appear in the March issue, currently at the printer.)

The Hitchens stories all share certain narrative essentials: politics, fierce argument, lack of respect for powerful and/or complacent people, and, most of the time, alcohol. A columnist for *The Nation* and *Vanity Fair,* author of numerous books on international affairs, Hitchens is a rocket-fuelled Socrates, a heedless and relentless debunker, a critic whose intellectual independence borders on self-sabotage. Those qualities alone would make him worthy of appalled fascination, a wild animal ever in the process of tearing itself to pieces, like the Tasmanian Devil of Warner Brothers imagination.

Hitchens is also a master prose stylist, modulating effortlessly between full-bore abuse and deft forensic evisceration. He makes his subjects more interesting, in the process of their knife-between-the-ribs defeat, than they ever were in victory. And his talent for amassing damning evidence is unsurpassed among practising political journalists. The present case against Kissinger, like earlier ones against Bill Clinton and Mother Theresa, is built on a swelling wave of argument and proof.

Significantly, those who deny this—and there are many—always do so not with counter-argument but with self-contradictory splutters of insult: Hitchens is a Maoist; Hitchens is a drunk; Hitchens is a terrorist. They have apparently learned nothing from watching a real case being constructed. Note to right-wing columnists everywhere: this is the real world; you have to advance arguments, not just sling epithets.

Hitchens is not a nice guy. He is riddled with personal faults and abrasive qualities, especially that form of character deficiency which means he really does not care what other people think. We often applaud this condition in theory, but in practice it is a different matter, as anyone who has tried it will know. Fearless is often another name for inconsiderate, and Hitchens is nothing if not fearless. That, too, is a narrative essential.

The best-known Hitchens story right now is probably the one Martin Amis tells in his memoir, *Experience*. On their way to dinner with Amis's mentor and father-figure, Saul Bellow, Hitchens truculently agrees not to utter any "sinister balls," code between the two old *New Statesman* buddies for, as Amis tells us, "vehement assertions of left-wing tendency." But under pressure of company and argument, Hitchens cannot contain himself. Ignoring Amis's barrage of shin-kicks, he launches into a 90-minute denunciation of Israeli aggression and a defence of the Palestinian intellectual Edward Said, repeatedly berating his Jewish host along the way.

At the end of it, "utterly sober" according to Amis, for once stretching the reader's credulity, Hitchens breaks a deadly silence by saying, "Well, I'm sorry if I went on a bit. But Edward is a friend of mine. And if I hadn't defended him … I would have felt bad."

"How d'you feel now?" Bellow wants to know.

You might wonder how Amis manages to stay friends with Hitchens, but the second act tells us: he tortures Hitchens through their long car-ride back to Cape Cod, refusing to pull over even though his friend's bladder, primed by many large drinks at lunch, is ready to burst. Amis finally stops by slamming on the brakes, with predictable and hilarious results. In short, the two deserve each other.

Lewis Lapham, the editor of *Harper's*, tells a similar story of perverse Hitchens outrage. In Berkeley, California, where Free Tibet flags waft atop three-car garages, Hitchens appears at the University of California journalism school and calmly denounces the Dalai

Lama as "a stooge for Hindu nationalism." Lapham is sharing the stage with him. "You have to understand, this is Berkeley," Lapham says later through a cloud of cigarette smoke. "Hitchens calls the Dalai Lama a stooge. Men are jumping to their feet, shaking their fists. Women are fainting dead away in the aisles. It's nearly a riot."

Afterwards, Hitchens moves through the Berkeley campus, swigging from a bottle of scotch, pursued by a series of angry interlocutors. He happily argues with all of them. He happily offers all of them a drink from the plastic-bag clutched in his fist.

My own Hitchens story is a little less colourful, if only because we happened to agree about the bizarre public canonization of Princess Diana, subject of a joint television interview. In the green room beforehand, he made a series of expensive long-distance calls and somehow managed to extract a drink from the producer. He seemed to become even drunker on the air, though I can't imagine how. It might just have been his drawling, sleepy-eyed demeanour, the quiet menace occasionally exploding into vivid excoriation.

Afterwards, in a nearby bar, he was certainly drunk, or getting there. I ordered a martini. He looked at me with a nostalgic air, poured himself another full glass from the bottle of red wine at his elbow, and said, "Ah, Mark, you remind me of my younger days, when I could drink."

It is probably too much to hope that Hitchens's work on the Kissinger case will destroy the strange but widely held perception that the former Nixon associate is a great statesman. Which means we will have to content ourselves, for now, with the very real courage of a writer with a rare talent for pissing people off. Like all originals, Christopher Hitchens is both irritating and inimitable. For once the old adage is appropriate: if he didn't exist, we would have to invent him.

✦

British are no longer masters of their fate
22 February 2001

London

British Prime Minister Tony Blair flies to Ottawa today, first stop on a North American swing whose main purpose is, of course, to curry favour with the new American regime of George W. Bush. Blair exuded confidence before he left from Heathrow on his chartered private plane, referring jauntily to the traditional "special relationship" that still exists between the British and the U.S., but he should take some cues from his Canadian hosts and learn the hard truth of 2001: the Americans now have a special relationship only with themselves.

London, still one of the greatest cities in the world, can be a hard place to see this. Immersed in its heady mix of history, culture, and literature, with the sharp tang of money and power in the air, you can forget that this is yesterday's world. It's been a long time coming—say, since American productivity overtook Britain in the 1920s and the imperial balance finally shifted—but the verdict is now crashingly obvious to all but a few. Britain is fallen Greece to America's ascendant Rome, and with the same consequences. It was fashionable for wealthy Romans to have Greek tutors and servants, and if English butlers are no longer the measure of New York high society, weekend trips from JFK to take in a West End show and maybe do some shopping at Harrod's or Fortnum's certainly are. Madonna and Candace Bushnell come here to get away from things, not to find excitement.

Naturally, this country of 59 million isn't happy with the idea that history has left them behind, along the way reducing their beautiful country to the largest theme park in the world. The novelist Julian Barnes parodied the cultural property of "Englishness" in *England, England,* about an elaborately twee interactive museum in Cornwall, but his real irony is that such a thing is hardly necessary: England fulfills the function just as it is. The newspapers here are full of politicians and columnists uttering what can only be regarded as the last bleats of a once-dominant country fallen on hard times.

"We are not simply an aircraft carrier for America," one Blair aide defiantly informed *The Observer* the other day, implying that Britain may not fall into line with Bush's controversial National Missile Defence project, which threatens the existing Anti-Ballistic Missile Treaty with Russia. But attentive readers caught the echo to George Orwell's *Nineteen Eighty-Four,* written a half-century ago, in which Britain is renamed "Airstrip One" and exists purely by virtue of its strategic value in a geopolitical situation controlled from elsewhere. The Americans don't really care that Blair disagrees with NMD, or that he wants to include Russia, China, and Continental Europe in any new nuclear umbrella plan. Why should they?

The received wisdom is that Britain can gain new influence by entering more enthusiastically into the European Community, adopting the Euro, and generally being the world's gate to the United States of Europe. Such a result isn't likely, though, given the persistence of Little England traditionalism, which abhors the idea of standing shoulder to shoulder with the French and Germans. (Conrad Black, a transplanted British Euroskeptic, thinks Britain should join the North American Free Trade Agreement instead—a position for which he would seem to be the sole advocate.) And even if unity were possible, it would not solve the structural-inequality problem. British supporters of a united Europe should note that Washington is all too keen on Britain being part of a tighter Europe.

Why? Washington's idea is that, with Britain as a bridge to unified European markets, there would be no need to shift existing American investment from London to Brussels. Of course, if shifting is what it takes—if conservative nationalism and ethnic prejudice keep Britain isolated on the wrong side of the Channel—then sooner or later the dollars will indeed leave here for greener financial pastures on the Continent. The relationship is special only in the sense that the more powerful partner can cancel it at any time. Britain is dating a commitment-phobic Terminator, a Dumpmeister.

Which all goes to show that the British are no longer masters of their fate. It's a condition Canadians understand very well, and that's what Jean Chrétien should perhaps press upon his visitor from London. You can rail and waffle and talk tough all you want, but that won't change the facts. The United States wields its vast economic, cultural, and military power in the punishing form of exceptionalism and isolationism. Its leader is a man famously untravelled and, like too many of his fellow citizens, happily ignorant of the world beyond the country's borders.

There is a second-order response to the situation, of course. It's the one where purveyors of the historical long view note that, no matter how powerful or apparently unassailable, empires always fall. The existing American regime will sooner or later crumble too, the result of economic overstretch, distant military entanglements, or simply paying too little attention to the web of global capital it helped to weave. Students of history know that financial or environmental crises in distant, unpronounceable places have an alarming tendency to radiate trouble all the way back to the centre of the imperial universe.

So that's what the smart people are saying, here in the land of the lost, where a mighty empire once stood. Trouble is, it doesn't help much. In the end, an American collapse will bring down Britain just as surely as anyone. As we Canadians know, to belong to an American satellite state in these opening days of the twenty-first century is to experience a peculiar form of depressed powerlessness. We can cheer or we can complain, but either way the ship has already sailed, and we're on it. Telling ourselves that one day it will surely sink is the coldest possible comfort.

✦

Apocalypse now? You got a problem with that?
7 March 2001

London

In Caryl Churchill's latest play, a one-act *tour de force* called *Far Away* currently showing in London's West End, three isolated characters meet and struggle over what appears to be the end of the world. In the final scene, they describe a landscape of total social collapse in which a swirl of strange alliances and topsy-turvy enmities threaten everyone, daily life reduced to a series of paranoid risk-assessments:

Todd: "But we're not exactly on the other side from the French. It's not as if they're the Moroccans and the ants."

Harper: "It's not as if they're the Canadians, the Venezuelans and the mosquitoes."

Todd: "It's not as if they're the engineers, the chefs, the children under five, the musicians."

Harper: "The car salesmen."

Todd: "Portuguese car salesmen."

Harper: "Russian swimmers."

Todd: "Thai butchers."

Harper: "Latvian dentists."

Todd: "No, the Latvian dentists have been doing good work in Cuba. They've a house outside Havana."

The play is funny and bizarre and, ultimately, harrowing. It is also, right now, eerie. The images of recent livestock funeral pyres, as Britain and Ireland struggle to contain the worst outbreak in decades of hoof-and-mouth disease, have played across the television screen like dispatches from the Apocalypse. Against this background, scanning the newspaper headlines becomes an exercise in compounding unease: another suburban school shooting in America, destruction of ancient holy sculpture in Afghanistan, new evidence of atrocities in Chechnya, pilgrims trampled to death in Mecca. The current winter seems bleak and interminable, every one of us caught in an extended bout of the blahs. Things pretty much suck: it feels like the entire culture has a hangover.

You might say it was ever thus, of course, especially in the world of journalism, which necessarily thrives on human tragedies large and small. (It is an ugly truth that some people are more busted up about the demise of Tom and Nicole than about the tortured Chechens.) But we should be wary of that shrugging dismissal. What if our unease speaks to a deeper issue? What if feeling dismayed and desolate in the face of the world's depravities is not so much a problem to be avoided as a human duty to be pursued?

I know, I know: this is the point at which another article on this page looks suddenly more interesting, or your arms begin their impatient twitching to turn the page. But before you go, consider a few questions. Was boredom a factor in the shootings in Santee or Columbine? Is anyone at all capable of torture? Can television or heartbreak drive us into madness? Is the relentless falling snow outside a mocking, evil image of your own soul's lonely terrain?

Mad-sounding questions. One nice thing about being a professional philosopher is that there is ample justification in the tradition for foolish, world-ending inquiry, starting with that irritating old bastard, Socrates. He would have known that apocalyptic literally means revelatory, tearing aside the veils of indolence and delusion and taken-for-grantedness. That's worth remembering, especially because it's still in the interest of many people to keep unsettling questions off the agenda.

A personal case in point. Some weeks back I raised in this column the ancient metaphysical issue of how we can know that what we perceive is actually real. (The occasion was the debut of various "reality-TV" shows.) In the *Ottawa Citizen,* a columnist replied by suggesting that "only a fool or a very young child" wonders about this; after all, we all know what is real! His article bore the (for me) keeper headline, "How we can really know that Mark Kingwell doesn't exist," and described me as both a "hip philosopher" and a "relativist," which are apparently equivalent terms in Ottawa. It was one of those runaway-logic things that started with a fact or two and ended with an unargued insistence on traditional moral values, whatever they may be.

For the record, I am not a relativist; neither was Descartes, whose version of the appearance-reality problem I was paraphrasing. As for hipness, it is probably, like beauty, in the eye of the beholder. But the deeper issue here is, what counts as a valid question, in a newspaper column or anywhere? Only a fool or a very young child wonders about some things, you say. So much the better. Descartes knew that his worries about reality would sound foolish to the merchants of common sense; he says so several times, almost apologizing for it. He also knew that he had to pursue those foolish worries if he was ever going to vindicate our knowledge of the world.

Descartes gets the world back for us, in the end (with God's help). But the skeptical procedure is a risky affair. Pursuing similar foolish questions led David Hume, for one, to the conclusion that we could not actually know anything except sense impressions. We couldn't even be certain that the sun would rise tomorrow, since our only basis for thinking so was that it always had—a crippling circularity. This, too, would sound foolish to most people, Hume admitted; he was forced to acknowledge that custom and habit count for more than reason in human affairs.

Hume was sometimes gloomy about his conclusions. "I am at first affrighted and confounded with that forlorn solitude in which I am placed by my philosophy," he wrote, "and fancy myself some uncouth monster, utterly abandoned and disconsolate. Fain would I run into the crowd for shelter and warmth." He resisted that temptation, and achieved a higher wisdom instead. Yes, philosophy is destructive of complacency: that is its point. But at the end of the day, there are still friends to love, meals to savour, diversions to enjoy.

At least, as long as the Latvian dentists don't join up with the Portuguese car salesmen and the ants.

✦

Romanticism is good, but get it in writing
21 March 2001

He was from the Baggy Sweater Brigade, one of those nebbishy academic creatures, prematurely old, who are to be seen palely loitering on university campuses the continent over. He hovered uncertainly on the outskirts of various clusters at the reception following the public lecture, in this case mine but potentially anyone's, exuding a pressing but unrealized desire to speak.

Finally he hurled himself across the social threshold and found voice. My lecture had argued that intellectuals, if they want to justify themselves, need to communicate their ideas to a non-specialist audience. He had a simpler concern: he wanted to know why anyone wrote anything. Ever. For whom, and to what purpose? Why?

As usual, this was less a question than an attempt to articulate a particular answer, namely his own. Maybe predictably, this involved something like what Yeats and his wacko Celtic-Twilight buddies used to call automatic writing, some form of quasi-divine poetic inspiration, with the Muse perched atop one's shoulder like a buccaneer's parrot, and extended bouts of self-obsession rendered into verse painfully wrenched onto the page in absolute solitude. He was, in short, that most hazardous of interlocutors, a Romantic.

I'm not a Romantic about writing, myself. Whether it's verse or a bandsaw operating manual or something in between, writing mostly seems to me to involve hard work and the struggle to communicate something, anything, to at least one other person. Inspiration may enter into it somewhere, and solitude is certainly a necessary condition, but there's nothing much divine about it. But then, I've always liked Dr. Johnson's remark about blockheads being the only ones who write for anything but cash; and admired the golf shirt a friend of mine used to wear, which sported the slogan, "Philosophy: I'm in it for the money."

Literary Romanticism is not just odd, it's self-contradictory. If, in the cherished tradition, the writing goes unread, the author unrecognized, then the writing has failed: it has not done the only thing it is meant to do. Undiscovered or unread writing is not better or worse than published writing; it is not writing at all. We may admire the weird purity of Kafka's desire to have all his manuscripts burnt, but if his friend Max Brod had not ignored that wish, we would not know who Kafka was. Kafka would not be a good writer or a bad one; he would not be any kind of writer. He would simply not exist.

The paradox at the heart of writing is that every writer writes at once for everybody and for nobody. All writing says (or maybe shrieks): *Here I am!* At the same time it whispers: *Don't ask me to pander, don't hurt me, don't get me wrong.* Writers can embrace this duality or they can ignore it. They can, like Nietzsche, reach a vast readership even while convincing each one that he alone is the chosen audience. They can even, as with David Foster Wallace and David Markson and Dave Eggers and other self-reflexive writers named Dave, make writing's paradoxes their theme. What they cannot do is outrun the deep irony of the act itself, a demand for worthy attention that can never be adequately met.

Thus the pathos of the unsuccessful writer, even or especially if his or her accomplishment is recognized post facto. Markson's own anti-novel *Reader's Block,* for example, lists tragic snippets culled from the history of Western letters: "Beckett's *Murphy* was rejected by forty-two publishers"; "Robert Frost had exactly five poems accepted in the first seventeen years in which he was submitting"; "Thackeray had to pay to publish *Vanity Fair*. Sterne had to pay to publish *Tristram Shandy*. Defoe had to pay to publish *Moll Flanders*." (All writing is about the writer: Markson's 1988 novel, *Wittgenstein's Mistress,* about a woman writing when there is no one else left alive, was rejected by an impressive list of 44 publishers.)

This kind of exercise is sometimes performed to give other writers hope—and incidentally to keep vanity presses in business—but it is really a catalogue of woe and should make sensitive people throw away their pens and keyboards. These genius-despised-by-his-contemporaries stories should always be accompanied by countervailing tales of once-famous writers now long forgotten, their impressive lifetime sales and soaring reputations wiped out by the inexorable passage of time and fashion. Attempts to rehabilitate forgotten writers should always be undertaken with a wintry air; they are, after all, exhumations.

People who don't write sometimes wonder why writers get so upset by bad reviews. Here, after all, is someone paying attention: surely that is better than being ignored? Well, yes and no. It's better roughly on the analogy of its being better to have loved and lost than never to have loved at all—with the rider that you didn't just lose but got clobbered. At such moments it can seem preferable, if one must write anything, to stick to academic journal articles, which have, according to a bleak statistic I once saw, an average readership of less than 1.0. Knowing that at best something like 0.87 of a reader is looking at one's latest effort on Husserlian phenomenology is, I believe, a species of comfort.

Indeed, academic obscurity and Romanticism about writing are related: they are both defence mechanisms against the inherent risks of human communication, which include not just being misunderstood but, alas, being understood all too well. Why write? There is, finally, no good reason, no reasonable reason. There is only the blind will to say something, to find out what you think and how well you can say it, to raise a chuckle or two and perhaps (not likely) make a tiny connection with another person.

Thin stuff, admittedly. But here's an even better question, which I leave as an exercise for those who made it this far: Why read?

✦

Let the protest pies fly
4 April 2001

I can't be the only observer of the Canadian political scene who wishes that Evan Wade Brown, the 24-year-old Charlottetown playwright found guilty yesterday of assaulting Prime Minister Jean Chrétien with a pie last August, had his own private jet-helicopter, a SWAT team of abseiling aides, and an inexhaustible supply of aerosol whipped cream. There are so many people out there who deserve pies in the face, from Toronto Police Chief Julian Fantino (for stupidly talking tough about yesterday's anti-FTAA protests), to Mr. Chrétien again (AWOL from Question Period for three days running), to Michael Douglas and Russell Crowe (I just didn't like the way they looked at the Oscars).

The tradition of throwing pies in the faces of celebrities and politicians has become an exhilarating sideshow in these days of mounting political protest around the globe, and I must say I'm happy about it. I'd like to see pies flying everywhere in Québec City later this month at the Summit of the Americas. There is something deeply satisfying, if admittedly infantile, in watching the smooth face of professional authority obliterated by the oldest sight-gag in the slapstick repertoire. I even like the verb *to pie*. It has a nice plosive ring to it: *Pie! Pie! Pie!*

As a political protests go, a pie in the face doesn't have much point beyond itself. It makes no arguments and offers no solutions. That is not to say that pieing lacks a theory. The Crown prosecutor in Mr. Brown's trial, Valerie Moore, has argued that he was influenced by members of the Québec branch of a loose international group of pie-protesters known as *entartistes*, who have pied many prominent figures, including federal cabinet minister Stéphane Dion, on principle. Apparently Mr. Brown's roommate told police that two *entartistes* from Québec met with Mr. Brown to discuss how to construct the pie and how to reach Mr. Chrétien.

Mr. Brown, for his part, says he acted alone and spontaneously; there is no word on whether he is still speaking to his roommate.

The real philosopher of the pie protest, however, the man who must be recognized as the Camus of cream, the Sartre of tart, is a veteran Belgian activist called Noel Godin, also known as *L'Entarteur* (the Pie Man). Among many other high-profile pie incidents, Mr. Godin was responsible for organizing a 30-person, 24-pie volley carried out against Microsoft chairman Bill Gates on February 4, 1998. Parts of four pies hit Mr. Gates in the face, and the images of his boyish mug slathered with whipped cream were instantly ubiquitous. (There is probably no causal connection, but the celebrated anti-trust case against Microsoft caused Mr. Gates's star to fall soon afterwards.)

"I'm part of a gang of bad hellions that has declared a pie war on all the unpleasant celebrities in every kind of domain," Mr. Godin told an interviewer, explaining what they had chosen Mr. Gates as a target. "He could have been a utopian but he prefers being a lackey of the establishment. The attack against him is symbolic: it's against hierarchical power itself. Our war cry was explicit: 'Let's pie! Let's pie the polluting lolly!'"

Their plan was simple enough: aided by a sympathizer within Microsoft Belgium, they waited on the steps of the building Mr. Gates was to visit in Brussels. "When he arrived with screaming sirens," Mr. Godin recalled, "he got out of his car, and as he was climbing the steps, several of our fighting units gathered and created a kind of pie whirl that fell on him."

Asked to describe Mr. Gates's reaction to the incident, Mr. Godin spoke in lines befitting a character from Alain Resnais's *Last Year at Marienbad*. "He had a kind of promotional smile," the Pie Man said, "that then became a smile made of sand."

The *entartistes'* targets are not restricted to politicians or business leaders. In November 1969, Mr. Godin and his associates pied Marguerite Duras, "whose work represented the 'empty' novel." Over the years, his "to-pie" list has included Tony Blair, Bill Clinton, Demi Moore, the Scientologists Tom Cruise and John Travolta, and the Pope, "a dangerous serial killer because he is against birth control." But he refused to pie Catherine Deneuve in Cannes, even for money. "We have never been pie mercenaries," Mr. Godin said. "I love Catherine Deneuve."

Mr. Brown is a worthy disciple. He made sure his own pie, constructed of artificial cream on a paper plate, would not harm the prime minister. ("The victim is injured only in his self-esteem," Mr. Godin has said. "We take a lot of care that the pies can't hurt physically.") In fact, Mr. Chrétien may even have been asking for it. Mr. Brown's lawyer, Jim Hornby, argued in court on Monday that

Mr. Chrétien actually consented to the action by saying, in the Québec newspaper *La Presse,* that many prominent figures had been pied and that it was "an honour and a distinction."

The Chrétien pie incident prompted a review of the security around the prime minister, who seems dogged by intruders and path-blockers. Chief Fantino, not to mention the officials in charge of security in Québec City—not to mention again the RCMP forces in Vancouver back in the APEC pepper-spray days—favour a different approach. Why review security after a harmless breach? Just close down all possible avenues of protest, exchange, discussion, or argument beforehand. Threaten and harass anybody not wearing a suit and tie. Make democracy into a gated community where authority is wholly immune, even from ridicule.

Then, the only smile made of sand will be the one on the faces of ordinary citizens who used to believe that democracy meant rule by the people. Who's laughing now?

✦

The cost of losing our public space
18 April 2001

Reading the Summit 2001 special supplement included in these pages the other morning afforded a rare treat: the glib rhetoric of neo-liberal economic justification was pushed far enough to emerge into open fallacy.

The McGill economist William Watson, editor of the magazine *Policy Options,* contributed a long and apparently balanced assessment of the FTAA, including some potted history and references to his appearances on television, and concluded by saying, "Sometimes you do not know how you feel about an idea until you see who is against it." His point: the FTAA is possibly unnecessary and probably unworkable, but since various "globalization Contras"—"tenured anarchists" and "mad-cow people" and other bugbears—are against it, well then, he's all for it.

Never mind that this is an "argument" that even the most impaired of my first-year philosophy students would recognize as ridiculous. What is more striking is the assumption of economic dominance that makes the claim possible—that makes it seem, no doubt, quite reasonable to some people.

It is precisely this assumption that is being challenged by many of the protesters who are gathering in Québec City this week, and the ongoing refusal of those inside to heed this deeper challenge is precisely what has made the string of protests from Seattle to Prague to Québec so necessary. (Just for the record, I don't know any tenured anarchists, but I can't for the life of me see why such people are self-evidently ridiculous. Even Mr. Watson must know that the only valid argument for tenure is that it protects academic freedom, including presumably the freedom to advocate radical government decentralization and the local organization of workers. Why not?)

"The FTAA is trying hard to embrace 'civil society,'" Mr. Watson wrote. "It has set up a committee on 'the participation of civil society' and it is making a great display of listening." But as Mr. Watson reports with some sadness, those outside are not impressed by this generous show of interest, this conversational largesse. "They are there to do one thing and one thing alone: Stop the liberal project."

Not at all. In fact, this gets it exactly backwards, in two related ways. First, the protesters are mostly there to *enact* the liberal project, not stop it, because the liberal project they believe in is the one where individual citizens get a voice in determining what happens to them. Second, and more deeply, they believe that economic policy should be determined by the interests of democratic decision-making, rather than having "democracy" and "civil society" tacked on as hasty addenda to the otherwise (as economists like to say) rationally inevitable demands of trade liberalization.

This philosophical dispute is the real basis of what will happen on the streets of Québec City this week, and anyone who spent time in Prague or Washington listening to the arguments, rather than simply dismissing the people making them as cranks and troublemakers (or, as another lengthy *Post* feature last weekend seemed to suggest, mere victims of fashion), would realize that.

What it really comes down to is the idea of public space, the space of democratic deliberation and debate. The much-discussed fence erected around the Summit site is just an expression, more straightforward than we usually see, of the current limits on such space. Most of the time, these limits are set instead by the commercialization of shared spaces in cities and towns, the soft dominance of overwhelming visual pollution and the numerous barriers to free passage.

What I mostly sense from the protesters, both those now gathering in Québec and the ones I've met in New York and Prague, is frustration. They feel alienated and closed off from decisions that directly affect them, and know that this is an obvious violation of the fragile democratic pact we all depend on. When faced with a fence keeping you from something that is properly yours, some anger is justified.

At the same time, many of them favour the wry humour and sly subversion that only a closed, surveillance-mad society of shrinking public space can arouse. The protest collective RTMark, for example, is erecting a Trojan Horse and a medieval siege tower and catapult next to the Québec City fence: "If our leaders and de facto corporate masters behave like medieval lords, they leave us no choice but to resort to medieval tactics," said the RTMark investor who is sponsoring the construction.

RTMark has also moved up their normal Phone in Sick Day from May 1st to April 20th, encouraging people to engage in the small protest of staying away from their routine functions in the exchange of capital. And for a hilarious response to urban barriers, including James Bond–like entry into forbidden places using such "credibility props" as clipboards and briefcases, see the online zine *www.infiltration.org*.

These are not arguments against private property. Private property is fine, but it should be an entailment of democratic participation, not the other way around—a point all too easily misplaced of late. Economists are hardly the only ones who let dubious early-liberal myths about the state of nature cloud their thinking about how property functions, and what it is for. We have property not by natural right but, instead, because there is a collective agreement among citizens to honour its conventions.

Those conventions are often enough good ones, and they probably allow us to do more of the things we care about than any other set we have so far imagined. They are not in place by divine fiat, whether your god is the Judeo-Christian one or the free-market one; they also display tendencies towards injustice that we, as citizens, have frequently noted and rightly attempted to regulate.

Is the FTAA such an attempt? Personally I doubt it; but I agree that we don't yet know for sure. What we can know for sure, and know *a priori,* is that it will only be such if it's undertaken on the basis of democracy, not in spite of it.

The world is becoming more and more private, individual, and driven by an insane quest for personal wealth. Is that just a natural development of the liberal project? Possibly, but before we simply succumb to it, why not stop and consider for a moment the costs of losing the very public spaces that made our sense of ourselves as private individuals possible in the first place. The protesters want us all to ask, *Who are we becoming?*

We all need to listen.

✦

Our motto: we want baseball back
2 May 2001

This is the story of how I discovered I was part of a secret society. Unlike the Masons or the federal Liberals, it's not a widespread conspiracy. There are probably no more than four or five members. You might better call it a cell, or a ring. At its centre is a smart, funny red-headed woman of a certain age with an appreciation of good gin, a store of salty anecdotes about the rich and famous, and reliable access to excellent baseball tickets. Oh yeah, and she has this awesome tattoo.

Last week, *Globe and Mail* columnist David Macfarlane wrote about our mutual friend, Alison Gordon, the baseball writer, mystery novelist, former president of PEN Canada, and all-round cool broad. I use the term "broad" here with prior approval: it's the only one that really meets the case. In another age, Alison would probably have been a *dame,* but nowadays you can't say that with any lively expectation of comprehension. My pals Ceri Marsh and Kim Izzo have just written an etiquette book for what they like to call *Fabulous Girls,* or FGs, but while Alison is certainly fabulous, she is no girl. Girls don't have the wicked wit; they don't know how to skewer male vanity with a look and a grin; they don't know where the bodies are buried. Alison Gordon is what an FG becomes when she grows up.

So anyway, in Macfarlane's *Globe* column it became clear that he too was part of the secret society, the mysterious cell, that revolves around Alison Gordon. His description of meeting her in a dim Toronto bar for several pre-ballgame martinis was eerily familiar—though he omitted the key detail that the bartenders are known to reach for the Gordon's gin bottle as soon as she crosses the threshold. His account of her eye-rolling campaigns against know-nothing fans and umpires might have been lifted from my own memory banks—though, again, he failed to mention her tactic of leaning over and cheering at high volume when somebody takes a cell-phone call during the game.

I've known for a while that Alison has this coterie of male friends she takes to ballgames, naturally, but never who else was part of the group. This seemed an essential part of the set-up. Lately, though, the contours of the cell are becoming clear. For instance, I mysteriously moved up the depth chart a few weeks back when a certain actor, stuck in rehearsals in Stratford, couldn't make it to opening day. (I could tell you his name but then Macfarlane would have to kill you.)

Normally this sort of knowledge would weaken a secret society, but these days we have a mission that goes beyond getting tipsy and yelling semi-coherent encouragement to tightly wound Blue Jays DH Brad Fullmer, or noticing that Raul Mondesi's feet seem to get smaller by the day. (Does he have to buy his spikes in the junior department?) Even tracking the emotional ups and downs of Jose Cruz Jr.—*now he's smiling! now he's sad!*—is no longer enough. We're coming out into the open. We're campaigning for Old Farts Day.

That's not what it will be called—Macfarlane suggested Tradition Day—but that's the general idea. Our aim is simple: we want baseball back.

Who can fail to notice that pro baseball parks like Toronto's SkyDome have become an all-out barrage on the senses, a relentless and inane symphony of noise, most of it commercial? Fans gathered there just to watch talented young men play the most difficult game ever devised by humans face a constant assault on their eyes and ears. A baseball stadium is supposed to be a public space, a small patch of peace carved out of the hurly-burly of life. Instead it is, for Jays fans, like being trapped inside a three-hour beer commercial set at maximum volume.

Hockey and basketball games the continent over are punctuated by the same brain-dead lighting effects and Cliché Rock playlist, of course, but the effect is most egregious in the summer game, the pastime. When the umpire commands time to begin, and the music and ads fall silent, fans are stunned and dumb, as if someone had just stopped hitting them in the head. The cavernous Dome echoes with the rolling aftershocks of the noise. Then, before we have a chance to recover, some huge electronic sign is telling us to cheer, some witless beer huckster is leading us in The Wave.

It's hateful, and antithetical to the leisure-time spirit of the game. It also has the unintended effect of making fans passive, doltish and isolated. (Or maybe *intended* effect: you can't rule out the possibility that this might be precisely the state advertisers prefer us to be in.) This is not the civil commons, a welcome respite from life's cares; it's just getting and spending by other means.

Now, I understand the economics of baseball. I'm not naive enough to think you could ever eliminate advertising from the game, or even would want to. No, all we're asking for is one old-school game a year: no ads, no contests, no air-cannon promotions, no aerobics, no music except an organ and "Take Me Out to the Ball Game" at the stretch. When the ceremonial first pitch is thrown, it should be thrown to the Jays catcher, not to the annoying mascot. While we're at it, no mascots.

We're not crazy. We don't want the DH rule eliminated (we'd miss Brad Fullmer, for one thing). We don't object to artificial turf or domed stadiums. We don't even mind paying $4.50 for a hot dog or six bucks for a beer. We don't want world domination, or life before the fall. We just want a decent baseball game.

And yes, this column is all part of the plan. But you knew that.

✦

Writers and the big, bad booksellers
16 May 2001

You know all the clichés about writers already, mainly because writers love to write about themselves, and each other. You know that writers are a sorry bunch, vain and touchy and bitter. You know they seethe with schadenfreude. And you know it doesn't really matter how acclaimed or successful a given writer is. It was Gore Vidal—a writer of early success and high earnings—who once said that when a friend of his succeeds, something inside him dies.

Here's part of a Clive James poem that was e-mailed to me yesterday by the independent Toronto publisher Sam Hiyate. It's called "The Book of My Enemy Has Been Remaindered."

The book of my enemy has been remaindered
And I am pleased.
In vast quantities it has been remaindered
Like a van-load of counterfeit that has been seized
And sits in piles in a police warehouse,
My enemy's much-prized effort sits in piles
In the kind of bookshop where remaindering occurs.
Great, square stacks of rejected books and, between them, aisles
One passes down reflecting on life's vanities,
Pausing to remember all those thoughtful reviews
Lavished to no avail upon one's enemy's book—
For behold, here is that book
Among these ranks and banks of duds,
These ponderous and seemingly irreducible cairns
Of complete stiffs.

There are very few things that transcend this grim rivalry, in my experience, but one of them is complaining about booksellers. Writers like to complain about editors too, of course, but it's not quite the same: you can avoid a bad editor, but you can't avoid a bad bookseller if you're going to sell your books at all. For the past five years, Chapters Inc. has been the bad bookseller no writer can avoid.

Indeed, Chapters provided the writers of this country with the best form of common cause since the Klingons decided the Romulans sucked even more than the Federation. (I was going to use a Second World War analogy, but then I'd be accused of being hyperbolic. For the record, I'm not calling anybody a Nazi, just a Romulan.) Tales of woe about the national chain—aggressive demands for steep discounts, massive returns, warehouse confusion, overdue bills, strong-arm tactics on small publishers—have circulated for some time, but only recently has the true extent of the damage become clear.

Now Heather Reisman and Gerald Schwartz of Indigo Books & Music Inc., who acquired the ailing rival company in February after a nasty takeover battle, are telling everybody that the carnage is going to continue. "I found deeper problems than I expected," Ms. Reisman said recently, adding that she plans to purge about $40 million of mostly book inventory and close or sell more than 20 stores when the merger of Chapters and Indigo is approved.

Which means that writers gathered in bars and cafés across the country will pause in their rounds of interpersonal complaint, their glee at somebody else's bad review or ill-advised author's photo, and join in one more chorus of hatred for Chapters. It's hard to derive joy from the remaindering of your enemy's book, after all, if all the other books, yours included, are being pulped, lost, or shipped back to the publisher.

To understand the anger, you first have to understand the strange business of publishing. Unlike most retail products, books are in effect consignment items. Bookstores purchase them, usually at 40-plus percent discounts off retail prices, and then try to sell them; if they don't move, or don't move fast enough, the bookstore simply returns them to the publisher. The publisher then tries to sell them to another bookseller.

Or doesn't. The dreaded practice of remaindering happens when a publisher decides it's cheaper to sell remaining stock at cost than to push it any longer, keep it in the warehouse, or destroy it. That's when you see hardcover books selling for less than their paperback versions. Writers get no royalties from remaindered books, so some writers have been known to buy their own remainders and destroy them personally, on principle. That may work for Gore Vidal, but it's not really an option for most authors.

In an industry like this, a really big retailer has disproportionate power. Their orders are so necessary that everybody has to play by their rules. Chapters was able to demand, and get, discounts above 50 percent and then to return between 50 to 65 percent of the books they were purchasing. (Normally returns run between 25 and 30 percent.) Meanwhile, publishers contemplating book projects sometimes thought it prudent to alter plans after a sales presentation to the mighty Chapters buyer.

After good initial sales in 1995 and 1996, the chain was hit with unexpected competition from online booksellers like Amazon.com and by Ms. Reisman's rival chain. Soon, to avoid financial collapse, Chapters was returning books faster and in greater quantities than ever, in effect dumping its money troubles on the already strapped publishers—who eventually passed them on, one way or another, to writers.

Ms. Reisman says it will take her at least 18 months to turn the merged company around, and she promises to abide by a code of conduct in her dealings with publishers. But it may simply be too late. Right now, Canadian publishing is wearing a brave face: lots of new fiction titles this spring, greater international acclaim by the day, parties nearly every week. If you look closer, the smile is strained. The most successful Canadian publishers are really just local shopfronts for transnational corporations. The authors who succeed need hefty American and British sales to do so. Small Canadian-only publishers—the ones who are supposed to nurture emerging talent—are a vanishing breed.

Canadian publishing will probably survive, if only because Canadian literature is so good (and because writerly resentment is, in its way, a sign of life). But the trust and goodwill are gone forever, and Chapters is to blame.

♦

The cart ruling: one golfer gets a free ride
30 May 2001

Kelowna
I have played golf exactly four times in my life, two of them enforced family outings this past week in British Columbia's sunny interior, so I have no particular stake in the ancient Scottish game. Nevertheless, yesterday's decision by the United States Supreme Court to allow golfer Casey Martin to use a golf cart on the Professional Golf Association tour strikes me as a serious and surprising mistake.

The 7-2 decision, based on the Americans with Disabilities Act, reasons that Martin, who suffers from a painful circulatory condition, is denied access to PGA tournaments if he cannot use a cart to get around the holes. Those who oppose his 1997 bid to qualify, including the PGA and and Martin's former Stanford University teammate Tiger Woods, say that walking the course is part of playing the game. Arnold Palmer has said that Martin's use of a cart would constitute a "competitive advantage." (Martin is currently playing in the Nike tour, and will not appear in PGA events until he qualifies in the normal way through sanctioned minor competitions.)

The decision hinges on the distinction between access to a golf course and Martin's ability to play the game. It says the cart is an enabling condition, not an advantage. The dissenters, Justices Scalia and Thomas—two men whose views I don't often find compelling—argued that the Court was being swayed by inappropriate considerations of "benevolent compassion."

The Court's level of compassion or propriety in legislating it are not the real issues, however. Nor is it whether one supports accessibility in general, which I certainly do. The real issue is that competitive sport is exactly the wrong place to make a stand about equal access. This decision is being viewed as a significant victory by accessibility activists, but it raises uncomfortable truths about the nature of human competition, and our interest in it, that won't be quelled by law.

Part of the difficulty in seeing this is owing to the haze of bad images that clouds the game. Golf clubs the continent over still support the proverbial cigar-chewing fat-bastard white guy who tools around manicured and heavily irrigated fairways, drunk on Chivas-and-soda and making off-colour jokes. Many private clubs still have unofficial colour bars or membership fees that act to create de facto gated communities; most or all consume vast natural resources to produce pleasure for a small minority. Less seriously—but still considerably—golf's fashion crimes are legion, from the fractal-pattern shirts and bright trousers to those ridiculous wide-brim straw hats that make even normal people look like overfed twits.

These are just a few of the reasons that have kept me from taking up the sport enthusiastically, despite concerted pressure from various people, including certain siblings and newspaper editors. But we need to separate, if only for a moment, the sometimes ugly culture of recreational golf from the often beautiful profession of competitive golf.

Whatever you think of the red-faced portfolio-manager duffers in their electric carts and heinous pants, there is something compelling and sublime in the spectacle of Tiger Woods or Mike Weir managing the mental and physical pressures of PGA golf. Of course a golf tournament is not a sporting event in the same mould as a basketball game, which demands so much more sheer athletic talent. But it is the concentrated exercise of high-percentile skill over a span of four days, one person competing at once only with himself and against a field of others. That is why it is worthy of our attention.

I have now played golf just often enough to appreciate this. The truism has it that hitting a Major League fastball is the hardest individual action in sports, but I would put hitting a final-round sand wedge 150 yards to the 18th green, maybe through a couple of trees, right alongside it. Golf is a stupidly difficult game, made all the more frustrating because the ball, its aerodynamic dimples presenting a study in apparent mockery, is just sitting there asking for it. People who are good at golf are rare; people who truly excel at it can be counted on a few hands. They are freaks of nature.

Because so much attention focuses on the actual golf swing, and because so many amateur players use carts habitually, we may forget that walking the course really is part of this unusual display of skill. Golf swings, like baseball pitches and boxing punches, start in the legs; the stress on those limbs and their muscles is more draining than non-players probably realize. Recreational golfers, deciding or ride rather than walk, are certainly free to make things easier on themselves by avoiding the wobbly knees that might otherwise appear on the 16th or 17th tee. But at the highest level this is not a concession we can or should make.

Competitive sports are by definition cruel and elitist; they do not tolerate weakness and they are not subject to compassionate intervention. Casey Martin is a good golfer who lacks one key aspect of success at the pro game; in this way, he is not unlike a decent pitcher who lacks a curve ball. The fact that Martin's condition is officially a disability rather than the result of an injury or sheer lack of talent is not relevant in the truly impartial court of physical achievement.

I said this was an uncomfortable truth, and it is. Egalitarian societies like our own are ambivalent about those aspects of our culture that still depend on, and demand, ruthless comparison. But we can't have it both ways: without that comparison there is no such thing as competitive sport, and everybody can be as good as everybody else—at everything. The wry Scots who invented golf knew better.

✦

Who's left? What's left? Left out. Left for dead
13 June 2001

For reasons entirely unrelated to a couple of porchside gin-and-tonics, I spent the past weekend nearly overcome with disorienting feelings of *déjà vu*. The New Democratic Party, official voice of the Left in Canada, is planning a major overhaul. Its paltry Parliamentary presence is lamented. There are calls for more youth involvement. A new leader. A better relationship with the traditional but disaffected labour constituency.

To call these cries and expressions familiar is to do a disservice to the crushing weight of inevitability and futility they truly evoke. So many times, and with such mounting boredom, have we been down this road before! The cartoonist Brian Gable, a satirical genius who happens to be employed by that other national newspaper, yesterday depicted an anesthesia ward in a hospital where a patient, stretched out upon a table, was made dead to the world through the recitation of old newspaper stories from a box labelled "Whither the NDP?"

Actually, I would take issue with Mr. Gable's conceit. The recitation would be, on the contrary, so painful as to obliterate all thoughts of imminent surgical incision. Anesthesia, maybe, but of a fairly drastic and unorthodox sort.

Don't get me wrong. I have been a stalwart supporter of the NDP in federal, provincial, and municipal elections my entire life. Luckily, I live in ridings where NDP candidates at least had a fighting chance. At the same time, I am not a member of the Party and the "Renewal Conference" I attended back in December of 1994, on assignment for *Saturday Night* magazine, was the first and only Party event I have taken part in.

I mention the conference because it evokes the eerie sameness of the current round of hand-wringing. Indeed, the situation creates a small-scale moral dilemma. If I were a different sort of writer, I might be tempted to cull about 900 words from the resulting *Saturday Night* article, which urged the NDP to become more ideological and less pragmatic, and drop it into this space without a qualm. But the editor who commissioned that piece seven years ago is now the editor of this newspaper, and he might conceivably notice. (I pay myself the compliment, possibly delusional, of thinking he reads everything I write with close attention.)

In the same vein, I might be tempted to pull a copy of the first article I ever wrote for this newspaper, back in January of 1999, which urged the NDP to become more ideological and less pragmatic. Changing a pop-culture reference or two, altering the date of Tony Blair's latest election victory, I could edit it to space, and once more walk away with a brisk step. But then even more editors, possibly some readers, might conceivably notice. (I know, I know: I flatter myself.)

You see the problem. For those of us on the Left, the NDP's woes are a recurring nightmare which no amount of the well-meaning therapy, or authoritative-sounding editorial opinions, will dispel. And there are only so many playful headline variations to be had on the double meaning of the word "left": *Who's Left? What's Left? Left Out. Left for Dead.*

Through no fault of its own, the NDP suffers from the same problem that currently afflicts the Right in Canada, namely that the Liberals are so good at stealing platform planks and moulding a soft-hearted yet hard-headed agenda that no other party has a look-in. Stockwell Day called, in vain, for a 90-day moratorium on criticism of his leadership. The fact is, 90 weeks wouldn't be long enough for the Alliance to get its act together against the all-powerful Liberals, and the NDP is likewise stymied on the other side.

Back in a first-year political science class, we were buried under a stack of articles that showed the causes of Canada's recurrent centrism: the fact that diversity and relative prosperity in a nation tend to converge on policies promoting social welfare yet grounded in reassuring fiscal conservatism. This elementary lesson seems lost on many politicians in this country. Note to would-be challengers on the Left and Right: Allan Rock and Paul Martin already have you outflanked. And Jean Chrétien probably has some sort of Dr. Evil plan to take care of them when the time comes anyway.

No, parliamentary success, even the Party's leadership, are less important to the NDP remaining a political force in this country than is regaining the moral high ground on issues such as environmental degradation, adult literacy, uneven wealth distribution, the health threats associated with privatization, and transnational democracy. This is even more true now than the first two times I argued it, in large part because democratic politics have taken on a new tenor during the past few years.

The NDP cannot look for youth renewal because political consciousness among young people is focused beyond national borders: they don't care about the fate of the NDP, they care about getting Mr. Martin's attention so he'll say the right things the next time he's talking to James Wolfensohn or Bono. Meanwhile, Maude Barlow and Naomi Klein, among others, have proven that one does not need parliamentary status to be a significant, globally-minded, leftist presence in national debate.

So here's my advice, for what it's worth. Abandon the project of reforming the Party with an eye to electoral relevance; unless it's on-target ideologically, cut Big Labour loose and suck up the resulting financial loss; and then embrace your fate. Leftist politics in this country are a leavening agent, essential in the clash of convictions that keeps politics from descending into mere management, but not likely ever to sway a majority. That's plenty, so do it with the most fire you can muster.

Svend Robinson can be leader if he wants.

✦

I watched Blind Date and now I can see ...
27 June 2001

So there I was, one day last week, in a dingy poolside room in the Trade Winds Motor Lodge in downtown Spokane, Washington, a place that feels like a clapped-out post-industrial town mysteriously transported to the middle of nowhere. (Feels like? Is.) Spokane is the sort of place that likes to say it's seen better days, but can't remember which days those were and whether it was sober at the time.

The Trade Winds, for its part, is just your average bad motel with the added attraction of some half-hearted and inexplicable pieces of Polynesian decoration: a black-velvet island-chief painting here, a shield and crossed spears there. Trade winds. In the near-desert of eastern Washington State hundreds of miles from the coast. Why?

Anyway, my kind of town, my kind of motel. There was no particular reason I had driven four hours to get there from Seattle, or would drive another four to get away from it the next day, but there I was. I was drinking beer, eating taco chips, and watching demeaning late-night television. And yes, I admit it, I was lying on the unmade bed clad only in a pair of tartan boxer shorts.

I was also laughing uncontrollably, because the show I was watching was "Blind Date."

If you haven't already seen it, and become an unwilling addict, let me explain the show's sly premise. Various men and women, all of whom have vied for the privilege, are set up for an extended date. There was an earlier British series, and various cities, including Toronto, have been used as sites, but the Los Angeles version is the best. Typically the pair will spend the afternoon together doing something odd—attending a puppet show, meeting a cook who specializes in deep-fried chicken wings—and then go out for drinks and dinner. Accompanying cameras capture their every move and comment.

The point of "Blind Date" is simple: to decide whether the two will hit it off, and consider going out again. Of course, this being television, that's just an excuse. Billed as a kind of romantic matchmaking service, the all-seeing electronic yenta, "Blind Date" is in fact a purveyor of everyday emotional torture, a televised psycho-logical experiment. We watch as two people, hoping for happiness, subject themselves to all manner of humiliation and insult, all the while smiling gamely into the camera.

What makes "Blind Date" so compelling is its imposed narrative structure. With six or seven hours of tape, the producers can edit down the dates into miniature essays in romantic futility. They then add various pop-up features: cartoon thought-bubbles attributing baffled or snide reactions to the participants; subtitles that mock bad conversational gambits or rack a running tally of flirty *faux pas*. This is what becomes so bleakly hilarious, because now you're not only inside a bad date, you're inside a bad date with a devastating running commentary.

It's easy to judge the people who take part as desperate losers, and the producers wicked exploiters of their weakness, but that misses the show's deep lesson. Underneath all the preoccupations and diversions of modern life, all the appurtenances of First World afflu-ence, ordinary people seem more miserable than ever because, plain and simple, they can't find love.

Forget politics, international news, the issues of the day. What people really care about is whether they're going to meet someone special—and maybe get some regular sex. A story in yesterday's paper reported that 28 percent of Canadians are having less sex than a year ago. Thirty-seven percent expressed a desire to have more sex, while a sad 23 percent said they had not had sex during the past year. At the same time, three in four Canadians are currently in a relationship, which means that, statistically speaking, meeting someone is not necessarily the route to satisfaction.

Nevertheless, we go on thinking it is; that's why there is so much dating talk everywhere you turn. Newspapers like this one are full of it. A few weeks back, a long excerpt from Ryan Bigge's clever but sad book about male loserdom described how to manage a date like a stock portfolio. Just last Saturday, an extended piece, with a big colour picture, by my young colleagues and friends Rebecca Eckler and Lauren Mechling detailed their attempts to meet eligible men in Toronto bars. (Ms. Mechling had already, in another long article, outlined her fondness for single men in their late thirties: SMILTs.)

We can complain that this is just white-space-filling drivel, but people are mad for it. Ms. Eckler told me she received more than 75 e-mail messages in the two days after her story appeared, most from guys asking for dates or explaining that men are just as insecure as women. That's more than any other story she's written. (The picture probably helped: both writers are better looking than print journalists have any right to be.)

It sometimes depresses serious thinkers that humans are, on the whole, more preoccupied with sex and their personal lives than with the Great Questions. Gossip and speculation rule conversation far more than thought or analysis. But I don't worry about it myself. Sooner or later, every one of us has moments of crisis when the larger issues of mortality and human purpose impose themselves. Try as you might, you cannot avoid forever the question of how to live, of what life means.

Against expectation, "Blind Date" raises those questions. One after another, the hapless contestants parade across the screen, trying and failing to find happiness. Their plight is our plight too. We laugh both at them and with them. Romance is futile, romance is inevitable, romance is our lifeblood. This is TV's version of Proustian reflection, leavened by the latter-day equivalent of Cervantes' irony or Rostand's wit.

Of course, I'm just a beer-swilling SMILT watching TV in his underwear, so what do I know?

✦

You have now heard of Empire. Empire is over
1 July 2001

Michael Hardt is an unassuming 41-year-old literature professor at North Carolina's prestigious Duke University, a place known in some circles for producing Blue Devil basketball teams that are NCAA Tournament perennials, but in others for housing a different kind of blue devil, high-flying smart guys like Stanley Fish and Fredric Jameson. Mr. Hardt is the new point guard on that team, a quickly rising academic star.

The reason is his latest book, a thick tome on globalization called *Empire* that is being hailed as the Next Big Thing in intellectual circles. Published last March by Harvard University Press, translated into 10 languages since, and the subject of both graduate seminars and coverage in the *New York Times, Empire* was co-authored by the Italian philosopher and suspected terrorist Antonio Negri. (Mr. Negri is currently serving a 13-year sentence in a Rome jail but presumably negotiated e-mail access as part of his deal.)

It is a sprawling, bold work which posits the existence of a radically new form of social organization: an imperial structure with no single power centre, a kind of self-organizing postmodern super-system. "Empire creates a greater potential for revolution than did the modern regimes of power," the authors write, "because it presents us, alongside the machine of command, with an alternative: the set of all the exploited and the subjugated, a multitude that is directly opposed to Empire, with no mediation between them."

Which means, as far as I can make out, that globalization is okay because its very success at linking up markets and nodes of power, moving goods and money around the planet so that we in the developed world have vastly more than we need, creates opportunities for resistance in (as theoreticians like to say) the resulting interstitial spaces. Critics have complained that the book is vague about how that actually works, and may be simply mistaken about the shape of things to come: nation-states, for example, are still far more influential than transnational structures.

None of that really matters. As the *Times* pointed out, there is currently a dearth of Big Ideas in the humanities. The once-fashionable theories of structuralism, deconstruction, poststructuralism, psychoanalysis, postcolonialism, and new historicism have all run their course, and nothing seems poised to generate the sort of excitement that formerly swirled around the merest utterance of Derrida or Foucault or Lacan. (Stanley Aronowitz, a sociologist at the Graduate Center of the City University of New York, was more forthright: "Literary theory has been dead for ten years.")

Hence the excitement over *Empire,* which has the good fortune to appear just when there is a buzz-gap that needs filling, and when globalization is the topic of the moment. The book nicely satisfies four basic conditions of any intellectual Big Thing, namely:

(1) Global scope. We all crave simple categorizations that schematize the entire world. Case in point. A friend of mine likes to play a mean-spirited but entertaining party game in which acquaintances are sorted into groups: Pretty, Smart, Both, or Weird.

As with party games, so with theories. Conceptual bigness is the first ingredient of a Big Idea.

(2) It's big in the other sense too. At more than 500 pages, the book is a doorstop. That is intimidating, and therefore good.

(3) As a result of (2), people are talking about *Empire* without having read it. That includes me, right now. This is crucial: if people actually have to read your book before they can talk about it, buzz is impossible. (I'll read it later, I promise.)

(4) The theory is political without being, you know, *political*. Like lots of theoretical work done by literary scholars, *Empire* has good left-wing credentials in the form of support for resistance and denunciation of oppression. But it doesn't have much to say about things like unionization, wealth transfer, or taxation schemes. This is excellent.

But I have some bad news for Mr. Hardt and Mr. Negri. *Empire* doesn't have Next Big Thing legs. It lacks crucial parts of the formula, and so will soon fade from view as quickly as it appeared. In particular:

(1) It's too easy to understand. The really powerful global operating systems in the theory world are cheerfully impenetrable. You have to sweat through at least a graduate seminar before you can even claim to understand what's going on. *Empire* may be big but it's not hard—a fatal flaw.

(2) Coverage in the *Times*. This looks like a good thing but, like a *Sports Illustrated* cover story, it's really the kiss of death. In common with every other fashion system, the world of intellectual trends is ruled by novelty and cool. Novelty and cool function in constant self-cancelling spirals; things cease to be new and cool just as soon as they are labelled as such. You have now heard of *Empire;* ergo, *Empire* is over.

(3) Mr. Hardt is a nice guy. This will never do. You have to be eccentric and caustic, reducing the psychoanalytic hour to five minutes, as Lacan did, or refusing to answer all challenges because they are self-evidently foolish, as Derrida did. Even Mr. Negri, suspected of inciting student violence during the 1970s, seems like a fairly charming and modest person. No no no.

(4) Neither of them is Parisian. Enough said.

In fact, I suspect all this talk about *Empire* being the Next Big Thing just obscures the deep truth, which is that there is no Next Big Thing coming. Or rather, the Next Big Thing is already here, and its message is this: Big Things are over.

Don't be fooled into thinking you understand what that means, however. It's all a great deal more complicated than it looks. And any day now, when I have a minute, I'll get to work on *The Theory Theory*, my massive, irritable, syntax-mangling monograph explaining why.

♦

Two dead people
25 July 2001

Like many another sensitive soul, I spent much of the past five days noting the various reasons that the death of Carlo Giuliani, the 23-year-old anarchist from Rome slain by two bullets and a reversing Land Rover during the G8 Summit in Genoa last week, is insignificant. Worry not, the news coverage implied, there's no reason to be upset that the escalating anti-corporate protests have finally claimed their first victim.

Why not? Simple: because he wasn't a victim.

Columnists and panelists alike sounded the mitigating bleat of privileged condescension. Mr. Giuliani, they noted, was a thug, punk, or hooligan (take your pick). He was a convicted petty criminal with a history of violent behaviour. He was part of a group of wild protesters with no constituency and no legitimacy. His violent methods bespoke only stupid disaffection and irrational rage, and were anyway condemned by other sectors of the anti-globalization movement.

Even if they hadn't been violent, furthermore, his protests were entirely misplaced since they did not address the realities of Third World poverty, which will only be alleviated by giving everyone the chance to own a Land Rover. Oh, and he wore black clothes, a balaclava, and combat boots.

There may be a few others I missed, but that pretty much covers it. Be my guest: clip-and-save the last two paragraphs for future reference. If you're an editorial writer at a North American newspaper, tape them over your desk against the next time somebody has the bad judgment to get themselves killed at a globalization protest, and you find yourself momentarily lost for words. (Though I doubt that happens very often in editorial conferences. Anyway, metaphor-challenged hacks can always fall back on the Right's favourite Lenin quotation and call opponents "useful idiots," after the manner of the Amiel-era *Toronto Sun*. That never gets old.)

Mr. Giuliani didn't exactly deserve to die—we don't say that kind of thing here in the liberal West—but, really, what can they expect, these thugs, punks, or hooligans, when they take to the streets that way? What was he thinking, putting his head in the way of bullets like that? And then just lying there when the Land Rover changed gears?

But, as the result of one of those media-driven confluences that novelists would be embarrassed to invent, I soon realized that none of this really matters. The chief reason Mr. Giuliani's death is insignificant is because he was not Katharine Graham.

It was hard to miss this über-lesson of the past week's political events. "Kay was a spectacular dame" read the headline on page three of this newspaper yesterday, reporting on the life of the former owner and publisher of the *Washington Post*. The accompanying story painted a thrilling picture of Mrs. Graham's star-studded funeral, attended by a range of wealthy and influential Georgetowners whose presence served to confirm her place in history.

There were politicians and power-brokers, obviously: Dick Cheney, Bill and Hillary, Ted Kennedy, Alan Greenspan. There were journalists, just as obviously: Diane Sawyer, Tom Brokaw, Tina Brown. Microsoft honcho Bill Gates came with his wife. Former British prime minister Sir Edward Heath flew in from London. Noted humanitarian Henry Kissinger was there, and gave a speech. Yo-Yo Ma played some Bach on his cello and made everybody cry, "bringing many handkerchiefs to averted gazes," as our correspondent delicately phrased it.

That made me want to avert my gaze from the page, but never mind. The real story here becomes evident: Mrs. Graham matters and Mr. Giuliani doesn't. In fact, the more you think about that, the more obvious it becomes. Mrs. Graham was rich. She knew a lot of people. When she wanted to change the world, she didn't don a black mask and set fire to things. She did what any sensible person would, and inherited a big newspaper.

And yet, she was modest about her life, just an ordinary mortal like the rest of us. The best part of the Graham funeral was when her daughter, Lally Weymouth, read a passage of startling banality from Mrs. Graham's living will. "Death is as much a reality as birth, growth, maturity, and old age," she had written. "It is the only certainty." In case you missed it, our faithful correspondent hammered the lesson home. This, he said, gave Mrs. Graham not only the last word but also the most universal one: "death comes to everybody, even the rich and powerful crowding the pews."

Sure, though putting it that way risks recalling Anatole France's tart assessment of equality before the law, that it forbids rich and poor alike to steal firewood or to sleep under bridges. And Mrs. Graham should perhaps have consulted the *Letters of Benjamin Franklin* when she was drafting her will, in particular the one from 13 November 1789, to Jean Baptiste Le Roy, where he suggests the only certainties are death *and taxes*.

That clear-eyed reminder that politics is everywhere would have been unseemly, maybe, since it dates from a time when the American republic still acknowledged its own roots in anarchistic political activism, before it became a cozy globe-dominating oligarchy that somehow still manages to pump out rhetorical hot air condemning the very idea of government. In those days, violent demands for representation, the basic first-person claim to be taken seriously as someone affected by policies and schemes drafted elsewhere, were not just accepted but celebrated.

We wouldn't want those uncomfortable thoughts crowding the vaulted expanse of Washington National Cathedral, of course. No, far better to reduce everything to diverting, sanctimonious platitudes about our shared existential fate. Mr. Giuliani and Mrs. Graham are both dead; the democratic myth says they each counted for exactly one. We all know that's not true, but what fun, now and then, to pretend it is.

✦

Mild rebukes, half-baked criticisms
8 August 2001

I've been thinking about the many ways the $10-million spent on the Hughes Report on the APEC pepper-spraying scandal might have been put to better use. Because, really, it's hard to argue with Jaggi Singh, the much-arrested anti-globalization protester, that the report is a useless "historical artifact" whose findings have been overtaken by recent events. "What was a scandal in 1997 is the norm in 2001," Mr. Singh said, adding that the report is "a good lesson in how governments engage in cover-ups."

True, Ted Hughes, the former B.C. judge who authored the 453-page document, had some harsh words for the RCMP and its amateurish, violent handling of events on the UBC campus back in 1997. Removal of signs and flags, the strip-searching of arrested female protesters, and the celebrated pepper-spraying at Gate 6 of the APEC fence were all inappropriate, Mr. Hughes decided. On top of that, officials from the Prime Minister's Office should not have used their influence with police in an effort to spare then-president Suharto of Indonesia, a delicate soul, from the embarrassment of seeing actual protesters.

At the same time, it was okay for the RCMP to use pepper spray after a section of the perimeter fence fell—though it was a bad idea to let the situation get that close in the first place. This logical poser came hard on the heels of another, even more twisted one: it was inappropriate for the Mounties to arrest Mr. Singh the first time, when he was carted off by plainclothes officers in an unmarked car, but it was fine to arrest him the second time, when he violated the conditions of being released from the first arrest, namely that he keep away from the protests.

That kind of inventive *Catch-22* thinking makes for mildly diverting reading on a hot August morning, and Mr. Singh must be getting used to these pre-emptive kidnappings by undercover police (a similar thing happened to him in Québec City earlier this year), but in the end it just points up the silliness of this report.

The protesters are unimpressed with Mr. Hughes's half-baked criticisms: Prime Minister Jean Chrétien, whose relationship with the dictator Suharto lies at the heart of the whole APEC mess, is nowhere blamed. Judging by their enthusiastic teargas performance in Québec City, the RCMP are likely to be just as unimpressed in a different way. Probably the only person who can take solace from the report is Staff Sergeant Hugh Stewart, affectionately known as "Sgt. Pepper" for his much-aired performance on the CBC wielding a can of pepper spray the size of a household fire extinguisher, who got off lightly. He "made some unfortunate decisions," Mr. Hughes wrote, but that's because "he was placed in a situation that was unfair to him." Like having to do his job under pressure, I guess. No fair.

Worst of all, of course, is that this long list of mild rebukes, tangled mitigations, and toothless recommendations will be delivered to—who else?—the same government whose bad conduct is glossed over by them. We all pay the bill, Mr. Hughes goes off to Yukon to adjudicate another conflict, and one more expensive Canadian avoidance-ritual is neatly concluded.

Which is why I think, with all due respect to the protesters' valid claims that their constitutional rights were violated, we should have spent the money on something else. I have drawn up a list of possible candidates:

(1) The Jaggi Singh Scholarship Fund for Studies in Transnational Citizenship. Ten million dollars in principal throws off a decent annual interest income, and I figure there's at least a few students who could use some aid in their studies of how the globalization of markets is altering politics. The federal government keeps saying that education is the key to understanding our changing world, and being better citizens. Let's take those platitudes seriously for once. I volunteer to administer this scholarship at the University of Toronto. Really, it's no problem.

(2) Former president Bill Clinton just got $10-million (U.S.) from publisher Alfred A. Knopf in a big book contract for his forthcoming memoirs. $10-million Canadian isn't quite in the same orbit, but how about using it to ink a deal for, say, the memoirs of ex-president Suharto? Whatever happened to that guy anyway? I miss him. Personally, I'd like to know if he had a good time in Vancouver, whether he still has his Roots leather jacket, if he sends Mr. Chrétien a Christmas card, that kind of thing. If we get him for less than $10 million, we could always use the remainder to buy Roots jackets for everyone who comes to Alberta for the next G8 Summit.

(3) In part because of a jammed fax machine, the PMO did not receive the Hughes Report until after it had gone out to various media outlets, leaving aides scrambling to respond. Clearly the government's priorities are out of whack: it doesn't need more wishy-washy reports, it needs more fax machines. After all, you can never have enough 1980s-era communications technology.

(4) Am I the only one who thinks that maybe the feds should provide everyone in southern Ontario with aphid-proof breathing apparatus? Nice bonus if it also blocks teargas.

(5) Canadian athletes have turned in at best mediocre performances during the World Track and Field Championships in

Edmonton. We've been forced to cheer for a couple of arrogant, past-it sprinters and a marathon runner who hurled himself across the finish line in order to finish 42nd. Jesus, give the $10-million—while we're at it, a whole lot more—to amateur sport in this country. We'll never be as good as the Australians, but at least we could stop embarrassing ourselves on the world stage.

I mean, at least until we host another gathering of world leaders.

✦

Boom-zines bust, like the industry
22 August 2001

I got the call about two in the afternoon, which means it was still morning on the West Coast. It was Alex, my editor at *The Industry Standard,* the weekly tech-sector magazine which had, a few weeks earlier, commissioned me to write an essay about design technology and democracy.

Alex, like all magazine editors on the West Coast, sounds like a 19-year-old surfer who downloads Link Wray singles from a comsat database while putting out an urban anti-surveillance zine and modelling part-time for Diesel. The other editor I worked with at *The Standard,* writing a piece on why wealth doesn't equal happiness even in Silicon Valley, was called Luke. Luke sounded like someone who lettered in volleyball at UCLA before going on to a brief stint playing rhythm guitar for Everclear. Last year I wrote an article for *Forbes* ASAP and my editor there was somebody named Rodes Fishburne. Rodes Fishburne! He looked a little like Peter Tork of the Monkees.

Anyway, Alex is a cool guy and a very good editor, and he had some bad news for me, the kind of news that no editor likes to deliver. Not only was my story not going to run, nobody's stories were going to run. The entire magazine was folding up like a pup tent. The industry had finally caught up with *The Industry Standard*. Like so many of the companies they had covered in the tech heyday, they were overextended, about U.S.$50-million in debt, and leased into cavernous, expensive properties in San Francisco to the tune of another U.S.$60-million.

It wasn't exactly a surprise. The magazine had been slashing staff and costs for months, watching its once-massive issues dwindle to wafer-thin pamphlets. A staff of more than 600 employees had been cut to 200 by the time the end came, and the chart-topping Y2K revenues of U.S.$140,000 had quickly dwindled as the magazine's ad base collapsed. Ad pages were down more than 75 percent through the first half of this year, with most of the former advertisers no more than wispy memories of barely-existent companies. The game staffers carried on assigning and editing as usual, but with a wintry demeanour even in the dog days of August.

Now it was over. The publication was sunk.

The irony was not lost on observers. Writing in the pages of this newspaper over the weekend, University of British Columbia business professor Paul Kedrosky was smug, even gleeful, about the turnabout. "Like the companies it covered, *The Industry Standard* knew how to promote itself, and its management (and staff) knew how to turn a phrase, but they didn't know much about running a business. Like most journalists, however, they sure could talk a good game."

Mr. Kedrosky came not to praise the genre of tech-sector magazines—"boom-zines," he called them—but to bury it. He noted that *The Standard* was just the latest casualty on a dismal list that includes

Wired, Fast Company, Business 2.0, eCompany Now, and *Red Herring.*
All but the last are gone or substantially changed, second-order victims
of the sharp economic adjustment that popped the New Economy
balloon a year ago. None of them, with their aggressive technological
rah-rah and move-it-or-lose-it confidence, would be terribly missed.

Now, I had no particular fondness for *The Standard* as a magazine,
but I did appreciate the effort to include some philosophical reflection
in their pages. John Battelle, the former *Wired* editor who took over
The Standard, may have been no management genius, but it's hardly
fair to blame him—still less the staff under him—for being caught up
in what has amounted to a tectonic shift in the economy. Short of
deciding not to exist in the first place, no amount of editorial acumen
could have saved *The Standard* once the tech market turned south.

Still, the grave-dancers had a point. Lots of people went a bit nuts
in the Bay Area during the 1990s. I've now lived long enough to
observe two boom-and-bust cycles at fairly close range, first in New
Haven during the *American Psycho/Bonfire of the Vanities* M-and-A
craze on Wall Street, then in Berkeley when Silicon Valley reached its
millennial peak and started to plunge. It's instructive to see a boom
in full swing, especially from the relative safety of a nearby college
town, which provides at least the illusion of above-the-fray wisdom.

I never got invited to any of *The Standard*'s lavish parties, as it
happens, but I did attend some glossy black-tie events back in late-80s
Manhattan where people made disturbing comments about the joys of
capitalism. I was disappointed when I couldn't go have dinner last
summer with Rodes Fishburne and Tom Wolfe at Elaine's—that
would have been a bicoastal Boomtown double-play. In San Francisco
I listened with frank astonishment as 25-year-olds explained to me that
the continent of Africa was "non-viable" and should be abandoned.
Great idea, I thought. Continental fire sale! Everything must go!

Hubris and selfishness were certainly key features of the tech economy, and the miniature millionaires who crowded all those pan-Asian restaurants and cocktail bars in San Francisco were indeed irritating. But what I'll remember is the e-mail traffic I got after my essay on wealth and happiness ran in *The Standard* last year.

"Your piece struck a chord with me," one young software designer told me. "I keep wondering what all this money is for." Exactly. Booms come and go, maybe faster now than ever, but the project of living a good life doesn't get any simpler for any of us— including the people caught up in them.

Now the only question is whether I'll get my kill fee from Alex before the creditors close in.

✦

Convergence should mean I get a TV show
5 September 2001

One downside of being a freelance newspaper columnist, especially one like me whose day job involves academic scholarship about the nature of truth and justice, is that you don't know anything about what's going on.

Sad but true. I was at a Blue Jays game the other day, a hot end-of-summer contest which the Jays managed to give away to the hateful New York Yankees, when a noted Canadian publisher and businessman (okay, it was Avie Bennett) asked me what the new regime at the *Post* was going to mean.

Mean? Regime? New?

All right, I'm being disingenuous. I knew what Mr. Bennett was talking about. Who doesn't? Conrad Black, scion of conservatism, has left the *Post* building. Izzy Asper, scion of something or other, is now the majority shareholder of this newspaper. Nobody knows what the deal was worth, or what Mr. Asper has in mind for editorial changes, beyond a hatred of red ink that reputedly borders on mania. (Mr. Black hates red ink too, but was willing to spill lots of it in a righteous cause. For a while. Then he left.)

I say nobody knows, but of course that hasn't stopped the furrowed-brow club, both inside the paper and out, from airing its opinions about Mr. Asper's connections to the Liberal Party and his Prairie common sense, whatever that means. The *Post* was born on a crusade to break the media monopoly in Canada, which it did mostly by giving more jobs to journalists in Toronto, and has continued on a crusade to decry the brain drain, diss the dollar, and unite the Canadian right, with what results we all know.

If it were my call, I'd say this was a crusade that ought to look for greener pastures. And maybe that's just what Mr. Black thinks too, which is why he's bailing. Meanwhile, Mark Steyn, writing on this page last week, speculated that the editors of the paper might now, under Mr. Asper's influence, try to find some common cause with the right-wing of the Liberal Party.

I don't know about that. In fact, the more people ask me about all this, the more I realize I don't know. I have never been to the *Post* editorial building, located in a distant part of Toronto known to its prisoners as Mills-and-Mills. I have never attended an editorial conference. The last time I saw my editor in person, she bought me a drink at a high-end minimalist bar located far downtown. I went to a party at Christie Blatchford's house last week, but I hadn't actually been invited. (For the record, it was a good party. There was a band and the police came; it felt like Mississauga, circa 1978.)

Under normal circumstances this deflection from the centre of all things Postal is useful, even necessary, for clear thought. Newsrooms are bizarre, toxic places, full of politics and resentments and pheromones. They give the people inside them a false and danger-ous feeling that they're at the centre of something. But when Avie Bennett asks me what the new regime is going to mean, I start to get anxious. Especially because, among other things, he seems to be asking me if my job is safe.

Well, until Roger Ebert starts writing every single story in the paper, as opposed to just half of them, I suppose the answer is yes. Sooner or later, though, somebody in Mr. Asper's orbit is going to notice that I'm not fitting in as well as I might. They might think talk of transnational democracy and David Hume is out of place on this page, maybe dispensable. The axe will be raised.

But I have a plan: That's when I demand my own TV show!

Yes, because yesterday I discovered the one thing I think I do know about the new regime: convergence. You might have missed it, flipping through the thin, holiday-staff paper, but there it was on page A6: an unreasonably gushy story about CanWest Global's new national news broadcast, Global National, hosted by erstwhile brain-drainer (or maybe face-drainer) Kevin Newman. And riding above it a box advertising the fact that the *Post*'s Julie Smyth would be on TV that very night to talk about ... well, whatever. Doesn't matter. The point is: Global National-National Post-er, Global Post.

I was on the phone the other day with my friend Rebecca Eckler, girl reporter, when she interrupted me to take another call. (She's like that.) When she came back on the line she told me it had been someone from Global National telling her about her new video camera. Rebecca is getting a video camera! Now, when she goes surfing or looking for dates or putting her dog on a bus, she'll be able to tape it for viewing on TV.

Television, not any political agenda, is the cornerstone of the new *Post* regime. Sure, the whole Liberal Party thing is in there some-where, but we all know that Canada is rapidly becoming a post-ideological state, not just a one-party one. Here, genuine political differences and the conflict of ideas are blandly glossed over. No opinion has greater weight than any other because none of them really matter. The post-ideological state is perfect for television, the medium of smooth contiguity.

I don't want just a camera, though. I want a whole show to myself. I figure it's the least Mr. Asper can do for me. On the show, I will interview my friends and we will talk about transnational democracy and David Hume. Every now and then, we will look straight into the camera and say, "Turn the TV off. Stop surfing the Web. Read a book. Subscribe to *This Magazine,* the award-winning left-wing journal now celebrating its 35th year of publication."

We'll call it Global Divergence TV.

✦

What September 11 was not about
26 September 2001

Last week, instead of writing my column for this space I decided to take some time to reflect on the difference between Socrates and Plato.

In contrast to his ironic, inquisitive teacher Socrates, Plato is a creature of certainty. The Socrates we encounter in his dialogues is, sometimes, the mouthpiece for a conviction that the real Socrates did not favour. Socrates wondered, probed, and interrogated; the only thing he was certain of was his own ignorance. He knew wisdom begins in uncertainty.

You wouldn't know that from the rush to judgment that shaped the past two weeks. Middle-aged white men, writing in newspapers or appearing on television, leaped to offer their brand of instant wisdom. This was, they said, a moment of absolute clarity. The path was clear, the task certain.

These pronouncements had a Platonic air. The hay-making, axe-grinding pundits, using terrible events to advance their political agendas, were gripped, like Plato, by moral certitude. They saw the truth and the truth was theirs. This was good for them, I suppose, but very bad for the rest of us. A full catalogue of their various blame-laying exercises would take too long to sort out here, but let me offer a list of things the current situation is not about.

(1) It's not about taking sides, if taking sides means turning off our brains. From President Bush on down, we have been told that we are either for them or against them. This is effective, well-worn rhetoric in times of trial, but it is also dangerous—and contrary to the principles of an open society. Those who seek understanding of motives or causes are, Charles Krauthammer wrote the other day, "too philosophical for decent company." Really? That just sounds to me like stamping out intellectual challenge and dissent.

(2) It's not about Left versus Right. In times of crisis, debate gets quickly polarized and nuance, not truth, is the very first casualty of war. Old binary oppositions fell into place and, amazingly, 70s-era phrases of abuse came roaring back. If people once more get to say "bleeding-heart liberal," I figure it's only fair if we start calling it "the military-industrial complex" again. But you know what? None

of that helps us understand why this crisis has come, or what we can do about it.

(3) It's not about whether we are anti-American. Agonizing over our relationship to the United States has become a distracting sideshow, a theatre of stupid self-hate. Smug excoriations of the Canadian soul were offered under cover of patriotism and solidarity, a twisted logic that reached a pinnacle when a *Post* editorialist argued that we actually deserved to be snubbed by President Bush last week because we were such bad friends.

This is the tortured reasoning of the jilted but still obsessed ex-girlfriend. Please stop it. The Americans take us for granted; they always will. Being pro- or anti-American is simply irrelevant because they just don't care about us. We can't curry favour by self-abasement, and there's no point in being angry about it. Time to move on.

(4) It's not about the death of irony, the end of postmodernism, the demise of relativism, or the decease of postcolonialism. A couple of weeks after David Letterman cried on TV, irony is alive and well, thank you, and allied as always with a kind of moral seriousness that Socrates understood perfectly. Irony moves us beyond the given categories of received wisdom, the rigidities of the already-thought. In a healthy society, irony never goes away; it just becomes more militant.

As for postmodernism, which the *New York Times* gleefully autopsied the other day, it depends what we mean. If we're talking about the fashionable literary and philosophical theory that seduced the souls of various ambitious academics a while back, it was already long dead. If we mean, instead, the insight that people now perceive what they call "reality" through the surreal lens of media exposure, and have their emotional experiences as a form of bizarre collective spectacle, I invite you to reflect on events of the last two weeks.

Relativism is the thesis that one idea (of truth, of rightness) is as good as any other. No philosopher I know, even those who happily call themselves postmodern, would endorse such a thesis. For one thing, endorsing it means contradicting it, since the endorser thereby offers a non-relative truth claim. Truth isn't relative, but it is often local. We in the West have been trying to export our truths for some time now; obviously not everybody is convinced.

Postcolonialism says that a heedless imperial power will, sooner or later, face frustrating and perhaps devastating attacks launched from the margins of its bland influence. Over?

(5) It's not about manliness or patriotism. We've heard a lot about heroism during the last fortnight, and seen many examples of ordinary people doing extraordinary things. But courage comes in many forms, as Socrates once again knew very well, and speaking your mind is neither weak nor disloyal—on the contrary. The first duty of democratic citizens is not obedience but criticism. Without that, the very things that make Western society worth defending are reduced to nothing, and the attackers win again.

(6) No matter what people say, it's not about good and evil. Presidential rhetoric has backed off from the Christian fundamentalist tone that coloured so much of the initial response to the attacks, but the vestiges of the deepest polarization of all still linger. But calling something evil doesn't make it more clearly wrong, it merely throws up a cloud of emotion. And it's a game all sides can play.

Eduardo Galeano, in a recent essay called "The Theatre of Good and Evil," noted that Henry Kissinger had called "those who provide support, financing, and inspiration to terrorists" as guilty as terrorists themselves. "If that's how it is," Galeano wrote, "the urgent need right now is to bomb Kissinger. He is guilty of many more crimes than bin Laden or any terrorist in the world."

Is that a good argument? If not, why not? Let's start with questions like that and see where we get.

✦

We're experiencing an existential crisis
10 October 2001

You have to admit, the image of packaged (vegetarian) food sailing down from the sky even as cruise missiles and smart bombs were obliterating deserted (but nevertheless strategically important) training sites had a certain unignorable *Dr. Strangelove* quality. I couldn't help thinking of some perverse comedy sketch in which a lowly shipping clerk slapped the wrong labels on the payloads as they were off-loaded from a Skymaster somewhere in the desert, on their way to hang from the hardpoints of F-16s or drop from the cargo bays of C-130s, respectively. Devastating C-ration attacks! Nutritious humanitarian airstrikes!

Now I understand that humour, even black humour, has been ruled out of court by the rhetorical watchdogs who dominate the space above my little head there, so let's leave the Strangelove imitations to the politicians, whose deadpan delivery is beyond improvement, and the directions for how to fight the war to the hawkish pundits, who are so good at knowing better, and think about our dreams and nightmares instead.

What are the basic dreams of the modern West? First and foremost, to overcome death. Sure, we talk about individual freedom and personal happiness, but what we really want is individual immortality and some form of *perpetual* happiness. Technology in all its forms, materialism in all its glory, consumerism in all its excess—the point of these forces is to dominate and control nature, to eliminate the irrational, and to shore up shiny objects against the contingency of life. In their essence, they dream of punching through the limits of existence.

This dream always fails, for there is no bandwidth wide enough or processing chip fast enough to evade our natural limits. There is, furthermore, no bomb smart enough to eliminate the unresolved, chaotic remainder of anti-modern fanaticism, the dialectical flip of our dream: the nightmare that is dreaming's immanent opposite. We have evolved rules to manage ethical and political conflicts, institutions to distribute and guarantee personal liberties—truly great achievements, I believe, things indeed worth dying for—but they are not themselves greater than death.

Then there's history. It's been said, with some justice, that recent events are a reminder that not even America's comfortable Promised Land is immune from history—usually still meaning by that History, as in the slaughter-bench which Hegel said would produce world events, great personages, and a bloody but inexorable march towards Rationality and History's transcendent End. But that progressive view of History is another great dream of the modern West. The attacks are really a reminder, Francis Fukuyama notwithstanding, that history has not yet reached its end—and never will. A slaughter-bench, perhaps, but never a rational one.

And what of politics? The dream of all liberalism is that any disagreement can and will be accommodated by a larger scheme of agreement. Usually that agreement is procedural or minimalist, a cluster of rules and rights and responsibilities. Sometimes, with great luck and skill, we produce a wider and richer agreement that allows not just co-existence but a thriving community. But always there is a presumption that, if the rules are extended far enough and the basic equipment of the game made available to all, everybody will want to play. Why wouldn't they?

This is a worthy and powerful dream, but a dream nevertheless—a vision just as utopian and unreal as anything imagined by the socialist left. Not everyone wants to play our dream-game: not because they want more prizes but because they find the game rotten to the core. We can point out the contradictions inherent in Osama bin Laden's Casio watches and satphones and television broadcasts, but the bottom line is, *it doesn't make any difference to him*. No synthesis is grand enough to encompass his beliefs, no historical progression sufficiently rational to take him in.

What we are experiencing now, in other words, as we lash out at the spectral enemy who has infiltrated our dreamspace and made it so nightmarish, is nothing short of existential crisis. We are being forcibly reminded that there are limits to our aspirations, our power, our ability to control. Our dreams are in danger of being shattered.

The essence of terror, both individual and collective, is the destruction of security. But terror is also about creating massive, unresolvable frustration, a feeling of powerlessness that is corrosive of personal identity. We begin to wonder, in those grey post-oneiric hours of dawn, what it all means, what we're up to, why we do anything. There is no defence against this crisis except toughness of mind, and no offence against it which is not, always and already, compromised by ineffectiveness. We all know "America Strikes Back!" is just a slogan, suitable only for the bottom of a television screen.

Does saying that mean we shouldn't strike back this way, that we should seek peaceful negotiation and a conviction in the international courts? The question is beside the point, and not merely because the missiles have already been launched. The West's psychic integrity has been challenged and badly damaged. Attempting to kick and scream our way out of this nightmare is not a choice; it is just what we will do.

We have always had trouble accepting this. I recently met a born-again Christian who professed himself untroubled by the conflict of cultures in which we find ourselves, this battle for Western self-regard. He said that human justice was fallible and so God's justice alone was equal to judging the good and evil in the souls of both sides (or however many sides there are).

I listened to him carefully and thought: human justice is fallible, certainly, but it's the only kind there is. There are always too many gods, or too few, to save us. It is terrifying to realize we are all on our own, down here in the land of the mortals. But sooner or later, we have to grow up and look after ourselves, cherishing what is good in our dreams and bracing for the nightmares that must come, from inside as well as outside.

And then, as we all know but pretend not to, we die.

✦

Freedom, not security, is fundamental
24 October 2001

My buddy Todd, a criminal lawyer, got married not long ago and the other night he and his wife had a party for their friends in Toronto. During the speeches one of the guests remarked that Todd likes to tell people who find his job distasteful that it amounts to "quality control on the state"—defending those whose guilt had been unofficially assumed or bad character pre-decided. Yes, some of his clients are unsavoury types; and yes, some of them eventually go down to conviction for theft, assault, or even murder. The point is that they all deserve an able defence.

The same guest, also a lawyer (there were a lot of lawyers there), went on to say that this job has a special relevance now that the government is poised to deliver the legislative equivalent of the Chevy Corvair—though the Ford Pinto might provide a more apt comparison. The sweeping new security bill, C-36, currently under the scrutiny of a Special Senate Committee, is an example of what happens when the state makes law in reactive mode. In Canada's peculiar form of cozy oligarchy, where the doctrine of parliamentary supremacy is really just another way of saying the Liberals can do whatever the hell they want, quality control is more necessary than ever.

Personally, and I may just be giving in to cynicism here, I don't look to the Senate to provide it. Among other things, their review is supposed to confirm the government's claims that the bill has been "Charter-proofed": that is, worded so it won't violate the guarantees laid down in the Charter of Rights and Freedoms. The government doesn't want to be fighting a lot of expensive legal cases arising from C-36. But really—being cynical again, sorry—neither the senators nor the government's inside Charter "experts" inspire a lot of confidence about the wisdom of this bill.

The commonplace has it that the recent terrorist attacks have forced us to reconsider the implicit commitments of our way of life. Like many commonplaces, that is both true and false. Yes, we've been thrown back on ourselves and forced to consider what matters to us. But, as so often, it has become easy to lose focus and descend into a haze of sentiment and flag-waving and talking tough. The really important commitments are to much more abstract things, things it's hard to get emotional about but which nevertheless provide the basic structure of our lives.

I mean things like the rule of law, the idea of an open society, and the ongoing, fractious nature of genuine democracy. And, somewhere in there, the special status of civil liberties.

It's a persistent problem in liberal societies that people have trouble distinguishing Hobbes from Locke. (I realize they may not put it to themselves that way.) It's easy to see why. Both philosophers offered state-of-nature thought experiments, the founding myths of the liberal state in the West. Both considered contracting individuals the basic building-blocks of a society. Nevertheless, writing less than forty years apart and with England's Glorious Revolution in between, they define the opposite poles of political justification in the early modern period. And their ghosts are with us still.

Hobbes's Leviathan (1651) offers a terrifying picture of a natural state where, famously, human life is "solitary, poor, nasty, brutish, and short." The only solution to the perpetual war of all against all, Hobbes suggests, is the creation of a sovereign monarchical power with absolute authority; only through a sacrifice of complete (but self-defeating) liberty will we secure the conditions of peaceful co-existence. Or, to put in the terms offered recently by one of my students, security trumps freedom.

Locke, by contrast, begins his *Second Treatise of Government* (1690) with a picture of the state of nature that is less stark but no less untenable: individuals in this natural condition have powerful reasons to want to move out of it, not least to secure private property. The main difference is that the resulting social order is founded on an agreement that, as with all true contracts, can be rescinded at any time if the terms are broken. Unlike the absolutism of Hobbes's monarch, Locke's democracy is subject to constant vigilance by citizens and the possibility of revolution should the state exceed its justified limits. Here freedom, not security, is the foundation of a well-ordered society.

In times of trial, when the Hobbesian state of nature seems to threaten, we need to remember this relationship of priority. In reality, there is no such thing as the state of nature, nor a natural right to property; there is only the more or less successful attempts of human beings to arrange their political affairs as best they can. But a liberal society that puts freedom second—even for a moment, let alone three years—is one in danger of self-contradiction.

All law is a tightrope walk, a contingent and revisable attempt to hold in balance various kinds of goals: freedom, security, equality, justice. It is never perfect and, as I argued in my last column, it will never extend as far as we wish it to. The kernel of truth in the Hobbesian vision—a point made powerfully in the last century by thinkers like Carl Schmitt and E. M. Cioran—is that politics is always about conflict. Sometimes we manage that conflict, sometimes we avoid it, and sometimes, most rarely, we resolve it. But it never goes away for good.

Freedom entails many associated risks, first among them the possibility that elements both inside and outside the liberal state will find reasons (or, as we know, motives beyond reason) to resort to violence. We must protect ourselves from those threats, and liberalism, as the McGill University philosopher Charles Taylor has insisted, is "a fighting creed," but not at the cost of the one piece of moral authority liberals can claim for themselves, namely that they still put freedom first.

Right now, the Liberals are not being liberals. It's time for all of us to insist they get back to their own—our own—first principles.

✦

The Richler: a font of distinction
7 November 2001

The only time I ever attended the Giller Prize dinner, pinnacle of Toronto's literary party scene, was the year Mordecai Richler won for his novel *Barney's Version*. Like everyone else who was there, I have a vivid memory of Mr. Richler ascending the stage, black tie undone and tuxedo shirt unbuttoned at the collar, to accept the award. Along the way, he lamented the fact that he had never won the award he always really coveted, namely the Cy Young.

For those of you whose lives are impoverished by a want of baseball knowledge, the Cy Young Award is given every year to the best pitchers in the American and National Leagues. Cy Denton True Young was born in Gilmore, Ohio, in 1867 and set the modern standard for pitching, recording a total of 511 victories between 1890 and 1911, a mark that has not been equalled since and probably never will. In 1904, Cy Young pitched the first perfect game in modern baseball history. He died in 1955, when Mordecai Richler was 24 years old and about to publish his first serious work, *Son of a Smaller Hero;* his breakthrough novel, *The Apprenticeship of Duddy Kravitz,* would follow four years later.

What was endearing about Mr. Richler's comment was its boyishness, the infantile wish for a form of achievement that is simple and obvious and, after its admittedly insignificant fashion, heroic. In a year when the World Series, especially the ratings-topping Game Seven between the Arizona Diamondbacks and the New York Yankees, managed to be both intrinsically excellent and resistant to television's regnant jingoism, a boy's dream of growing

up to be a great pitcher is salvational. Innocence frankly acknowledged has its own kind of heroism.

The Giller Prize was awarded again in Toronto last night, but to my
mind the more interesting book-world announcement this week was
the news that Random House and the Giller Prize people had unveiled
a new typeface named after Mr. Richler. The new design includes those
little symbols that typographers call dingbats, used to separate or deco-
rate blocks of text. In this case, they illustrate aspects of Mr. Richler's
life and enthusiasms: cigars, whisky, baseball, fly fishing.

It's not the Cy Young Award, but for some of us it ranks up there.
In fact, the next time I get any kind of award I'm going to accept it
by noting that it's nice, but not as nice as getting my own typeface.
(I gave up on the Heisman Trophy a while ago.)

To be sure, Mr. Richler might not have been quite so enthusiastic
about this somewhat recherché form of tribute. "What would
Mordecai have thought?" wondered the Knopf Canada editor and
publisher, Louise Dennys. "He'd probably have been shocked.
He'd probably think we'd all gone crazy." She said that, unlike
some writers who want to influence type design for their books,
Mr. Richler was not "picky about that sort of thing."

Applied to writers by an editor, "picky" is a word that is really
code for "crazy and demanding." So it's another form of accolade to
note that an author often thought to possess a prickly personality
was so agreeable about something that makes lesser writers—I'm
thinking specifically of myself here—become deranged.

That's the way with enthusiasms: they can shade over into obsession, sometimes unpleasantly. For whatever complex of pathological
reasons, I love type design beyond all reasonable proportion. If a
typeface is ever designed for me, it will have to cope with the possibly self-defeating task of including a dingbat celebrating type design,

which would risk looking just like a letter. (That little conundrum would also satisfy another enthusiasm, namely for philosophical puzzles concerning sense and reference, use and mention.)

Anyway, back to Mr. Richler, baseball, and whisky. The same day we learned of the new typeface the papers also reported that sad news that the Montreal Expos are on the chopping block as Major League Baseball considers a contraction from 30 franchises to 28. Other teams at risk as the owners meet this week in Chicago include the Minnesota Twins and the Florida Marlins, both owners of past World Series titles. The Expos never won a title. Their best season, 1994, when they boasted a 74-40 record in August, ended prematurely because of a players' strike. The shrinking fan base and weak dollar mean the team is no longer viable.

Mordecai Richler could have written a brilliant novel about a city like Montreal losing a franchise like the Expos. I'm not sure any other contemporary novelist could, or would want to. Mordecai's Montreal is no longer with us, and it seems largely unlamented in the cultural power centre that is Toronto. And baseball hardly inspires romance right now. Other issues on the agenda at the owners' meetings are the perennial depressives of stadium relocation and a possible players' strike.

Even the Diamondbacks, the new World Champions, look like a franchise without a future. Their veterans, like Mark Grace and co-MVP pitchers Randy Johnson and Curt Schilling, are past their primes—which, significantly, they spent with other teams. Like the Marlins a few years ago, the Snakes are post-modern champs, the kind of cobbled-together team that exists in a B-list market and somehow manages to make a run for the title in a lucky year.

Don't get me wrong. It was a terrific series, and I'm glad the D'backs won—not least because I had a massive bet with my brother

Steve in Seattle, who for some reason took the Yankees. But it's hard to feel good about baseball right now, hard to feel good about Montreal and the loonie. It's hard to feel good about a lot of things.

Which means there's never been a better time to sit down, tumbler of the Macallan in hand, with a copy of *Cocksure* or *St. Urbain's Horseman,* typeset (for preference) in Richler. You'll feel better, believe me.

✦

There is no normal for the world to get back to
21 November 2001

George W. Bush spared the life of a turkey called Liberty the other day, as part of an annual little jape ceremony in the White House Rose Garden that is one of the underestimated perks of presidential office. The turkey, for its part, took the liberty of attempting to gobble Mr. Bush's genitals—or so, anyway, it appeared from the photo that ran alongside yesterday's news item. The Reuters report described the groin-area attack as "a few nervous pecks" which Mr. Bush "dodged."

An alternative bird called Freedom was absent from the ceremony, prompting Mr. Bush to make a ponderous joke alluding to the recent security-related scarcity of his vice-president, Dick Cheney. "Freedom is not here," Mr. Bush told the gathered children and reporters, "because he is in a secure and undisclosed location." Good one, George! Bahahaha!

It's American Thanksgiving tomorrow, and the traditional football-and-turkey holiday is somehow signalling that enough time has passed since September 11—and of course enough bombs fallen—for Americans to reassess their position in the world. Thanksgiving is the traditional beginning of the Christmas shopping season, marked of old by the Macy's Parade and the lighting of the Christmas tree in Rockefeller Center. Never mind that toy giant FAO Schwarz, whose flagship store dominates the corner of Fifth Avenue and Central Park South, has just been sold off and downsized. What with the successful Northern Alliance advance on Kabul and the 21.1 percent recovery of the Dow Jones industrial average, there is suddenly a sense of restored confidence.

In fact, Canadians can do our part to help things along, and not just by buying as many consumer goods as possible in the short month left before Christmas. Yesterday, *Financial Post* columnist Diane Francis urged Canadians to throng to New York for a "Canada Loves New York" rally on December 1st. Travel and accommodation discounts are ready. Roots, Inc. souvenirs are available. McDonald's Canada honcho George Cohon, a Chicagoan who is now (like Ms. Francis) a Canadian citizen, has been a big part of organizing the rally.

"We've got to struggle and fight and be strong and go after these terrorists, but we have to fight to get back to normality," Mr. Cohon said. "This rally is partly to show solidarity but it's also to get our psyches into doing stuff like this."

A trip to New York is never a bad idea, of course, and there are few cities in the world that look so good just before Christmas. But let's take a minute to remember what was supposed to be the deep lesson of the September attacks, namely that there is no normal to get back to. How many times have we been told during the past two months that the world was changed forever, that history was revisiting the prosperous West's pocket of smooth complacency, that the inevitable advance of globalism had to be rethought?

Now, scant weeks later, the prevailing wisdom seems to be that shopping and football and pardoning turkeys can set the world aright.

I was in New York myself 10 days ago and was struck by what many others have noted already, the amazing resiliency and good humour of the city's citizenry amid their eerily altered landscape. Personally, it makes me nervous to have a shaven-headed 19-year-old with an M-16 and a steely gaze watching me empty my pockets at airport security, and the makers of the HumVee must be delighted with the sudden ubiquity of their ugly machines, but mostly the effects of attacks were subtler.

I was in town to meet with editors about a book project, and together we gamely tried—and mostly failed—to imagine what the political world might be like 18 months from now, when I might conceivably deliver the manuscript. In the middle of one meeting with Doug Pepper, a transplanted Canadian editor who is also an old friend, we had to evacuate the building because of a phoned-in bomb threat. It was the fourth threat in 24 hours, and the occupants of the building wearily trooped out onto Park Avenue and mostly decided to call it a day.

It wasn't clear, by the way, whether the threats had been prompted by the UBS Warburg offices in the same building, some kook who appeared to be obsessed with the legendary editor Sonny Mehta, or some other kook who had been standing in front of the building with a sign reading "Random House = Elitism." (To nobody's surprise, that guy turned out to be a rejected author.)

This was the weekend that Mr. Bush addressed the United Nations and, for those who haven't already forgotten, it was the weekend before the Monday morning that saw another airplane crash into the fabric of New York City—this time, only an accident. Only.

It was also the weekend of a massive memorial service for the fallen firefighters of September. Doug and I went in search of a bar where we could continue our meeting and found them all jammed with burly, moustachioed firefighters from all over North America, many of them looking very Norman-Rockwell old-school in their double-breasted dress tunics, white gloves, and round hats.

Later, on Fifth Avenue near St. Patrick's Cathedral, four and five deep on the blocked-off street, I watched all these big-hearted tough guys weep openly as the air filled with the heart-tugging skirl of bagpipes. I watched them salute the slow procession of pumper trucks, lights flashing, as they floated silently down the avenue.

That was a Thanksgiving Parade, if you like—one filled with memory and mourning and a sense of history. One that loves New York, and human courage, without saying anything at all about things returning to normal. What we used to call normal is now, to paraphrase, in a secure and fully disclosed location. It's the same place you can find the dead, on both sides of this nasty and inconclusive conflict. It's known as the irrecoverable past.

Pardon me for saying so.

◆

A happy time for public education
5 December 2001

What an odd sensation to see the headline that dominated the front page of yesterday's *Post*! In big caps, we were told that Canada's public schools performed extremely well in a recent Organization for Economic Co-operation and Development study, scoring top-five grades in most categories, including second in reading and fifth in science among 15-year-olds from 32 industrialized countries.

Canada's public school performance vindicated by an international study? The news reported in the boy-this-country-sucks national newspaper? I thought I must be dreaming. Then I was overcome with a mild but unmistakeable feeling of happiness—not a common reaction to the front page of this paper, at least for me. For obvious reasons, including what looks like a lifetime career commitment, I like to think Canada's education system is among the best in the world. It seems I was right, and that's occasion enough for a little pre-holiday toast to the value of public education.

I don't teach 15-year-olds, indeed often have the feeling that by the time the students reach me the good effects of their secondary schooling have somehow worn off, replaced by surging hormones and an overpowering desire to make inane cell phone conversation. But that's probably just the result of early-onset crankiness, an occupational hazard. I have taught undergraduates in three different countries, including some gifted Ivy Leaguers, and the truth is that Canadian students are excellent—even if they can't always master the subjunctive or remember that the past participle of drink is drunk. (You'd think that one would be easy.)

It's the last week of fall classes at the University of Toronto, where I teach philosophy, and the usual end-of-term feelings are in the suddenly temperate air. For the students, a lot of stress about deadlines and juggled assignments, required readings skipped but now about to resurface on final exams, and thoughts about just how closely their family holidays might resemble the emotional train wreck depicted in Jonathan Franzen's *The Corrections*.

Not exactly a happy time, in short, especially if you are averse to piped-in Christmas carol medleys, Holiday Blend coffee specials, and the unwitting sadness of Christmas lights. And yet I have always loved this time of year on campus, both as a student and a professor. There is something of that feeling the novelist E. L. Doctorow associated with another outwardly idyllic scene, the late-summer picnic in Central Park: "We stroll around, watch some softball, find a grassy spot for ourselves, unwrap the deli heroes, uncork the Snapples, and prepare to have one of those balmy, ritually relaxing Sundays when the sense of loss is in every heart and a nonspecific melancholy seems to permeate the air."

This year in particular the term has been a period of strange, dreamy anxiety. It's not just the September temperatures that make the past three months feel like they passed in a slight haze. Nor does it help that, in politicians' speeches and television coverage anyway, the current melancholy (and anger and hatred) seems very specific indeed. Classes started this year on September 10th and they have, in ways both obvious and otherwise, been dominated by what happened the next day.

I am teaching two undergraduate courses this semester, one a short introduction to philosophy and the other in the philosophy of art and beauty. Both are second-year level but draw students from all over the university population, scientists and humanists, teenagers and retirees. Both have been lively and challenging and full of surprises. (Both have also demonstrated the seemingly insuperable tendency of some students to arrive late for class, doing so with a consistency and lack of apology that would have made an earlier generation of university professors apoplectic. But that's another column.)

I wondered, in both cases, how to talk about the terrorist attacks and the ongoing issues of retaliation, conflict between values, and propaganda. Contrary to what Margaret Wente apparently thinks, university classrooms are not sites of quasi-Marxist indoctrination where failed domestic revolutionaries get to twist the minds of hapless youngsters who just want to get a job. They are, at their best, places where the kind of questions that do not get asked elsewhere can receive an airing.

In the intro class we were reading Plato's *Republic* and the celebrated debate in Book One between Socrates (representing rational commitment to justice) and the Sophist Thrasymachus (representing a morally skeptical political realism). Justice, says Thrasymachus, is simply the advantage of the stronger; it is decided by conquerors and implemented on the weak. Making a connection to what was then being called Operation Infinite Justice was not difficult—though sorting out the resulting arguments was, as always, much more so.

In the aesthetics class the task was harder still, and arguably riskier, since I decided to poll the students on whether they had found the images of the exploding World Trade Center towers beautiful. (Mostly they opted for what seemed to me less troubling words, like "spectacular" or "overwhelming.")

You never know where a discussion like that will go—that's both the danger and the pleasure of teaching. You likewise never know who you will reach, or how deeply, or even when. The slouching smirker at the back of the room, constantly checking out the pretty field hockey star in the front row, turns out to be a brilliant logician. The young woman who always ate her lunch during class is the one who comes up to you at the end and says she won't think about the world the same way any more.

Sooner or later they'll all be job-seekers, yes, but before that they need to become citizens of the world. That's what public education is for, and that's what the citizens of our provinces pay for. Don't let anybody tell you otherwise.

✦

Football fan rage
19 December 2001

Seattle

There are two things you have to remember about the bottle-throwing incident that marred the end of the Cleveland Browns game against the Jacksonville Jaguars on Sunday before it gets blown out of proportion.

First, it gets cold in Cleveland in December, which means that even the hardiest fans are prone to irritation. And second, those bottles were made of plastic. One of these caveats arguably negates the other—frozen plastic bottles might be as painful as glass ones—but I don't think the fleeing referees were ever in serious physical danger. Nevertheless, the ugliness of the reaction should prompt a long-overdue elimination of the replay-challenge rule, a blight on the game.

For those who missed the mêlée, here's what happened. With less than a minute left in the game, Cleveland down 15-10 on fourth down, Browns quarterback Tim Couch threw to wide receiver Quincy Morgan, who appeared to catch the ball at the Jaguars' nine-yard line for a first down, goal to go. Crouch, who had no timeouts left to use, lined up his team and spiked the ball, stopping the clock. (For non-fans, this is standard practice: you burn a down to get a de facto playclock timeout while you consider your next play carefully.)

Meanwhile, however, the referees had called for a review of the previous play—a right they have under a three-year-old rule that is the NFL's equivalent of a Scrabble challenge. The coaches buzz the ref on a belt pager, like an errant limo driver, and he looks at a replay on a TV camera. If the call is reversed, the challenging team gets whatever advantage accrues (in this case, possession on downs); if the call stands, the challengers are punished by losing one of their timeouts. The Jacksonville challenge made perfect sense even if the Morgan catch was uncontroversial: they had timeouts to spare and wanted to stop what might be a game-winning Cleveland drive.

Now, Morgan's catch was in fact controversial—the challenge was mandatory given the time left, and the referees then reversed the completion call, starting all the ruckus. But it needn't have been. From the gamesmanship perspective, a well-placed challenge on even a mildly contentious play can halt the momentum of an opponent's drive and mess with their heads. The same thinking prompts a timeout before your opponent attempts a long field goal: you want the kicker, notoriously fragile of psyche and probably from some warm soccer-playing nation, to get cold and rattled.

The justification for the much-disliked instant-replay rule is that fans and players alike want to see the correct decision made, for the sake of the game. But that all depends on where you're sitting: inside a warm living room or in the stadium. I wouldn't go as far as Browns president Carmen Policy, who waved away the fans' reaction as mere enthusiasm, but pro football, always the most made-for-TV of sports, should take the opportunity to check its priorities.

I missed the Cleveland bottle-throwing incident because I was in the stands at Husky Stadium, the amenity-challenged University of

Washington facility that is the Seattle Seahawks' current home. The Seahawks were playing the hateful Dallas Cowboys, the New York Yankees of football.

For those of you who don't watch the Weather Channel or have friends in Vancouver, it's worth knowing that the Pacific Coast was in the grip of a major winter storm at the time. That means rain and wind beyond the imagination of even someone like me, who lived in Edinburgh for two years. It rained for hours and days together; it rained hard and it rained soft; it rained enough to float an Ark and then sink it. And all the time, the wind howled off the Pacific and stirred up dark-green chop on Lake Washington.

Though my friends laughed at me, I went to the game. I went alone, because my brother had suddenly remembered a party he had to attend in Vancouver. I put on two sweaters, three jackets, two with hoods, and a baseball cap. If I'd had waders or gaiters or plastic pants I'd have worn them too. Even so, I was badly equipped. In the stands around me, there were guys with more foul-weather gear than a SEAL strikeforce. These guys had camouflage bodysuits and collapsible windscreens; they had triple-layered waterproof ponchos and close-hooded Gore-Tex parkas; they had thick rubber electricians' gloves and heavy molded-sole duckhunting boots.

I was soaked through from the waist down by the end of the first quarter. By the end of the first half, when the last two minutes of play took about half an hour to get through, I had no feeling in my toes and was being buffeted around like a plastic scarecrow. Umbrellas were exploding in the wind. It was raining so hard you could barely see the ball.

Happily for all of us there, Seattle played well in a game they had to win to stay in even theoretical playoff contention. But what if the game had been close and the officials started messing with instant replays? What if a potentially game-winning drive had been halted—yet again—by the demands of television?

It's bad enough that the only person in a football stadium who really controls time is not the head referee but a TV-network official with a pair of Day-Glo orange sleeves. He's the guy who calls the "TV timeouts," otherwise known as commercial breaks. By now fans at the stadium know two other things: (1) they are a necessary part of the hugely profitable spectacle that is sold to television every Sunday; and yet (2) the League doesn't really give a damn about them.

You can't get beer at Husky Stadium, in plastic bottles or otherwise. The strongest drug on offer is caffeine, and I doubt a shower of styrofoam Starbucks cups would kick up the same stir as the rain of bottles in Cleveland. Next year the Seahawks will move into a brand-new stadium. But you know what? Calls made on the field should stay on the field. The instant-reply rule isn't good for football, it's only good for TV. High time the League spared a thought for the monster fans, not the sofa spuds, and ditched it.

✦

The meaning of icing
6 March 2002

New York

"I think this is a group that thinks the rules as they are are just fine. These meetings will be more philosophical talks about changes than actual changes."

—Chicago Blackhawks general manager Mike Smith

"The rules are just fine," remarked Bettman, as he and the Thirty Tyrants strolled through the public square of Naples (Florida).

"But come, Bettman," I said, plucking his sleeve, "you cannot actually hold such a view. We have only recently seen the Olympians play, and everyone agrees it was awesome. We must now take the opportunity to ask what hockey really is. Surely it is not a simple thing, like a carpenter's hammer or a horse's fetlock, but instead a complex one, like the harmonious chord produced by a happy marriage of musician's skill, well-tuned instrument, and hearer's pleasure."

"What?"

"I mean," I said, "that the fans are part of the game. Also, there are issues of balance and degree. For instance, you will perhaps tell me it is universally known a man may not cross into the zone ahead of the puck."

"We call it offside."

"Assuredly you do. But recall the tag-up exception, which possessed force until recently. If the attacker dumped the puck in behind his forwards, they could swiftly retreat to the blue line and attack again. No offside was called!"

"So?"

"Does an exception not prove that a rule is the changeable creation of men, and by men can be changed? The blue line would seem to be a fluid and contingent thing, not the necessary essence it appears to be when painted straight across the rink. Or do you not agree?"

"Whatever. I just think things are fine the way they are. The tag-up rule actually meant more dump-and-chase, because defencemen didn't have to carry the puck in. Plus, guys kept getting injured on the opposite point when the puck was fired around the boards. A couple of defenders were always waiting to crunch them."

"Ah," I said. "But you will, I think, grant me that dump-and-chase sucks? That it is a degeneration of capital-H hockey? Of hockeyhood? Hockeyness? Hockeytude?"

"Stop it. Yes."

"So how can you evade the argument, now commonly to be heard among us, that the red line should be eliminated? Did you not see the long grace of those Olympic passes, the thrilling end-to-end breaks? Even you must have noticed how the Swedish torpedo made the Canadians look stupid in the first game. If the blue line is mutable then surely the red is all the more so?"

"Yeah, well who won the gold medal?" Bettman replied without relevance. "Anyway, people seem to forget that the red line was introduced in 1943 to speed games up, not slow them down, and to reduce offsides. It works because not every team, or every line, is as good at passing as those Olympic teams were."

There came a chorus of agreement in the small square.

"If there's no red line," said the disagreeable one from New York called Sather, "there would be 40 icing calls a game. And not nearly as much forechecking as now."

"No red line will not do what people think it will do," added Lamoriello, who lived across the river from Sather in New Jersey. "You'll see the trap more and more. I like to see quick skating and passing." Lamoriello blushed slightly as he said this, since his own team was notorious for favouring this very same trap; but I let the contradiction pass.

"Eliminating the red line will eliminate physical confrontations," said Smith. "In the city in which I work, the fans like physical confrontations."

There was general laughter at this remark, because it is well known among us that the citizens of Chicago could make even Spartans quake in their boots if they came to town for an away game.

I was not put off by their objections, however. I felt that we had not yet touched on the fundamental questions of time and space.

"But surely," I began, "the Olympics taught us that a truly exciting contest takes place within two hours, not the three or more we now often see. And the larger ice surface acted not unlike a thaumaturge's spell, liberating every aspect of the game. Gentlemen, you must grant me that shorter and more exciting games are what the fanciers of hockey deserve? And while we're at it, how about a no-fighting rule so players can exhibit athletic prowess instead of getting mauled by goons like Brashear?"

Bettman started shaking his head in a world-weary manner. I sensed that my many cogent arguments had somehow failed to penetrate his soul.

"We think fans like fighting," he said. "We'll probably try some version of the 15-second faceoff rule, maybe 20 or 25 seconds. But you have to remember, this is a commercial enterprise. We have ads to sell and need breaks to do it in. And those 15 extra feet of ice, even if we could do it in some of the buildings, which we can't, equal a lot of prime seating." The Thirty Tyrants all nodded sagely.

"It's the quality of the players that makes the tournament, not the rules," Smith said, repeating their favoured sophistry.

I gazed at them in consternation. "You are confusing commercial motives with what is good for the game," I said. "You are forgetting the fans. Surely it was truly said that the physician acts to heal not when he is concerned with money, but only insofar as he exercises skill for its own sake? Is it not the same in hockey?"

But Bettman was already moving off, followed by the others. I called after them: "You can't go yet, gentlemen. We haven't even discussed the meaning of icing!"

They did not heed my call.

✦

Let glass and steel scrape the sky again
20 March 2002

New York

On a Monday, six months after the destruction of the World Trade Center, the crowd at the summit of the Empire State Building, now Manhattan's tallest, is scarce. The longest wait is for security clearance at the base of the tower, and the usually interminable queue to buy tickets, where punters are bombarded with hectoring calls to spend more of their money on package deals and filmshow extras, is mercifully short.

You take the first elevator 80 floors up. Then another one climbs the final six storeys and opens onto the clean lines, criss-cross steel fences, and art deco details of the Observation Deck, a place wrapped in layers of cinematic memory and popular mythology, the ghosts of Cary Grant and Deborah Kerr, of Meg Ryan and Tom Hanks, even (if you've been paying attention) of Michael J. Fox and a couple of his "Spin City" character's ex-girlfriends. Not to forget King Kong—in the early versions anyway. As with so many parts of New York, even if this is your first visit, you know you've been here before.

Or, if you have in fact been here before, maybe when you were young and in love, this time feels different. Of course it does. It is a cold clear day and visibility is superb. Unlike the commanding vista once offered by the Twin Towers, which made the whole of Manhattan stretch out in front of you like a triangular urban landscape, with undulating densities and craggy peaks, including the Empire State itself, this picture is a composite. You must walk around all four ledges to put the city together, piece by piece.

The south side is crowded. People point out to each other what is actually unmistakeable, the hole in the sky where the Twin Towers used to stand. Absence as presence, a kind of retinal after-image whose wavering spectral outlines the mind seems unwilling to accept. A big American flag hangs on the building near City Hall whose height blocks the view of Ground Zero itself.

People gaze out as well as down, and you follow their looks into the bright sky. Airplanes are making their way across the domed air, deceptively stately, even peaceful, at this distance. Visually, they don't give away their terrific speed and power, their coiled kinetic energy and bombloads of jet fuel. Just streaks of lovely silver leaving trails of vaporized fluid behind them, thin straight lines of possibility.

Standing there, cold and alone, you can't help imagining the converging vectors, the bending flight paths that would connect one wonder of twentieth-century technology with another at the point where you stand.

"The skyscraper and the airplane were born side by side, and ever since then have occupied adjacent rooms in our collective unconscious," the critic Adam Goodheart wrote not long ago in *The American Scholar*. "Before the fire, before the ash, before the bodies tumbling solitary through space, one thin skin of metal and glass met another. Miles apart only moments before, then feet, and then, in an almost inconceivable instant, only a fraction of an inch. Try to imagine them there, suspended: two man-made behemoths joined in a fatal kiss. Fatal, fated: perhaps even long foreseen."

Perhaps, though that sense of precious fatalism misses the wonder, the mechanical joy, of these two quintessential inventions of the passing epoch. Their collision six months ago marks the end of an era and a reminder of the clashing fundamentalism between two world religions (one of which doesn't see itself as a religion), but it cannot diminish the soaring beauty that was turned so heinously to destruction. Technology abused is no argument against technology.

Architects suggested then that the era of the skyscraper was over for good, but you cannot believe it. Born in the congested real-estate of Manhattan and Chicago, built to new and almost unfathomable heights in Hong Kong and Kuala Lumpur, the skyscraper is, as a nineteenth-century engineer said, the evolution of building from crustacean to vertebrate. Steel beams give us the ability to construct spines and hang floors from them; elevators the chance to reach beyond the six or eight storeys of human fatigue.

Sometimes desire rises to mad levels of transcendence. Fantasy skyscrapers of the early modern period show whole country estates lifted into the sky on steel platforms, the transported comforts of home built into thin air where, in fact, only the pressurized, womblike airplane can really go. The human need to rise up, to touch or even inhabit the sky, does not cease. A fatal collision may be implicit in the two beautiful machines, the pillar and messenger, the Atlas and Mercury of our world, but so are the deepest aspirations of human life.

Now, six months on, the love of the skyscraper and the airplane is surging back. Long paeans to the chunky Woolworth building, or the light-absorbing Seagram, appear almost weekly in the press. Habitually jaded New Yorkers, principled opponents of looking up, can be seen gawking openly as late-afternoon sunshine lights up the tough volume of the Empire State, or nighttime mist transforms the Chrysler Building, William Van Alen's unimprovable art deco rocketship, into a romantic Tim Burton vision, a peerless symbol of Gotham.

Meanwhile, the forces of memory and money, the public and private interests, try to make sense of that tear in the fabric of Lower Manhattan—so far inconclusively. Memorial or replacement? Building or monument? Today, when darkness has fallen on this half-year afternoon, two beams of light will pierce the sky to heights much greater than the lost buildings themselves. And you, because the day's airplanes stayed on course, will be able to watch from the ground, down there with all the other aspirants inhabiting the grid.

And the next day, rising in an airplane over the wounded island, you will think: Build high, architects; scrape the sky again. New beauty, a wonder of glass and steel, is the best memorial.

✦

Dihydrogen monoxide and the city
3 April 2002

New York

Today begins the second week of a Stage One drought emergency in New York City and, seven days in, I still can't get anyone to talk about it.

"The city reservoirs are usually 92 percent full this time of year," I said to the guy at the deli downstairs, getting my coffee one morning. "Right now they're at less than 50 percent."

He looked at me with no particular expression on his face. "Bagel?" he said.

"Not since 1989 has a drought emergency been declared in the city itself," I told a cabbie on my way uptown for a dinner date. "This has been the driest winter in decades, with an average of just 8.21 inches of rain. That's half of what's normal. It's also, just so you know, 21.35 centimetres."

He stared straight ahead. "You want me to stay on Sixth or go over to Park?"

"The city uses something like 1.2 billion gallons of water a day," I told my roommate, an Italian fashion photographer. "The mayor is hoping restrictions and voluntary constraint will draw that down to a billion gallons a day."

"I can't hear you, Mark," she said. She was running a bath.

"The drought conditions extend all the way from Maine to Georgia," I informed my political theory class. "The federal government has issued warnings for the whole Eastern Seaboard. New Jersey imposed statewide restrictions three weeks ago. In addition to the emergency in the city, which also affects Westchester, Putnam, Ulster, and Orange Counties, New York has placed drought warnings on 21 other counties."

"Will this be on the exam?" one of them asked.

Now, I understand that crisis is a fact of life in New York, and the cultivation of insouciance a general imperative. It is considered deeply, paralyzingly uncool to show concern for anything that might excite notice or fear in normal people. For instance: when the man on the sidewalk in front of you begins screaming and climbing the lamppost, or if a piece of the street suddenly falls away in a subterranean dropout, your preferred move is simply to walk on by, perhaps humming a tune. On no account should you acknowledge a problem, or indeed that anything at all is happening.

At the same time, incredibly trivial things, things that people in other parts of the world would consider beneath interest, should call forth a psychotically extreme response. An absence of skim milk at the coffee prep station. A hesitant driver who causes you to break stride and lose precious nanoseconds crossing a street against the light. Once you grasp this reversal of polarity, much of the apparent oddness of New Yorkers disappears.

But the lack of reaction to the drought emergency seemed to go beyond even this. Water is, after all, the essence of life. Humans cannot survive without a steady, clean supply of it. And New York's water system is one of its great infrastructural success stories. For a city so big and complex, the drinking water is remarkably plentiful and clean; it tastes good even without a filter, and won't hurt you. I've tried in vain to visualize what 1.2 billion gallons looks like—a 12-foot-deep swimming pool the size of Central Park? an aqueous version of the Empire State Building?—but I do know that it's *a hell of a lot.*

Now that supply is dangerously low, and nobody seems to care. Ironically, the first few days of the emergency were marked by fairly intense rainstorms—not enough to make a significant difference, especially upstate where the reservoirs are, but further eroding any sense of urgency. Car washing and lawn watering were being restricted throughout the city, but those are activities that, in my part of lower Manhattan anyway, seem impossibly suburban and alien. It must suck not to be able to water your lawn up in Westchester, but really, who cares? Here, you turn on the tap and water still comes out. Where's the crisis?

Some people even began to wonder if water was really so great anyway. Since the drought emergency began, New Yorkers have been passing around the address of a spoof website that details the dangers of the toxic agent known as "dihydrogen monoxide" (www.dhmo.org). "Each year," the site says, "dihydrogen monoxide is a known causative component in many thousands of deaths and is a major contributor to millions upon millions of dollars in damage to property and the environment."

Some of the associated dangers include: "death due to accidental inhalation of DHMO, even in small quantities" and the fact that "gaseous DHMO can cause severe burns" while "prolonged exposure to solid DHMO causes severe tissue damage." The chemical is used, among other things, to assist in abortions and improve the performance of elite athletes. Meanwhile, the Environmental Protection Agency "refuses to deny" it is involved in a coverup of the toxin's dangers.

Around this time, the shower in my somewhat shabby West Village apartment malfunctioned. When you turned the handle, brown sludge dripped from the showerhead. The bath still worked, so my roommate was unperturbed, but to me it felt like a special warning. Should I step up my efforts? Did I have a mission as the harbinger of drought-danger?

But no. I had it all wrong. In the economy of doom that is modern urban life, this isn't a crisis at all. The mayor can say emergency if he likes, and hand out fines to people washing cars, but it's not like there's, you know, an emergency. We've got nine or 10 months of supply in the reservoirs. The rain will come sooner or later. We can always drink the Hudson.

Meanwhile, there's war in Israel, war in Afghanistan, what to do with Ground Zero, and the prospects of Yankee pitching. In New York, even doom has to wait in line.

✦

When the pact of civility breaks down
17 April 2002

New York
In the new film *Changing Lanes,* Samuel L. Jackson plays Doyle, a reformed alcoholic having a very bad day. There's a moment when he is tempted to drink a glass of bourbon. He calls his AA sponsor

and instead of downing the shot he opts for multiple verbal and physical assaults, destruction of property, creating a disturbance, resisting arrest, and attempted murder.

I badly needed a drink myself at one point in this movie. Well, no; there was more than one. But the biggie was when Amanda Peet, as the gorgeous young wife of a slick lawyer played by Ben Affleck, advises her husband to stay in the legal game even though he's suddenly discovered rampant corruption in his tony Wall Street firm.

"I could have married an honest man," Peet says, and you think, well sure, because she's so good-looking she could have married anybody. "I could have married a professor of Middle English, with tenure at Princeton. But I married a Wall Street lawyer."

I'm not sure what got me most: the implication that teaching Middle English at Princeton is somehow boringly honest, or the sure knowledge that Amanda Peet will never go out with me because I have tenure.

I know, I know: it's just a movie. But where was my whisky? I was powerfully reminded that the *New Yorker* critic Anthony Lane, reviewing the other urban-paranoia movie now in theatres, *Panic Room,* confessed a desire for strong drink during its viewing, though for evidently different reasons.

Panic Room and *Changing Lanes* are both tales of conflict at the margins of society, both take place in New York, and both flirt with the idea that social order is fragile. One is small, even claustrophobic, and succeeds as pure thriller. The other tries to be larger, even cosmic, and becomes sick comedy; it makes reflection on the social covenant into *The War Between the Tates.*

Changing Lanes, co-written by Chap Taylor and Michael Tolkin, who also wrote *The Player,* shows how a routine event—a fender-bender involving two men both late for court dates—could easily escalate into a terrifying confrontation not only between them but with law, order, divinity, and the very idea of goodness. This morning you failed to exchange insurance information; by the afternoon you are the victim and/or perpetrator of attempted murder and million-dollar fraud.

This is mostly silly. "Sometimes God likes to put two guys in a paper bag and let 'em rip!" Affleck's character yells an hour in. At a priest. In a confessional. On Good Friday.

We understand: he is frustrated.

The two men, so stereotypically different in age, class, race, and intelligence, are nearly identical in one respect. They are both borderline sociopaths who amply deserve each other. Bourbon or no bourbon, Jackson's Doyle is addicted to irrational rages. His AA sponsor knows it, and his estranged wife goes so far as to say that's exactly why she's taking their two kids to Oregon, where there are "thousands of dull bearded guys." (Portland's cool quotient just went way down.)

Affleck's Gavin isn't hysterical, just naive to the point of idiocy. Is it really possible he reached the age of 29, and a law partnership, without acquiring either more guts or more savvy? Either way, he's a dork. His father-in-law, the firm's sleazy senior partner, is played by Sydney Pollack. Did Gavin miss *Eyes Wide Shut?* You never trust Sydney Pollack when he's wearing Armani and talking about sailboats.

There's a moment, about five minutes from the end, when the two men meet and realize that events and other people's decisions have outpaced their revenge-becomes-redemption storyline: off battling each other, they've been snookered. The film should have ended there, with the two of them battered, dazed, and not one whit wiser. That would have been cool. Instead, inevitably, we endure a denouement involving Gavin's late-hour power play at the law firm (now coerced into some pro bono work) and Doyle getting his kids back. I felt like booing. Doyle's a raging nutbar! Gavin lives in moral infancy! Did we all suddenly forget that?

But the real problem is the suggestion that New York is where the pact of civility is most likely to break down. Michael Tolkin has obviously been spending too much time in Los Angeles, where everyone drives. It's way too easy to go morally nuts in a car. Here you have to walk, and the sheer proximity of eight million other people elevates social interaction well beyond some Hobbesian state of suspended war into a daily triumph of cooperation. This city is a throbbing success story, not merely of competitive individualism but of its twinned opposite, shared aspiration.

You miss this if you focus on the alleged rudeness of New Yorkers. Sure, some New Yorkers are rude. But there are rude people everywhere, and lots of apparent rudeness is really just the verbal equivalent of a high five. Walking in Manhattan always reminds me of an old cartoon in which two New Yorkers pass each other, both saying "Fuck you!" even as their thought-bubbles say "Have a nice day!" In the second panel, two Los Angelenos pass each other and the sentiments are reversed.

Changing Lanes begins with a set of crude premises about human nature and proceeds to get tangled up in its own illogic. In this nightmare world, the advocates of civility are either sanctimonious (William Hurt as the AA sponsor) or ridiculous (an overly earnest law student). Genuine civility is neither; it is, instead, the most mundane and demanding of virtues, a daily attempt by imperfect beings to make space for each other.

On my way home from the theatre, three people apologized to me when, lost in thought, I bumped into them. I used to think that only happened in Canada. "Fuck you!" I said to them happily.

✦

Left, right, left, right, fly a kite
1 May 2002

New York

It's May Day so, like any self-respecting left-wing wacko, I rose this morning with a glad heart, sang the *Internationale* in a loud voice, and ran downstairs to lecture the guys at the deli about anarcho-syndicalism.

"Die Strasse ist dialektische!" I cried, indicating the tree-lined street outside, which could so easily be turned into a barricade. "Revanchist lackeys!" I yelled at the colourists and razor-cut specialists from the beauty parlour next door. "You are mired in laxity and eclecticism!"

Then I read the papers and my sprightly mood was broken. Seems Canadians can no longer tell their Left from their Right, if they ever could. Three-quarters are dim or fuzzy on the whole thing and fewer than half, according to the new Compas poll, correctly identified the ideological bearings of the Canadian Alliance.

That's no surprise, really, when you think about ... well, whatever the hell the Alliance has done. (Don't worry, it won't take long.) The more troubling issue is what the results mean for the rest of us. Herewith, a summary:

(1) It's a great opportunity to blame the French. I know everybody's doing it right now, but don't let that stop you. They invented the Left/Right business when they sat down in the new National Assembly of 1789, and even then they must have known it was a crazy idea. Blaming the French also creates amusing strange-bedfellow moments, like finding myself in agreement with Mark Steyn, who had himself a good time the other day blasting the

"Eurosnots" for, I don't know, supporting fiscally responsible democratic socialism or something, and carefully correcting those of us who misunderstand the politics of Jean-Marie Le Pen. Mr. Steyn demonstrated that M. Le Pen is not an extreme right-wing madman—a designation the writer reserved for himself—but a nationalist socialist.

Good to know. Furthermore, and deftly anticipating the Canadian poll, Mr. Steyn advised that we "might as well throw away the compass" when it comes to French politics. An electoral choice between President Jacques Chirac and Prime Minister Lionel Jospin "boils down to a candidate who's left of right of left of centre, and a candidate who's right of left of right of left of centre."

Okey-dokey. Just remember: Stupid French. Stupid, stupid French.

(2) Unfortunately for them but very good for the rest of us, the poll results put most of Mr. Steyn's fellow right-wing madmen out of business. They can no longer use the terms "left-wing," "lefty," or "left-leaning" as handy pejoratives whenever they happen to disagree with somebody. John O'Sullivan, writing recently in these pages about M. Le Pen, is in even more trouble. Inventing desperate new labels—post-fascist, post-communist—he indulged a flurry of derangement about the current mood of voters in the land of Descartes and Derrida. It's really much simpler. Repeat after me: Stupid French.

Of course, I will have to curb my own use of "right-wing jerk" and "fascist asshole." But I got over that a while back, right around the time I realized that most people who use "left-wing" and "right-wing" without irony are boring—a far more important designation, and one most Canadians have no trouble making.

(3) The after-poll hand-wringing suggested the results were a function of ignorance. "In 20 years of teaching at Canada's top

research university I have never assumed that first- and second-year students have understood the left-right spectrum," said Sylvia Bashevkin, a political scientist at the University of Toronto. "There is a lamentable lack of political education in the school system."

No, there's a lamentable lack of education in the school system. If we started doing polls on all the things people don't know, we'd be buried in paper before the end of the summer. Besides, see (1) above: Mark Steyn says throw away the compass, and who are we to disagree?

If you want to try a new and improved compass instead, you can always take the test on www.politicalcompass.org, a British website that plots your answers to various questions along two vectors: economic (left/right) and social (authoritarian/libertarian). As the site says, this can help explain reactionary socialists like Robert Mugabe as well as reform-minded fiscal hardliners like Margaret Thatcher.

For the record, I took the test and scored minus 6.75 on the first scale and minus 7.13 on the second, hanging me in the far bottom corner of the resulting biaxial diagram, well to the left of "Red" Ken Livingstone, Mayor of London, and decidedly more libertarian than Mahatma Gandhi, that fascist asshole.

(4) Does this all mean that Canadians don't care about politics? Well, let's be charitable: call it a mixture of apathy and bafflement.

The bafflement is widely shared. Michael Bérubé, writing in *The Chronicle of Higher Education* this week, gamely tries to untangle the ideological differences between Christopher Hitchens and Tariq Ali, both prominent "men of the left" who debated each other in Washington last month. "The Hitchens left is soft on American imperialism," Bérubé writes, "and the Ali left is soft on Islamist radicalism." After that, it all gets a little cloudy, with mounting tensions and comical contradictions reminiscent of that scene in Monty Python's *Life of Brian* when the People's Liberation Front of Judea breaks ranks with the Judean Popular People's Liberation Front.

That joke is never as funny when applied to political reactionaries, for some reason—maybe because they are off building F-16s and making loads of dough instead of arguing doctrinal differences. But clearly the real issue here is the drive in all ideology for a foolish consistency, what William James once called "the hobgoblin of little minds."

See, once you give up trying to fit the contents to the package, you have to get down to the business of actually debating issues, one by one. It's hard work. In baffled post-ideological Canada, that fiscally conservative social welfare constitutional monarchy, we take a smoother road. We just elect the Liberals and forget about it.

✦

Has Chirac anointed a French philosopher-king?
15 May 2002

New York
One interesting wrinkle from the recent French presidential election, the one between the crook and the fascist, is the appointment of the philosopher Luc Ferry as education minister in the new Chirac cabinet. (For those keeping score, Chirac is the crook. Probably.) This is of course less bizarre in modish France than it would be here in Imperial Gumpland, say, where stupidity and virtue are widely considered identical. But it's still raising an

eyebrow or two. Is M. Ferry, a Sorbonne professor still young at 51, angling for the job of philosopher-king? Does he have transcendental ambitions beyond the youth, education, and research portfolio?

Immediate reaction to the appointment centred on M. Ferry's politics, variously described as "right-wing," "neo-conservative," and "liberal-democrat." Employing the Marky-Mark Steyn/Kingwell triangulation method, I figure that places him somewhere in the region of Isaiah Berlin or Colin Powell. M. Ferry is mostly known for his attacks (with co-author Alain Renault) on the four main icons of what is boringly but inevitably called "postmodern radicalism": Derrida, Foucault, Bourdieu, and Lacan. M. Ferry and M. Renault suggested that these influential purveyors of "68 thought," though ostensibly revolutionary, were really just intellectual nihilists, marching in a kind of late-Marxist lockstep devoid of positive purpose or coherence. In the process of laying bare power's social construction, the intellectual heirs of 1968 had cut the ground out from under themselves.

A good deal of this critique was motivated by sheer resentment, I imagine, or by that form of patricidal bloodlust common in scholarly circles at least since Aristotle trashed Plato's theory of the Forms in the *Nicomachean Ethics*. But some of the points are well taken. Foucault's attacks on the surveillance society, and its invisible structures of soft domination, can find spectres in every corner, in the process levelling the distinction between society at large and actual brute instances of domination. Derrida's theory of deconstruction is notoriously ambidextrous when it comes to real-world policy. And Lacan's psychoanalytic innovations contain very little political substance of any kind—though that is hardly a point against them.

Bourdieu presents a different case, since his consistent, Veblenesque sociology of power's masks and deceptions—always pointed, never silly—would be a breath of fresh air in any political culture. He also grappled with the issue that now most afflicts the new education minister: the inside-outside place of the intellectual in society. Bourdieu's most popular and successful book, *Sur la télévision,* was a spirited attack on mass culture and the made-for-TV intellectuals who courted it. But, in a typical twist, the argument of the book was first presented by Bourdieu himself in the form of a prime-time television program.

M. Ferry's entry into the Chirac cabinet takes to a new level the usual hazards of public intellectual life—the sort of thing analyzed with such heavy-handed disdain in Richard Posner's recent book, just the latest in a long series of complaints, arguing that public intellectuals are traitors to scholarship. Now M. Ferry is not merely in danger of being what Bourdieu called *"un fast-thinker,"* cutting his ideas down to sound-bite size and currying favour with the editors of *Le Nouvel Observateur* or *Le Point.* (Or, like Harvard-now-Princeton superstar Cornel West, cutting a rap album instead of lecturing to pesky undergraduates.) He is flirting with the much deeper, and more dangerous, contradictions of Plato's decision to leave the security of Athens and sail to Syracuse, there to advise the tyrant Dionysus the Younger on the creation of an ideal state.

The overpowering desire to put ideas into play, what the critic Mark Lilla has nicely labelled "the lure of Syracuse," is more common among philosophers, especially those devoted to political ideas, than many people realize. Fortunately for everyone, most of them never do much about it. Occasionally, with the right amount of fame and friends in high places, they get to stick their hands in the dirt, and this is mostly bad news. In a recent essay collection,

The Reckless Mind, Mr. Lilla details the disastrous political flirtations of various twentieth-century philosophers on both the left and right of that old ideological spectrum. (In practice, this means Marxists such as Sartre as well as Nazis such as Heidegger.) His conclusion is the perhaps obvious one that philosophers need to master "the tyrant within": that restless urge to take hard-won abstract truths and make them concrete.

Plato himself, after a couple of disappointments with the well-meaning but ruthless Dionysus, came to the same conclusion. His celebrated defence of the philosopher-king in *The Republic* is much better read, as Allan Bloom and others long suggested, as an ironic warning to ambitious young proto-philosophers to steer clear of politics. The same erotic urge is at work in both the philosopher and the tyrant. They both want, in a sense, to master the world. But when the line between love of truth and love of personal satisfaction blurs, the results range, on the evidence, from the inept to the heinous.

Luc Ferry is no idiot. I'm sure he knows all this. I just hope he remembers it, and avoids the delusion of thinking he can solve one of human thought's oldest paradoxes. Philosophy, dedicated to getting things right, is always coming up against its own limits. Its task is by nature both infinite and outcast, and therefore cannot be translated into policy or power. At the same time, the desire so to translate is embedded in philosophical thought itself; but that translation would, in turn, undermine the original validity of the thought; and so on, to the end of the world.

A philosopher can certainly enter politics, even do some good there, but the hard truth is that he must, in so doing, give up being a philosopher. Thinking otherwise means politics and philosophy both lose—and so, in turn, do we all.

✦

This is not a column about the Middle East conflict
29 May 2002

New York

As one of my colleagues pointed out on this page last week, I was recently included in a list of columnists who had, according to a press release from the Canadian Islamic Congress, "directly or implicitly suggested ... that Palestinians, Arabs, and Muslims are most to blame for the Middle East conflict." The reasons for this remain murky, since (as the writer noted) I have "meticulously stayed away from" the subject of the Middle East.

That made it sound as though I have no opinion on the insane mess in the Middle East, though, and of course such a thing is intolerable to any self-respecting purveyor of instant op-ed wisdom. The other writers indicted by the CIC, many of them members of the Moral Clarity Brigade, a couple of former or quasi-Canadians living in Washington and New Hampshire, have not dropped the ball in such an egregious manner. Indeed, in the months since last September their rhetoric about this, that, and the other has only grown more self-assured and peremptory. The depravities of the Israel-Palestine quagmire have been assessed in their turn, and explained with the rigour and simplicity of a problem in trigonometry.

This is excellent, because that's what commentary journalism is supposed to be. Like so many other grateful readers, I turned with relief from the news pages and television broadcasts, where all is mayhem and confusion and dead bodies, and found solace in the smooth definite phrases of condemnation. I was made to understand that suicide bombings undermine all possible claims to grievance, maybe the very idea of a claim itself. I came to see that self-defence is a value whose authority necessarily extends to bull-dozing homes, aggressive sniping, and erecting barbed-wire fences pretty much wherever you want.

So far, so good. But then doubts crept in, the feelings of certainty grew wispy, and the mathematical proofs came apart in my hands. Awkward facts obtruded, such as the knowledge that Israel has never formally recognized the right of a Palestinian state to exist anywhere—the sort of concession that might be thought basic to, well, pretty much anything else.

And that's when I realized that most examples of op-ed clarity, dispensed in wet brightly coloured spurts, like aerosol cheese, were no longer doing it for me. After all, a truly reasonable position about the Middle East conflict reduces quickly to four, maybe five, linked propositions. Namely:

(1) Suicide bombing may be, in the words of the bitterly funny online comic strip "Get Your War On" (www.mnftiu.cc), "literally the freakiest human act possible. Seriously, what could a human do to themselves that would be more bizarre and scary?"

Indeed. Part of what is terrifying about that form of terrorism—all terrorism—is that most of us simply cannot imagine what would lead someone to do it. We try, and we fail.

"Would you suicide-bomb yourself if it would also kill Osama bin Laden?" one character in the strip asks another. "Hell no! The whole point of killing Osama bin Laden is that it increases my chances of staying alive!"

(2) Partly as a result of (1), the Israeli leaders are not going to compromise. At the same time, the Israeli people, maybe especially the young men and women in their absurdly youthful citizen-army, are sick to death of all the death.

Listen, for example, to nihilistic voices of the teenage soldiers who patrol the Occupied Territories, as recorded the April issue of *Harper's Magazine*. Here extreme moral hollowness is experienced, and expressed, in the flat tones of a television talk show. "In Hebron I shot the legs off two kids, and I was sure I wouldn't be able to sleep any more at night, but nothing happened," one 19-year-old paratrooper said. "You become so apathetic you don't care at all. Shooting is the IDF soldier's way of meditating. It's like shooting is your way of letting go of all your anger when you're in the army."

(3) Thus the American position on the Middle East, that long military and political support of Israel would underwrite a position of moral suasion when the Bush Administration stepped in to regulate the conflict, is revealed as wishful thinking. They can't abate the crisis any more than you or I or Spider-Man.

(4) This means lots more people are going to die horrible deaths in the weeks and months ahead, blown to bits in random restaurants, or picked off haphazardly in rounds of what the IDF likes to call "punitive shooting"—better known to the rest of us as raking anything that either (a) moves or (b) doesn't move.

(5) Damn.

Not much of a position, I grant you. Where are the answers? Whither the polished phrases and solid laying of blame?

As the CIC communiqué proves, however, it doesn't really matter. Like most writers, I am familiar with the weirdly vertiginous experience of having thoughts imputed to me which I do not hold, have never so much as entertained. This is usually a matter of distorting some actual writing, but obviously it needn't be. The CIC may even be on to something. If you can be condemned for writing a column you didn't actually write, you could also write a column without actually writing it!

So, just for the record, this was not a column about the Middle East conflict. It was not a column at all. I do not have an opinion on the conflict there. Neither do you. In fact, why stop? The Israelis say the Palestinians have no right to exist. It follows that they do not exist. Therefore there is no occupation, no resistance, no conflict because there cannot be.

Very satisfactory. Just don't forget to check the headlines for the tally of people who died today on both sides of the wire.

✦

The thief, the thinker, and his identity
12 June 2002

New York

The other Mark Kingwell was a cheeky bastard. After a three-day shopping spree at various stereo outlets, home-supply stores and discount jewelry joints, racking almost 20 grand in components, power tools, and diamond chokers, the other Mark Kingwell stopped to get some cash. He wanted a little walking-around money, a bit of dosh, some peeling paper, some cake.

The other Mark Kingwell wasn't going to stop just anywhere to get the cash. The other Mark Kingwell was no run-of-the-mill grifter, some cheap punk on a mindless blowout. No, he was a criminal mastermind with a comic-book sense of humour, the Lex Luthor of credit-card fraud. Or maybe he was just an idiot. Anyway, he used the ATM in the deli at the corner of the street where I, the real Mark Kingwell, lived. There it was on the statement,

MasterCard cash advance, three hundred dollars, deli. And then the other Mark Kingwell went and had a couple of martinis.

Reading the printout of recorded expenses, plotting the other Mark Kingwell's journey through the cash nexus of modern urban sprawl, was the only time I laughed during the disturbing experience of having my identity stolen. Otherwise it was long, frustrating phone conversations with suspicious security officers, some mid-level "X-Files" paranoia about the wobbly infrastructure of the postindustrial state, and a few afternoons of wild speculation about who, how, and why.

Like other victims of credit card fraud, I alternated between being freaked out and surging with resentment. A couple of weeks ago in the *New York Times Magazine,* a man called Adam Ray recounted his own version of this late-capitalist metaphysical nightmare when a fraud artist in Virginia applied for eight cards in his name. "In less than a month, this guy spent more than $40,000, a large chunk on stuff I'd never buy for myself, like Tommy Hilfiger and Nautica clothes and designer shoes," Mr. Ray said. "He also bought $5,000 worth of Zales diamonds, and while I don't blame the woman who got them, my wife was getting mad because I never bought her such nice things. All the gifts I'd given her suddenly seemed less special."

Mrs. Ray sounds a little, um, demanding, but you see her point. There's something galling about identity theft, especially if the thief proceeds to splurge by preying on your own good credit. At the same time, if the thief shops at places you don't frequent or care for, you feel oddly offended. I mean, maybe not Tiffany's, but couldn't he at least have gone to Birk's? And doesn't he realize that I myself, the real Mark Kingwell, have issues with how Wal-Mart treats its employees? Pretty soon you're wondering whether identity really is, as marketers insist, the sum of your shopping preferences.

Which just scratches the surface of the philosophical mysteries here. People tend to take their personal identity for granted, but that's simply a mundane refusal to engage the deep questions of existence. Who are you? How do you know? How can you demonstrate it? Are you the same person from one moment to the next? In ancient Greek mythology, the warship of the minotaur-slaying hero Theseus was, over many years, replaced plank by plank. When every single plank had been replaced, was it still the original ship? If the removed planks had been secretly stored and later assembled, was *that* the original ship?

Questions best left for the seminar room, you say, but I can tell you that once the consensual fiction of identity is fractured, and somebody else is in possession of your numbers and passwords, things get weird. It is, for example, remarkably difficult to convince a credit agency that you are who you say you are. You keep shouting, "But I'm the real Mark Kingwell!" and "Of course I know my mother's maiden name!" even as you realize that this is exactly what the other Mark Kingwell would say. Before long, you feel like you're in one of those "Star Trek" episodes where you have to prove you're the real Kirk by knowing which way Sulu parts his hair or refusing to shoot McCoy with a phaser.

It doesn't help if you have now and then committed details of your personal life (and drinking habits) to paper. For a while, I wondered if the other Mark Kingwell was indulging in a witty deconstruction of the appearance/reality distinction, or making fun of my "media personality." But then I saw that this was pointy-headed crap, and thinking I'd been specially targeted was just another illusion of identity. I'm merely a statistic in one of North America's fastest growing crime waves. U.S. attorney-general John Ashcroft says he wants to make identity theft a federal offence, which would add two years to any conviction, but as deterrents go, that's chump change. Mr. Ray's impersonator, for example, who bilked more than 50 people out of a half million dollars, got a mere six and a half years on a plea bargain, and he only got caught because he was greedy and stupid.

Meanwhile, the vertigo about personal identity, once experienced, never fully subsides. In "Listening to Bourbon," his sly satire on personality-altering drugs, Louis Menand offers this compelling assessment of the ancient philosophical puzzle: "The sexual stallion and future world-beater of nineteen, for whom three pizzas and an accompanied hour in the back seat of a car are just the beginning of a decent evening, and the sagging commuter of twenty-five years later, who staggers home hoping only to have the stamina to make it through the first half hour of Charlie Rose, are nominally 'the same person'. But by virtue of what? Of having the same Social Security number? Identity is the artificial flower on the compost heap of time."

That, as Mr. Menand says, is why people need bourbon. Or in my case, as the still-at-large other Mark Kingwell apparently knows, a martini.

◆

Americans aren't so exceptional
26 June 2002

New York
It really wasn't fair, but on a recent final exam for a course in human rights theory I offered my students a series of semi-serious two-point

bonus questions. Some were obvious jokes, things no New Yorker could admit to knowing even if he or she did: the name of the Toronto Maple Leafs' head coach, the capital city of Saskatchewan. Others, like the rights covered in the Second Amendment and the wording of the Declaration of Independence, proved surprisingly elusive. And just one student in the whole class knew where the newly created International Criminal Court will hold its trials.

Standard stuff, you say, and frankly no big deal anywhere off the set of "Jeopardy." But the Dutch capital of The Hague may yet become a household name in America, especially if U.S. troops have to drop in and rescue Henry Kissinger or some hapless peacekeeper from the evil clutches of the ICC, which officially convenes next week. To hear commentators in Washington (and this newspaper) tell it, the new war crimes tribunal is the scariest thing to happen to individual liberty since Stalin decided due process was useful window-dressing for terror. "Certainly, there can be no serious doubt that crusading European jurists and anti-U.S. activists would try to haul Americans before the ICC on trumped up charges of crimes against humanity," our own goggle-eyed editorialist warned.

Oh, please. Never mind that, under the Rome Treaty, the Court has no power to investigate or prosecute any American if the U.S. asserts jurisdiction and takes on the case in good faith. Where are these scary jurists and "activists" with their necromantic power to "haul" innocent Americans before anything? The spectre of capricious prosecution is pure invention, designed to serve the increasingly immoral demands of America's isolation from the rest of the world.

What is worse is that, in the post-September 11th shakedown, Washington's desire to hold itself aloof from the international community has become not merely unseemly but self-defeating. The Bush Administration has carved out a position where its own actions undermine the very demands for justice used to validate the war against terrorism. Instead of trying to subvert the ICC, the U.S. should be taking a leading role in it.

Of course, just try selling that idea down in humid D.C. these days. The myth of American exceptionalism is so strong that nothing, not even the goal of coordinated international law, can make headway against it. The United States is that unique and maybe unprecedented thing, an imperial power whose existence is predicated on denying its imperial status. American power-brokers invoke the idea of "the West" when they're trying to get allies on board the troopships to Afghanistan, but that's pure expediency. Nobody of influence in this country seriously doubts (to use the handy editorial jabber) that America is in this, as it's been in all things, fundamentally self-interested.

Former president Bill Clinton signed the Rome Treaty two years ago, raising brief hope that the U.S. might decide to join the international community in a meaningful way, but realists know that countries often sign treaties they have no intention of ratifying. President George Bush has made it clear he will not ratify Rome, and the Administration announced last week it will refuse to participate in United Nations peacekeeping operations as long as the ICC claims jurisdiction over U.S. servicepeople. Congressional opponents of the Court, meanwhile, including House Whip Tom Delay and Senator Jesse Helms, have gone so far as to draft the American Servicemembers' Protection Act, otherwise known as The Hague Invasion Act, which would authorize the President to use "any means necessary" to secure the release of an American citizen detained by the Court.

Hence the paratroopers-descending-on-Holland scenario. Attached as an amendment to a veto-proof bill authorizing billions of dollars to combat terrorism, the invasion bill is not yet law, but it has already aroused protest from the Dutch Parliament. The foreign ministers of the European Union, understandably distressed that the U.S. might decide to buck all conventions of law and use military force to shut down the proceedings of the Court, issued a statement of "particular concern," which is diplomatic language for "bloody hell!"

Silly them. At this point, the pro-Washington toadies just call them Eurosnots or Euroweenies or something equally hilarious and get into a short-order pissing contest about sovereignty, which the U.S. inevitably wins. I mean, who really cares what the foreign minister of France thinks about this or anything? He's probably a snooty intellectual wearing an expensive suit and a necktie, and anyway how many aircraft carriers does he have? Throw in a couple of insults about the feeble nightlife in Brussels, the rarefied dinner-table conversation of Parisians, and the case is closed. When you're the lone superpower on the planet, what's a little compromised Dutch sovereignty?

The problem is not really American arrogance, though there's plenty of that to go around, or even the stupid spectacle of competing Western sovereignties in a global world. It's rather that Washington's refusal to co-operate with the ICC—not to mention its past delinquency over UN dues even while occupying a seat on the Security Council—indicates a failure to understand the moral basis of justice. As Immanuel Kant argued two centuries ago in one of the foundational texts of the modern world, the essence of justice is universality. The basic insight is even older, ably defended in Plato's *Crito:* exceptions to the rule of law tell everyone the law is not to be taken seriously.

American exceptionalism is regrettable at any time, insulting to the efforts of lawyers around the world to bring war criminals and genocidal tyrants to justice. At a time when the cries for justice come most stridently from the one voice refusing to endorse that effort, exceptionalism moves beyond self-serving to cynical, short-sighted, hollow, and wrong. You might even say it's criminal—except that the Americans are doing their level best to drain all meaning from the word, except when it suits them.

✦

If you're serious about God, this is a disaster
10 July 2002

New York
When is God not God? When He's blessing America, apparently. Or when in Him we trust. Or when this big old imperial power is one nation under Him. Take your pick. Philosophers have puzzled over the question of God's nature for centuries, reaching various entertaining or desperate conclusions, and yet the answer was right there in front of our eyes all the while—God is a Yankee.

Not even Nietzsche could have killed God off any more effectively than the Supreme Being's annexation to American patriotism. Yes, it's true. In the flurry of controversy over the recent Ninth Circuit Federal Court ruling that reciting the Pledge of Allegiance violates the U.S. Constitution's separation of church and state, nobody seemed to mark the passing of God as, you know, *a god*. The ruling, from what has been consistently described as the "notoriously liberal" West Coast court, was instantly ridiculed on op-ed pages and talk shows from coast to coast. President Bush stood up and took issue with it. It was, everyone said, certain to be overruled by the Supreme Court.

No doubt. But that's because the Supreme Court doesn't really believe in God. If they did, they would realize that the current wording of the Oath, whose god-free 1892 version by Francis Bellamy was altered by Dwight D. Eisenhower's administration in 1954, does indeed cut against the Constitution's famous—you might say notoriously liberal—division between worship and government. It is only by invoking what the higher court has called "ceremonial deism" that any of the ubiquitous God-talk of American public life is saved from legal incoherence.

Trouble is, that doesn't save it from logical incoherence. Deism is the thesis that there is a God but "he" is neither interventionist nor, in some versions, an entity of any kind. The god of deism is more a philosophical principle, like Aristotle's Unmoved Mover or the fixed point of causality. In the seventeenth century, when smart European philosophers were trying to reconcile reason with faith, often in order to avoid persecution and punishment from the Christian authorities, they constructed deistic theories as a way of keeping God in a picture without giving up the hard truths of science. Deism meant you could sign on to religious doctrine without actually allowing that Christ was God, that there were miracles, or that God cared a hoot what went on in this intricate clockwork universe. Deism suggested that if there was a Great Clockmaker, he was, so to speak, off in another room having a glass of iced tea.

Most theologians and the vast majority of ordinary Christian believers wanted nothing to do with the idea. The "god of the philosophers" has been ridiculed and rejected by orthodox Christians for centuries, not least because it takes all the interesting divinity out of the Creator. You might as well construct a religion around natural selection. So when the Supreme Court invokes it to keep God in the patriotic picture, there are only two possibilities: either they know their position is unconstitutional and are using obfuscation and semantic trickery to keep that under wraps, or they haven't done their homework and are confusing two very different notions of what "God" means.

How convenient. This God-not-God move is the same mealy-mouthed rationale you hear everywhere now, as God is invoked more and more often as a token of post-9/11 American righteousness. Earlier this year, a worker at a Home Depot in Long Island was enraged when his large "God Bless America" sign was removed from the store window because it violated company policy against religious signage. "It's not religious," he said angrily to the television reporters.

If it's not religious, what is it? If he doesn't mean the Christian God of the scriptures, why does he even care?

In this country you get used to seeing God, of course. In my neighbourhood, nearly every storefront and pizza box sports a stars-and-stripes motif and the "God Bless America" injunction. I was at Yankee Stadium the other day and everybody got up during the stretch to sing the same sentiment along with a scratchy recording of the late lamented Kate Smith. (God had other plans that day, though: the usually hapless Toronto Blue Jays racked an 8-3 victory.) Every piece of currency, from the lowly Lincoln penny up to the Benjamin, says "In God We Trust"—an inclusion that President Theodore Roosevelt, for one, staunchly opposed because he thought it debased belief in the deity. The same motto will soon appear in every public school-room in Michigan, Virginia, and Utah, with other states certain to follow. And every morning since 1954, schoolkids across the country have risen and pledged their allegiance to an indivisible nation under God.

Does any of this matter? Well no, if you're prepared to reduce God to a neutered and empty synonym for, say, Powerful Force We Really Hope Likes Us. But if you're serious about God, this is actually a disaster.

As so often, the devout and pragmatic landowners who founded this country, not to mention their far-sighted successors, knew better: they kept God out of the Constitution precisely because they took belief in him seriously. God is invoked in the Declaration of Independence, an explicit expression of hope (it also contains the lines about life, liberty, and the pursuit of happiness), but is conspicuously absent elsewhere. Christian believers all, the Founders nevertheless knew that a state-creating legal document had to be neutral on the issue of religious faith if the country was ever going to realize the liberal dreams they had inherited from some of the very same philosophers who, a generation before, had struggled with faith and reason.

"It will never be pretended that any persons employed in that service had any interviews with the gods, or were in any degree under the inspiration of Heaven," John Adams wrote of the founding in his influential *Defense of the Constitutions of Government of the United States of America*. "Thirteen governments thus founded on the natural authority of the people alone, without a pretense of miracle or mystery … are a great point gained in favor of the rights of mankind."

Adams was an intelligent and perceptive statesman, but he was wrong about one thing: that very thing gets pretended every day, from the President and the Supreme Court on down.

✦

Greed will save the markets, again
24 July 2002

New York

Bernard Baruch, namesake of the college currently issuing my paycheques, is said to have avoided the worst of the 1929 Wall Street Crash by listening to his shoeshine boy. Stopping one morning to renew the glow on his wingtips, Baruch was offered unsolicited stock tips by the shammy-snapper tending his feet. He knew immediately that the bubble was set to burst. When even shoeshine boys are players, Baruch reasoned, speculation has gone too far. He called his broker and said, "Sell, sell."

The only shoeshine boy I know is not a boy but an old man, labouring away up at Grand Central, and I'd take stock tips from him anytime. He radiates understanding of the universe such as to shame mere philosophy. But I'm not sure even he could have predicted the past week's disastrous slide, which bears the usual hallmarks of human irrationality and fear, plus healthy doses of schadenfreude and bad faith.

In fact, listening to the experts pick over the implications of the crash, we see nothing less than a morality spasm dressed up as analysis. Markets are confidence games, wispy and bizarre, but the current one seems even more pathological than ever, with tipsters and authorities lately reduced to the status of therapists. "There is an absolutely clear sea change in the psychology of the market," one analyst told our reporter yesterday, as the Dow dipped below 8,000 for the first time since October 1998. "Instead of buying the dips, people are now selling the rallies. It's the dead-reciprocal of three years ago." Another added: "Sentiment is obviously negative, where bad news is bad news and good news is bad news. We're on that roller coaster where emotions are probably overtaking rational thought in some cases."

Ah, yes. The market clearly suffers from a form of bipolar personality disorder. Three years ago it was giddy, beyond all reason or sense, going mad as it topped 10,000. Now it is depressed and chastened, unable to see light even where the sun shines clear.

The received wisdom is that this bout of blues is rooted in distrust of corporations, with their mattress-padding stock option schemes, insider trading cabals, and creative accounting practices. As the $40-billion collapse of WorldCom comes hard on the heels of the Enron scandal, investors are jittery and disappointed. There is an "integrity crisis," and only the public appearance of justice will restore the faith that has been so cruelly tested. Thus the Simpsonsesque spectacle of pundit after pundit calling for the open humiliation of disgraced execs. "Do we need to see people being led away in handcuffs?" one anchor asked his expert analyst the other night, not kidding. "Yes, Brian," she replied. "Yes, we do."

Now, I'm all for the public shaming of white-collar criminals. And it's true that, so far, indictments have been issued only in the Arthur Andersen case, with the poor Securities and Exchange Commission presumably bogged down as more big companies crowd the doorway into Chapter Eleven. But we should see these calls for rolling heads for what they really are, the avoidance rituals of a hypocritical and delusional system.

Much has been made in recent days of Federal Reserve chairman Allan Greenspan's phrase "infectious greed," which he used to describe the corporate culture that produced the Enron collapse. Hailed as a coinage of Churchillian, maybe even Ciceronian,

174 ♦ Mark Kingwell

resonance, this routine banality has become the catchphrase of the day without much pause to examine its braindead assumptions. Let's correct the oversight.

Spastic late-hour moralizing aside, greed is not an excrescence on the true benign nature of markets, whatever that may be; it is their essence. Markets function to maximize individual or corporate self-interest. They are not collective undertakings, just semi-chaotic conglomerations of desire that supposedly act more efficiently than other schemes of human organization. To condemn greed in markets is as incoherent as damning the flow of water in turbines. The Enron guys will go to jail not because they were greedy but because they were careless, a sin no market will tolerate for long.

If this greed were not infectious, moreover, the market would be even less defensible than it is. Self-interested market actions are designed precisely to inspire similar behaviour in others. In the famous tit-for-tat solution to the problem of coordinated action under conditions of ignorance—otherwise known as the prisoner's dilemma—it is rational to co-operate at first, then defect if other players do. In other words, start off nice but don't continue so if others aren't. Call that infectious if you like, like an unwelcome viral invasion, but knock-on greed is no more than rational under conditions of market capitalism.

Of course at this point, it's a short step to a blanket judgment that markets are evil. Or, on the other side, to the insight that the non-market sectors of our economy—let's say, oh, government agencies—are mired in accounting boondoggles far more corrupt than anything the sharpies at Enron could dream up in a month of trying. The first claim is untrue, and anyway pointless; the second is true, but unhelpful. Both miss the point, which is that, like it or not, we're all in this together.

The biggest mistake we can make about markets, indeed—and it's one the latest skid has encouraged to the point of derangement—is to think of them as entities with a mind of their own. Markets have no mind, and so they have no psychology. They don't rise and fall for good reasons or bad. They are the sum total of millions of individual decisions made by millions of individual investors, each trying to get ahead of the others.

Remembering that won't solve the problems of a panic-induced crash, because panic is even more natural to humans than reason, and our entire culture is infused with the greed the market rewards. But it might just stave off the worst effects of a market death spiral, which at this point is in everybody's interest. I'm no shoeshine boy, but here's my advice for what it's worth. Hold on to your shares. Resist the temptation to bail, or freak, or lay easy blame. Ride out the storm, because it's a storm of our own making.

And if you have any spare cash, buy gold.

✦

What's a few stolen or missing firearms?
7 August 2002

New York
Memo to Glenn Fine, inspector general, U.S. Department of Justice; re. the lost guns: *I have them.*

Well, not all of them. After all, 775 weapons lost by various agencies, including the beleaguered Federal Bureau of Investigation, between late 1999 and last January, is a lot of firepower. I only have most of them, the Glocks and Uzis and a few crates of Street Sweepers. I also have most of the 400 laptop computers misplaced by the agencies during the same period, which may or not contain classified national security information. In fact, I'm writing on one of the laptops right now, a sleek titanium Mac PowerBook G4, which is pretty cool except it tends to freeze when MS Word runs at the same time as that Koran-based decryption software.

My message to you, Mr. Fine, is *don't worry*. Take it easy. Follow the president's example and go on vacation. Play a few rounds of golf. I'm not giving the guns and computers back, but I'm not selling them off to criminals either. They are probably way safer here in my Manhattan apartment than they would be in Quantico. Yes, I refused to sign that copy of the Pledge of Allegiance you kept sending me back in January, but that's just because I'm a subject of the Queen, and you know how she is about these things. You should relax. After all, that's what most of your agents apparently do.

"Some property theft and loss, to include guns and laptops, is inevitable," the FBI said in a statement responding to the Justice Department audit, made public the other day. "Indeed, the FBI's record in this regard compares favorably." You have to like that use of "to include," which makes this concession sound like a menu order. And "compares favourably" to what? To the Immigration and Naturalization Service, for one. The FBI claims responsibility for only 212 absent weapons, the INS for 539. That leaves the Drug Enforcement Agency, the United States Marshals Service and the Bureau of Prisons on the hook for just 24 lost, stolen, or missing firearms. Now that's outstanding!

In the old days, losing even one gun was considered rather shameful among law enforcement agents, at least in fiction. In the movie *Magnolia,* for instance, the police officer depicted by John C.

Reilly is so rattled by dropping his sidearm in a rainstorm that he spirals into a deep personal crisis. In Akira Kurosawa's film-noir homage, *Stray Dog*, a detective played by Toshiro Mifune has his gun stolen and then used in a murder. He becomes obsessed with recovering his gun, solving the murder, and assuaging his guilt.

The FBI and INS have found a better way. They're just not going to stress too much. Oh yeah, I know they've promised to review their inventory procedures and implement the "necessary reforms and policies" called for in the Justice report. But really, the underlying attitude is that misplacing a few guns and computers is, like losing track of your walking-around money while on vacation in New York, just the cost of having fun. Instead, agents can concentrate on looking good as they perp-walk WorldCom execs in front of waiting TV cameras.

That's why, even with all these guns in my possession, I confess I'm not reassured about the current plan to join the various security and intelligence agencies into a superbureaucracy called the Homeland Security Department. Senator Joseph I. Lieberman, main sponsor of the bill, has never quite come out and said that, when it comes to security, "homeland" just sounds better than "domestic" or "inland" or "national." Nor has he openly admitted that his push for the Department's formation is linked to his rumoured plans to go after the presidency in 2004.

What he has said is that current vulnerability of this country to further terrorist attack is the only argument needed to ram through the largest reorganization of the federal government since the U.S. Department of Defense was created in the 1940s. Initially, the bill's sponsors hoped to have the new Department up and running in time for a September 11th anniversary. That now seems impossible, in part because unexpected opposition has slowed its passage through Congress.

Senator Robert C. Byrd, of West Virginia, has been the most outspoken critic of the plan. At 84 years of age, the passionate Mr. Byrd, a Democrat like Mr. Lieberman, wants to know why a plan the Bush Administration designed "on the back of a cocktail napkin" should be allowed to breeze through the House and Senate.

"Have we all completely taken leave of our senses?" he said in a dramatic July 30 speech on the Senate floor. "The president is shouting, 'Pass the bill, pass the bill!' The administration's cabinet secretaries are urging the adoption of the president's proposal without any changes." But that is not the way constitutional democracy works, he said. "If ever there was a time for the Senate to throw a bucket of cold water on an overheated legislative process that is spinning out of control, it is now. Now!"

Yup—though, in the end, the Homeland Security Department will almost certainly pass anyway, and the resulting capacity for incompetence—to include loss of guns and laptops—will continue, if not grow. The only real snags to the plan revolve around such irritating labour issues as job security and due process. Phil Gramm, the Republican senator from Texas, is on record saying that fussy federal employees compare unfavourably to Marines, who go where they're told and can be summarily discharged for poor performance.

Mr. Gramm is right. Screw collective bargaining and workers' rights. I say, make the secretaries in Border Patrol, the paper-pushers over in the Bureau, do push-ups whenever they get uppity.

While we're at it, couldn't we get some of those pesky federal judges out of the way? Judge Gladys Kessler of Federal District Court in Washington ruled last week that the Bush Administration has no right to withhold the identities of people it has detained as part of the September 11 investigation, and she gave the government 15 days to release the names. "Secret arrests are a concept odious to a democratic society," she said.

Down and give me fifty, sister. I have a gun.

♦

Boredom is the parent of wisdom
21 August 2002

New York

The thing is, I don't feel boring. Five times a week, I bound into the lecture hall with the sprightly gait of Jim Carrey making a "Tonight Show" appearance and dilate on pre-Socratic fluxus or Heidegger's concept of dwelling. Which is why I read with such distress the news that University of Toronto professors—my esteemed colleagues and myself—topped a recent continent-wide student poll as the ones most likely to "suck all life from material."

This is quite a distinction. The poll covers 345 colleges and universities, expressing its findings in a series of Top-20 lists; Toronto and McGill are the only Canadian universities mentioned. To make a list of any kind, good or bad, a school has to generate a strong consensus. To rank first on a list is the statistical equivalent of the "jailbreak" double safety blitz: every attacker rushing to the same point on the field and burying the quarterback.

At the risk of boring you, I'll point out that actually, of course, it isn't. There is no sample-to-sample control in these results and therefore no rational way to compare findings. That is, while at least 300 students were polled at each institution, none of them is able to experience life at other places. The rank-ordered lists, while entertaining and profitable for author Robert Franek and his collaborators, are misleading. The only thing they tell us is that U of T is the school where students are most likely to say their professors are boring—not the most relevant factor in evaluating a post-secondary destination.

But even accepting that quibble, what could be the reason for the results? Well, it's certainly possible that U of T professors are indeed outstandingly boring. That was not my own experience: I was an undergraduate at Toronto before I became a professor there, and I remember a procession of brilliant teachers, including Alkis Kontos, Peter Seary, and Kenneth Schmitz, who inspired a passion for learning without which my life would be much diminished, if not unimaginable. Still, there were some real duds in there too, and my case may be a statistical anomaly.

On the other hand, maybe boredom is in the eye (or drooping eyelid) of the beholder. Maybe someone easily bored is someone lacking in imagination, or someone easily distracted by a cell phone text message. Maybe students elsewhere are taught by professors more willing to sacrifice substance for entertainment, thinking—as one of my recent American colleagues put it—that the only way to find favour with students is to imitate television. (Socrates had no such problem.) Or maybe today's U of T students simply haven't learned the deep lesson that a boring professor is a blessing in disguise, providing hours of fun in the form of imitation opportunities and beer-table allusions.

Still, cut as much mitigating slack as you like, it stings a bit to learn our students think us so dull. So here is my prescription for how we can do better next time round….

Oops. Just as I was writing that, the phone rang. It was my buddy Brennan, an actor, inviting me to come visit him on the set of "Law & Order." I hopped in a cab, zipped over to an office building on

Fifth Avenue, and the next thing you know I'm sporting a plastic set-pass and a pair of headphones, eating pastrami on rye as Jerry Orbach slouched by saying, "Where'd the sandwiches go?"

Brennan is playing a young computer jockey whose fiancée of one month has been found dead, so of course I figure he did it. He nailed his interrogation scene with the two police detectives in a few takes and then we went outside for a cigarette. I told him I was glad to be there but also how punishingly dull television production always strikes the outsider. An hour of set-up, five takes and nearly 30 minutes of taping, minute adjustments, untold minutes of just standing around and waiting for something to happen.

"Yeah," he said. "But if this was film, we'd have done 15 or 20 takes of that shot. And if it was Kubrick directing, we'd have done a hundred."

All that hurry-up-and-wait for one smooth 20-second piece of drama, one tiny degree in the arc of narrative. Eventually it adds up, and when you have the right eye, you can see that. The director has the eye; the bored set visitor probably doesn't. Whose judgment should be trusted? Could it be that the reactive desire to eliminate boredom has it all wrong?

Boredom, says psychoanalyst Adam Phillips, is "that state of suspended anticipation in which things are started and nothing begins, the mood of diffuse restlessness which contains that most absurd and paradoxical wish, the wish for a desire." The wish is paradoxical because it is tangled up in itself, does not know how to desire straightforwardly. We are waiting but we don't know for what; we want to want something but can't say what it might be.

Hence the peculiar paralysis of boredom, the "dreary agitation" and "cramped restlessness" which register as unpleasant moods but are really clues to our troubling immersion in aimless desire. Like all paradoxes, boredom pushes us past our routine expectations, builds to something bigger and more disturbing. At least, it does when given a chance. Boredom, like wonder, is the parent of wisdom.

And yes, there are still more connections between Jerry Orbach and pre-Socratic fluxus, but you'll have to come my lecture hall to find out what they are.

✦

Britain should stand up to U.S. war frenzy
4 September 200

London

It's always instructive to traverse the oceanic and cultural divide between New York and London, not least because it means you can brush up on true stories of American profligacy and strangeness, things that get ignored in the stateside press because they sound too much like parodies from *The Onion*. You have to come to England to find out about the 265-pound Bronx maintenance worker who is suing McDonald's, Burger King, Wendy's, and Kentucky Fried Chicken for making him obese, or the Illinois woman recently ordered by a judge to stop breast-feeding her eight-year-old son.

To which the only valid response is: since when is 265 obese? There are guys in my New York neighbourhood who weigh twice that and aren't even considered large-boned. And we all know the really interesting court case will come when that eight-year-old grows up and sues his mom for forceful ingestion of anabolic steroids or, I don't know, PCBs.

Even Londoners' head-shaking about the unthinkable fascism of mayor Michael Bloomberg's anti-smoking laws is hardly cutting-edge when everyone in Manhattan, from Eurotrash to New York's finest, already has it covered. The rather excitable Swedish actress Kerstin Sund told the *New York Times* last week, "I shake with anger when I hear the name Bloomberg. He wouldn't last a day in Europe with all his stupid rules." And when my buddy Adam was arrested recently by an undercover cop and fined $75 for smoking in an open-air subway platform, it was the bored, hulking cop who bitched about the mayor as he filled out a clearly quota-driven citation.

Over here, of course, the front pages are understood to carry far more serious fare: Posh and Becks calling their son Romeo; Lady Archer's spat with her former personal assistant. In short, the standard transatlantic move of mocking fat, weird, litigious Americans from a position of longstanding cultural superiority is still what it's always been, namely, a cliché dressed up as cleverness wrapped in baseless self-satisfaction.

But it's still shocking how much the British genuinely misjudge Yankee culture, especially when it comes to geopolitics. Prime Minister Tony Blair, in Johannesburg this week to appear at the World Summit—and tangle with an increasingly wacked-out Robert Mugabe—has become embattled over his position on a U.S.-led war with Iraq. He seems oddly surprised about it. Armchair hawks on this page and elsewhere have been insisting on this war for weeks now, despite well-reasoned caution from Colin Powell, James Baker, and others. Mr. Blair woke up the other day to find his Labour Party supporters and parliamentary opponents alike unhappy with the prospect of Britain sending troops on the road to Baghdad anytime soon.

These critics join most of the world. To oppose a hasty and ill-conceived Iraqi invasion is not to condone Saddam Hussein, or to suggest that no change of regime is necessary for regional stability. As Mr. Powell has made clear, further diplomacy and weapons inspection must be pursued before an attack can be remotely considered ethical. It would also be useful to see clear proof, as opposed to febrile rhetoric, that Iraq is implicated in the World Trade Center attacks.

There is some local support for a war, to be sure. A few right-wing pundits are, bizarrely, inclined to take President George Bush's recent Churchillian posturing at face value, comparing Saddam to the appeased Hitler. A little more plausibly, Iain Duncan Smith, leader of the Conservative Party, has argued that Iraq poses an independent threat to Britain—which means that submitting to American foreign policy is not craven bootlicking but, instead, hard-headed self-interest. Tony Blair must be kicking himself for not thinking of this dodge himself. He now faces the dilemma of swallowing the small pill of ideologically suspect realpolitik over the large pill of going on as Washington's toady.

Meanwhile up in Edinburgh, at the annual literary festival, the playwright Harold Pinter got a big ovation for calling Mr. Blair a war criminal and demanding he be put on trial in The Hague.

Now, Mr. Blair is many things, but a war criminal is not one of them. If anyone really thought such a charge was possible, it might mean reconsidering support for the International Criminal Court, which begins its controversial deliberations this week. But of course it isn't, and so it doesn't, and the only thing controversial about the ICC is that the Americans won't play. Just like they won't play along with the Kyoto Accord. Just like Mr. Bush wouldn't be caught dead attending the Earth Summit. One ironic consequence of recent events is that Mr. Bush, now ignoring his father's former advisers, detaining prisoners at whim, and looking to wage war without Congressional support, is in a position to teach Queen Elizabeth a thing or two about the joys of hereditary monarchy.

More than 18 months ago, I described in this column the lost-in-space mood of post-millennial Britain, at that time still trying hard to convince itself that American exceptionalism and Mr. Bush's famous foreign-policy vacuity didn't extend to London, gateway to Europe, partner in the special relationship. Mr. Blair was the leading cheerleader in that chorus of deluded colonial self-abasement, and events since September 11th have done nothing to minimize his submissive inclinations. But he was wrong that Mr. Bush cared about Britain, or Britons, beyond getting the Royal Marines and SAS into Afghanistan.

Now, a year on from those events, it's time for Mr. Blair to take a cue from his own people and grow a spine. He has parted company with Mr. Bush over Kyoto and Johannesburg, even at times over Israel. He must do the same over Baghdad. It might not work, so confirmed is the Bush Administration's go-it-alone blinkering, but British opposition might just tip the balance away from opening another front in this vague and ineffective war.

◆

Gulf War II—You heard it here first
18 September 2002

Readers of this column probably don't credit it with much influence in the corridors of the White House——an attitude shared, except in delusional moments, by the author—but news comes this week that provides hope. Scotland's *Sunday Herald,* one of the few actually independent newspapers left in the British Isles, published hard evidence that the Bush Administration was planning a "regime change" in Iraq even before the 2000 election and had a detailed plan in hand by January 2001. They also reported that the U.S. and Britain have been selling chemical weapons to the Iraqis since 1992.

I had to check the dates myself to be sure, but yes, there it was: in January 2001 I argued in this space that the easiest way to cement Bush Jr.'s all-too-shaky "mandate" was to start up the suspended war with Iraq. Gulf War II would have silenced domestic critics and galvanized public opinion; there was, I suggested, no time like the present. The ever-helpful headline-writer came up with something on the order of "Get on with it!"—which doesn't have the straightforward menace of "Let's Roll!" but it's pretty damn close. I even suggested Bush *fils* should ask his father for some of those sky-blue quasi-military shirts that presidents favour when visiting hot-climate theatres of war.

I was kidding, of course, but the Bushies chose to ignore that—one of the dangers of attempting satire in our political culture, where a scenario constructed to scare the bejeezus out of your average citizen just looks like a good policy option to your average politician.

And yes, it's proven a little more complicated for Mr. Bush than just doing whatever the hell he wants. It took him more almost two years to get his plan to topple Saddam Hussein really going, and he's had to invent comic-book rhetorical devices like "the Axis of Evil," speciously linking the Iraqis to al-Qaeda terror, to keep the fire high. His father's own advisers, meanwhile, have weighed in against the new war, surely complicating conversation over the family dinner table.

But the man is not for turning. And his latest moves display a degree of savvy that will force all of us to reconsider his mental abilities, at least in the service of self-interest. Mr. Bush's appeal to the United Nations last week was a stroke of genius. On the surface, it marked a significant reversal of all previous policy. Suddenly Mr. Bush is a committed multilateralist, a pillar of the international community! He comes to New York with political cap in hand, asking nicely for support against this evil man in Baghdad.

In reality, of course, it finessed the situation in a manner to please Thrasymachus or Machiavelli. Now brought generously into the war plans, the U.N. Security Council will find it impossible to resist the arguments of a suddenly compliant and co-operative Bush team. Meantime, behind the soft words is the hard truth that the U.S. will proceed with their war plans no matter what happens. In fact, in case anyone has forgotten, British and American planes are bombing Iraqi targets even now, war or no war.

If you doubt that this apparent change of heart was both sudden and cynical, note two things: Defense Secretary Donald Rumsfeld swiftly recalled a *Washington Post* op-ed justifying a unilateral pasting of Iraq just days before the 57th U.N. General Assembly opened last Thursday. Then Mr. Bush, after meeting in the morning with Secretary General Kofi Annan and learning of the tough anti-arrogance message the latter was about to deliver, hustled to revise his own speech in a way that would startle everyone up to his national security adviser, Condoleezza Rice, the Administration's late-model Terminator.

Spreading the largesse, Mr. Bush even offered to rejoin UNESCO, the U.N.'s social and culture organization which Ronald Reagan had quit almost 20 years before. Suddenly the U.N. is not the commie-haven and Third-World whine-fest we've been led to believe? Amazing! As the critic Ian Williams put it, "Perhaps not since the enemy changed from Eastasia to Eurasia in mid-oration in George Orwell's *Nineteen Eighty-Four* has there been such an abrupt about-face in a nation's foreign policy."

In the wake of the UNESCO announcement the Dow Jones Industrial Average immediately dropped 202 points, but this new Bush dodge is still the stuff of brilliance, a snookering to make Jean Chrétien's smartly executed freeze-drying of Paul Martin look like the work of an amateur. Naturally there was no mention of ponying up the U.S.'s long-overdue U.N. dues or accepting the authority of the International Criminal Court—those things might actually cost the Administration and its friends something. Instead there was a subtly effective soft-pedal version of the old sandlot threat to play nice just until I take my football and go home.

This is realpolitik for the New Age, a bland power-play deployed as a sincere request for help. The U.N., for its part, has no choice but to go along, since Mr. Bush is now doing exactly what they asked, talking their language and postponing (if not eliminating) the prospect of unilateral attack. And it all seems to be working nicely: Iraqi vice-president Tariq Aziz announced yesterday that U.N. weapons inspectors will be allowed unconditional access to sites in Iraq.

Is this a victory, however small, for multilateralism? Will the Bush Administration, faking it for now, someday actually come to acknowledge the value of an international community? Don't hold your breath. Washington rejected Mr. Aziz's latest offer just as they've rejected all previous ones. As Machiavelli warned, cynicism should beget cynicism. Mr. Bush's display of co-operation is a calculated sham, no more and no less; credit him with a change of tactic, not a change of heart.

✦

It's not un-American to oppose war
2 October 2002

Cleveland

Despite what you may have heard, there's lots to like about Cleveland, the definitive Rust Belt city on the southern shore of Lake Erie. It's not the coolest place in the world, and Lord knows not the most beautiful. But it has the Rock 'n' Roll Hall of Fame, the Browns and the Indians, and a pretty impressive art museum. Clevelanders love Canadians, which is nice, and they think Toronto is a great city, which makes a change from travelling within Canada. Above all, Cleveland has the kind of blue-collar good sense that helps put American foreign policy in perspective.

Cleveland is part of what Washingtonians surely mean when they talk about "the heartland," and it has both the virtues and vices of political American life: the work ethic, but also the string of anti-union leaders; the friendliness, but also support for the death penalty. Strange that in such a place opposition to the Iraq war should be so widespread, thoughtful, and firm.

Well, maybe not so strange. I came here to give a couple of public lectures, one of them rather unwisely titled "America's Role in the World." Just before I walked into that one, held in an overdecorated wedding cake of a hall, with purple and white plaster doodads climbing from floor to ceiling, I paced the hallway outside and briefly wondered what the hell I was doing. It's one thing to pontificate from the safety of the distant study, quite another to teach your grandmother how to suck eggs in person. An audience member approached me and pressed the point. I was going to talk about America's role in the world? And I am Canadian?

Yes, and yes. But I decided to make a virtue of necessity. A non-American friend of American ideals is maybe the very best person to address the topic of America's role in the world, I said. After all, no charge of treason can be levelled against him, no aspersions cast on the fact that he refused to sign a copy of the Pledge of Allegiance when employed by the City University of New York. And if he happens to come from right next door, in contrast to a distant Frenchman or Briton who might base his views of American life solely on imported sit-coms, he might just know America better than it knows itself.

It's a familiar argument to Canadians, of course, held responsible for everything from our ability to export newsreaders and comedians to the fact that some of the most quintessentially American music you'll hear at the Rock Hall was penned by people like Robbie Robertson and Jim Cuddy. Familiar, but with a deep root, which I believe is a sense of shared philosophical goals.

To judge the current war immoral and unjust, to condemn Washington's lack of co-operation with the International Criminal Court as contrary to the rule of law, is precisely to uphold the very ideals that underwrite all liberal democracies, including the United States. America's position as the most powerful example of the best political regime humans have so far devised gives it more responsibility for those ideals, not less.

What always gets obscured in debates about American military adventurism—what is getting lost every day on this page and elsewhere—is the fact that opposing American policy is not the same as hating America. Prime Minister Tony Blair, battered by his own party for the invasion of Iraq, lashed out with the usual tired charge of "anti-Americanism." Canadians are all too familiar with this braindead tactic, since versions of it dominated our national conversation in the weeks following September 11th, and never fully disappear. When in doubt, accuse your opponent of being anti-American. It's the transnational version of calling his patriotism—or his courage—into question.

What surprises me is that ordinary Americans rarely indulge in it. Certainly nobody in Cleveland ruled me out of court for daring to question American policy from an American podium. Instead, there was a sort of sigh of relief, a strange form of permission to express opposition once the window of dissent had been cracked. And if you're thinking that I was preaching to the choir because it was a university campus, let me say that I made the same points with people in bars, taxicabs, and the seats of Jacobs Field with the same results. (Granted, beer was sometimes involved.)

Americans are rejecting this war for all kinds of reasons from the pragmatic to the spiritual. Opposition has made for strange bedfellows, with conservative isolationists lining up, for the moment, with humanitarian multilateralists. Some people just straight up dislike tangled Newspeak bullshit like "anticipatory self-defence" and "forward deterrence." Others find it bizarre that President Bush's fixation on Saddam Hussein seems personal, irrational, and tangled in its own rhetoric. As *Harper's* editor Lewis Lapham recently pointed out, the only argument for going to war now is that Mr. Bush has said he would, and failing to do so would be a public relations disaster.

America's role in the world is systematically unstable. It is suspended somewhere between an existence as one republic among many and an imperial role predicated on explicit military supremacy. The Iraq war is a key test case for this wobbly condition.

What happens next, whether America openly accepts and defends its hegemonic status, or retreats and submits to the international community, will obviously make a difference to the people who live in places like Cleveland.

But it will make an even bigger difference to those of us who live outside the United States and can't directly influence its elected leaders. Whether we like it or not, we all have a stake in American foreign policy. Saying so isn't anti-American or anti anything else. It's something much simpler. It's standing up for the ideals of justice, equality, and peace that are the foundations of the modern political world, breaking a lance for those goals that seem, right now, pretty distant. It's being a citizen of the world.

You don't have to go to Cleveland to see that, but it helps.

✦

Drop the universal in university
16 October 2002

As so often when we think in reactive mode, the current panic over rapidly expanding enrolment in our universities has obscured the deeper question of what those universities are for. The coming double cohort in Ontario is larger than predicted! Demand for places across the country will leap by 30 percent within the decade!

These news items have generated the usual responses. In Ontario, parents and educators alike blame the provincial government for underestimating the size of the 2003 freshman class, which will see Grade 12 and Grade 13 students competing in the same pool. The provincial governments in turn blame the feds for lack of funding to cope with a growing system-wide surge caused by echo-boom demographic pressure. Professors are being hired and dorms erected at a brisk clip, but it might not be enough! What'll we do?

Here's a rude suggestion, one which might sound bizarre coming from someone who makes his wage as a university professor. How about some of those young people don't go to university at all? How about they immediately enter the workforce, read and travel for a while if they can afford it, maybe just move out and try living with a bunch of friends who want to start a webzine or recording collective?

In my experience, many students simply don't know why they're at university. Every year, I open a large introductory course by asking the cliché question of philosophy, *Why are you here?* The answers always range from the pious to the pragmatic, but I have noticed lately a funny trend: the answer is foreign sports cars, German for preference. Two years ago, it was a picture of a BMW that one student had taped to his binder with the caption *"telos."* (Not a make of car, just the Greek work for purpose or end.) This year, a student told the class she was there because she wanted "an Audi." At first I thought she said "an outie," as if she somehow believed philosophical reflection would alter the configuration of her belly button.

Students go because their peers do; or because it's the logical extension of high school; or because their parents did. They go because there is the prospect of a lively social life, with plenty of beer, chat, and sex. They go, most often, because they believe it is the best route to better financial prospects in life. (They're probably mistaken about any connection between philosophy and sports-cars.) Rare is the student who arrives at university with a clear sense of higher education's independent value.

But—and this is the main point—most universities demonstrate no clear sense of that. Let me put the point in the form of a counterfactual: if the purely social goals associated with university education could be realized by some other means, I suspect many students would forego the traditional route, especially if it was cheaper to do so.

At the moment, we have no such alternative route to success in early adulthood, if only because universities have been accommodating our young people in such large numbers for so long, along the way fudging their own idea of what they're up to. In the past, a frankly elitist university would have no enrolment problem like our current one for the simple reason that only the academically best would be admitted, period. If that meant that some good-not-great students were turned away, tough.

But the policy that has governed university education, in Ontario and elsewhere, is universal accessibility: if a student qualifies, there should be a place for him or her. It might be in Sudbury rather than Toronto or London, but never mind. And never mind, too, that such a policy inevitably encourages grade inflation in high schools, since teachers know their students will only be penalized later for tough standards now. University education is not a privilege but a right—if still a competitive one.

That reasoning, coherent on its surface, is why university education the continent over is in such a strange state, sprawling and confused and constantly moaning about declining standards even while scrambling to admit more students to ensure a steady flow of transfer payments.

Universities grew out of medieval monasteries and still retain some vestigial signs of these origins, not least in the form of useless (though never worthless) disciplines like mine. Every now and then we even dress the part, donning our gowns and hoods and reciting a little Latin. The reality is that the modern state-supported university is, by turns, a corporate-sponsored research wing, a quasi-parental holding tank for late adolescents, and a training institution for the ambitious.

Its purpose seems self-justifying, wreathed in the comforting folds of knowledge for its own sake, but in fact it is systematically unstable. Learning is cherished, but only intermittently. Intellectual freedom is defended, but too often succumbs to outside pressure. Many of my colleagues complain privately that their students today are less skilled than a decade ago, but no one can say publicly that this may be the entirely logical outcome of general accessibility.

We could of course bite that bullet and give up on evaluation, embracing our fate as socialization machines financed by taxpayer largesse and corporate interest. Or we could, on the other side, take our intellectual ambitions more seriously and crack down on admissions, along the way refusing entry to lots of people whose families continue to support us through their taxes. The resulting surge in personal attention would, I suspect, nullify the common charge that Canadian universities are alienating and even boring.

Neither option is politically viable, however, and that is why universities will continue to stagger along in their dazed state. Those of us within them know that we have the best job in the world. We get to read and write and teach for a living and, with luck, might even have something deep to offer our students. But I wonder what good things might happen if some of those high-school graduates now weighing their prospects looked up and said, *You know what? Thanks but no thanks. I've got better things to do.*

✦

Individuals commit crimes, not races
30 October 2002

The great German critic Theodor Adorno, a subtle and prickly observer of all things mass-cultural, argued that the basic appeal of reading your horoscope is the illusion of control. Like all systems of magical thinking, astrology is non-falsifiable but conceptually massive. It organizes a complex reality—basically, the human population and its behaviour—into a simple categorical arrangement with vast but evidence-free explanatory power.

We like this. In fact we crave it, for a simple, if perverse, reason. Somewhere in the corners of even the most credulous human mind lies the creeping suspicion that the universe *doesn't make sense*. We know astrology is not true; but we want it to be true; so we pretend that it is true; and then we try to make it true: pure magic.

In this case, the dangers are of course minor, running only to, say, an alarming first date with someone who takes their magic a little too seriously. And even otherwise rational people can desire the communion wafer of cheap insight dispensed by the morning horoscope. So what?

But what about other forms of magical thinking, based on just as little, that get a firmer grip on our imaginations—and our actions? Here's a radical suggestion: "race" as it is currently conceived, especially in the recent furor over crime profiling and suspect detention, is precisely that.

The evidence of biology shows that difference between what we call races is genetically scant. On the scale of the human genome, blacks and whites (to use the usual hot-button racial dyad) have vastly more in common than they don't. In fact, it's not even close: in the basic terms of physical science, race is hardly salient at all.

But it is, of course, socially salient. That's why the *Toronto Star* recently reported that blacks in Toronto account for a "disproportionate" amount of the city's violent crime. That is, some 27 percent of homicides, sexual assaults, and gun-related charges are associated with a group that represents just 8.1 percent of the city's population.

What do those claims mean? Look below the surface. They mean, foremost, that the presupposition of racial identity is assumed, not argued for. Now debate over racial profiling can go either way, because the main argument is already over. You can complain that the police are "targeting" blacks because of a racist presumption of heightened criminality (the crusaders at the *Star*). But you can also claim that a certain amount of targeting is "reasonable" because it narrows the scope of a search (Christie Blatchford in this newspaper).

Both positions are incoherent. They merely beg the question they purport to answer: is race a relevant factor in pursuing criminals?

The "reasonable" position would have us believe that stopping young black men in the wake of a crime wave by young black suspects is something most of would be prepared to accept. It is, allegedly, no different from stopping young blond men following a serial rape spree whose main suspect was a young blond man.

This is both true and untrue. The true part is that police are acting reasonably when they question people who match the description of the suspects. Skin colour is a relevant factor in that effort, just as hair colour and build are. But that is not the same thing as racial profiling, and the police exceed reasonable suspicion when they expand a search to young black men generally.

The deeper trouble with the "reasonable" position is that it can lead, soon enough, to the unpleasantly common charge, in Boston or Los Angeles, of *DWB:* driving while black. Here we mistake a certain minor descriptor for a total identity. And as long as we do, people both with and without that descriptor will have a social stake in keeping the mistake going. As Shelby Steele argues in the October issue of *Harper's* magazine, the current "age of white guilt" also means the "disappearance of the black individual": a loss disguised as a gain.

Which brings us back to astrology. Suppose three of the four suspects in the recent spate of shootings (three black, one white) were Piscean. And assume for a moment a small absurd condition, namely that astrological sign were visible to the eye, like skin colour. Now what? Well, we might well accept that police were questioning some more Pisceans than, say, Scorpios—always assuming, of course, that they met the rest of the description. But what we would not do is argue that Pisceans, as a group, were more prone to violent crime.

Or would we? Would we perhaps begin to think there were reasons, not all of them their fault, that Pisceans behave in violent ways. They go to Piscean dance clubs and hang out on the streetcorners of Pisces neighbourhoods. Pisceans view themselves as somewhat apart from the rest of society, a subculture with special Pisces advocacy groups and forms of dance and music they consider particularly Piscean.

And now, the feedback loop of magical thinking enters the imaginary picture. Because now, just as with some people and their horoscopes out here in the real world, baseless association becomes self-fulfilling prophecy. People born between February 19 and March 20 begin to take on stereotypically "Piscean" traits and attitudes. They think in Pisces fashion, speak a Pisces patois, feel touchy and disadvantaged. They get used to being treated differently by police and their fellow citizens.

Of course, we all know why race isn't the same as astrology. Skin colour is visible and racism has a long social history. But we do nothing to break the illogical hold of racism as long as we continue to use race as a magic category, from inside or out.

For the record, I'm a Pisces. My *Post* horoscope tells me I "enjoy the study of metaphysics, philosophy, astrology and especially paranormal psychology. Way-out subjects intrigue you. Mentally, you're not here, you're someplace else."

Call me crazy, but it's a place where individuals, not races, commit crimes.

✦

What keeps you up at night?
13 November 2002

Harold Bloom, whose hefty study of genius is being excerpted in these pages this week, is a chronic insomniac. He tells us so on p. 647 of the book, mentioning in passing that the affliction allows him extra reading time for the apparently unending task of being the world's best-read man.

Bloom mentions this in the context of a rare failure: insomnia notwithstanding, he hasn't managed to re-read all of Iris Murdoch's 26 novels in order to claim her as one of his "one hundred exemplary creative minds." He will have to focus on just a handful of the works. This confession is trademark Bloom, nicely capturing his fundamental presupposition, a neat always-alreadyness with respect to books: no work is ever merely read; it must always be re-read.

The attitude is warmly reminiscent of the fundamental dictum of all academic (and, to be sure, all other reactionary) politics, first noticed by the Cambridge classicist F. M. Cornford. In his little political satire, *Microcosmographia Academica,* Cornford immortalized it as The Principle of the Dangerous Precedent: "no action shall ever be done for the first time."

Variations on this kind of debate-killing critical apparatus are in good nick these days, with presumptive condemnation and rhetorical sleight-of-hand all the rage. Consider last week's U.S. mid-term election results, with their vanishingly small voter turnouts miraculously transformed into a new mandate for the Bush Administration. It used to be that supporters of the current arrangement would point to the validity conferred by people voting with their feet; now it's evidently enough that people vote with their asses. Here, a second non-mandate is used—hey presto!—to reinforce the legitimacy of the first non-mandate. Critics of the non-mandates are laughingly told to get over it, for preference as a message from "Earth" to the outer space of, I don't know, logic and constitutional integrity. Hilarious.

At the same time, the Democrats are ridiculed for being beaten by the man they consider inadequate to the office. "If Bush is too dumb to be President," Mark Steyn said the other day, "how dumb do you have to be to be consistently outwitted by him?" To which the only response is, if the Dems are too stupid to be taken seriously, how stupid do you have to be to stomp them in column after column, week in and week out?

But you knew I would say that, so back to insomnia and Harold Bloom—who, incidentally, shows himself a dedicated critic of the current Bush regime in his book's many asides and digressions. Maybe that's what keeps him up at night.

"Men who are unhappy, like men who sleep badly, are always

proud of the fact," Bertrand Russell notes in his book *The Conquest of Happiness,* and Bloom is no exception. Many insomniacs consider their sleeplessness a badge of distinction, something on the order of an unusual spiritual subtlety. Insomnia is, in this regard, the less dangerous cousin to artistic suicide, whereby overwrought musicians or novelists or painters hurl themselves from bridges or buildings owing to an excess of sensibility.

"Insomnia is not bad in itself," says Mrs. Hawkins, the narrator of Muriel Spark's novel *A Far Cry from Kensington* (not one of Bloom's choices). "You can lie awake at night and think; the quality of insomnia depends entirely on what you decide to think of. Can you decide to think?—Yes, you can."

But that makes it sound altogether too easy. Nighttime thoughts are sometimes unwelcome ones, and the choice of them not up to you. As Jake says in Hemingway's *The Sun Also Rises*—a work of genius according to Harold Bloom—"it's easy to be hard-boiled in the daytime." Not so at night. Awake at four a.m., our thoughts naturally turn toward darkness. The mind races. Anxieties small and large rise to consciousness like surfacing whales, only receding by an effort of will that is, after its fashion, a prolongation of the sleepless state. Bubonic plague in New York City! Republican smugness in Washington! Eminem a box-office star everywhere!

By now it is probably obvious that I'm an insomniac myself. With all respect to Bertrand Russell, I'm not proud of it; nor, *pace* Spark, can I simply decide what to think while in insomnia's grip. I used to combat creeping night thoughts by a not very successful manoeuvre which is undoubtedly a mark of the times. In a sort of video-game update of the old spiritual exercise in which one imagines the Kingdom of God as a house or castle, I would picture my mind as a forward fixed position held by enemy forces. My mental versions of Navy SEALs would assault room after room, trying to extinguish worries by shouting "Clear!" at the top of their voices.

Don't laugh; it's no weirder than other counter-measures developed by insomniacs everywhere. Roger Angell, the famed baseball writer for *The New Yorker,* wrote an affecting and very funny memoir, *Ainmosni,* in which he explains how he combatted insomnia by constructing palindromes and elaborate backstories to explain them. ("A dum reb was I ere I saw Bermuda." Tale of the Reconstruction? Alternative Napoleonic exile?) This after imagined rounds of golf and fantasy baseball games become hopelessly interesting and so failed to work.

Eventually, of course, the palindromes prove just as addictive and a sleepless Angell descends into field-reversing despair, prisoner of his nighttime obsession. Once formed, the habit of going from right to left cannot be broken. "'No!' I whimpered, burying my throbbing head beneath the pillows. 'No, no!' Half smothered in linen and sleeplessness, I heard my sirens reply. 'On!' they called. 'On, on!'"

My tactic's problem, in these terms: sniper peels ere sleep repins. Solution: now I just read the paper. Steyn, bard veritas? On? No. Satire v. drab. Nyets!

Works every time.

✦

Where my rights end—and yours begin
27 November 2002

Does a motorcyclist without a helmet pose the same kind of danger to others as a cigarette smoker? Is a bridge without a high fence the equivalent of leaving a loaded gun in the house? Is obesity on a moral par with child abuse? Is my suicide a form of harm inflicted on my parents?

These questions, none of them fanciful, concern individual freedom, the right to control my body and mind—what we might call individual sovereignty or the right to self-use. The classic statement of this right is J. S. Mill's *On Liberty,* that impassioned argument against tyranny of the majority. There, Mill draws on a tradition of personal ownership already established by John Locke, who made the body and its labour my first legitimate possessions.

"In that part [of conduct] which merely concerns himself," Mill writes of the free man, "his independence is, of right, absolute. Over himself, over his own body and mind, the individual is sovereign." There is no possible justification for infringing this power of self-use, including the alleged happiness, wisdom, or benefit to him and others. "These are good reasons for remonstrating with him, or reasoning with him, or persuading him, or entreating him, but not for compelling him, or visiting him with any evil in case he do otherwise."

The sole exception is what Mill calls self-protection: if the exercise of your liberty harms me, I have the right to curb it. Or, as we sometimes say, your right to swing your fist ends at the precise point where it meets my chin.

Which sounds simple. But even pure theoretical debates about self-use rapidly become a tangle of analogies and second-hand harms. You certainly have the right to kill *yourself* with cigarette smoke, but not to poison *me* with the noxious exhalations of your filthy habit. You have the right to drink yourself stupid, but not to drive afterwards and knock a teenage pedestrian to her death.

Add the real-world condition of a universal health care system and the equations immediately go quantum in complexity. Now the jerk tooling his Ducati down the 401 without a helmet isn't just a jerk, he's a potential drain on our tax resources. Your vast consumption of Timbits and Chicken McNuggets is suddenly my problem too, since I end up underwriting your long stays in hospital.

Now add new kinds of harms in the form of "psychological costs" or "social consequences": the suffering and neglect of the obese mother's children, the grief and self-recrimination of those left behind by a suicide. Finally, mix in some controversial claims about sanity or mental balance—which qualities, if we lack them, mean that our liberty is no longer our own affair—and you have a recipe for legislative disaster.

The liberal position, the one that Locke, Mill, and most Canadians favour in some form, is that you don't legislate rationality or morality—you don't lay down in law what counts as smart or good. Legislation may start off with reasonable measures to secure our rights, but pretty soon, mixing and jumbling factors, it leads us down the path to the notorious nanny state, or rule by what P. J. O'Rourke famously called "the Safety Nazis": some dull bureaucrat's milquetoast version of good sense. We begin by mandating seatbelts (costless, sensible, hard to object to) and soon find ourselves, bizarrely, banning perfume in public places or ordering Halifax police officers to tackle Polar Bear Club members trying to get a wintry dip.

O'Rourke's hard-libertarian position strikes many in this country as peculiarly American. And it is indeed a recurring theme in American culture; some disgruntled, funny, self-destructive guy—it's always a guy—launches a bitter riff against those who want to crack down on dangerous pleasures. (Denis Leary does a neat version of it in the action movie *Demolition Man* as the reluctant leader of an underground resistance movement.) Because individualism is so often defended and so deeply enshrined in American life, there is always—at least in theory—a healthy debate there about perceived state-backed encroachments on liberty.

Here in Canada, suspended somewhere between libertarian and socialist extremes in the political culture, we are more ambivalent. The received wisdom says we favour a greater degree of collectivism than our neighbours to the south. The Charter, product of a sprawling, pluralist post-war society, certainly enshrines more social nuances and communal goods than the U.S. Bill of Rights. And yet we don't pursue social democracy consistently, or against the deep individualism of the liberal tradition.

And of course Canadians know that the wholly sovereign individual is a myth, an essential piece of fiction we use to understand, and maybe extend, the value of our lives. We all exist as part of a community, a web of care that at once sustains us and inhibits us. We are free to jump off that web, but we ought to think long and hard before doing so.

The elaborate, and ugly, new suicide barrier along Toronto's Bloor Viaduct, whose metal stanchions weirdly resemble crucifixes, offers a case in point. The barrier is arguably, after its fashion, a form of Mill's remonstration or entreaty. It delays the moment of decision and so possibly keeps another sovereign individual, another experimenter in living, on the web. It says: *Of course you may go, my friend. I could not reasonably prevent you. But let's talk before you do.*

In fact, though, how voters respond to a legislated control on self-use often depends on how the issue is framed or what imaginary scenarios of disaster are constructed—those fictions that we in the philosophy business call "intuition pumps." If a proponent can present a catalogue of alleged potential harms, jumbling various principles and arguments, citizens may find themselves acceding to things that, in theory, they oppose: random searches without cause, for example, the basis of seasonal drunk-driving crackdowns.

More disturbing still, in the wake of last year's terrorist attacks, otherwise liberty-loving citizens, including many formerly Jeffersonian Americans, were suddenly shrugging off racial profiling, targeted extraditions, intrusive personal searches, and even, god save us, actual torture of captured prisoners.

The trouble with liberty is that it can't just be for us and not them, or for now and not later. You can't fight a war defending values that the war measures themselves flout. And we should always remember that it's not such a long step from the complacent mantra of today's lengthy security lines—"If you've done nothing wrong, you have nothing to worry about"—to the collective surveillance programs and state-rewarding snitching of Orwell's imagination.

The point of liberty isn't merely that we enjoy it, that we might just get our kicks by feeling the wind in our hair or biting down on juicy red meat. It is also that individual liberty is the only principled route to the kind of diversity of personal projects that is human life's glory. Innovation in life, like innovation of all kinds, happens at the margins. There, where people are engaged in experiments in living—altering consciousness, altering bodies, testing the limits of experience—lies the future of our species. Some of those experiments will fail, and there will always be costs that trickle down to the rest of us in some form. But there will be benefits too.

The battle over mandatory seatbelts is over, probably for the best. In the battles still to come—over new drugs, new thrills, and maybe new spills—the onus is always on the state to show why law should ever extend to protecting us from ourselves.

◆

The man who doesn't read is unforgivable
11 December 2002

My old friend John Allemang, writing in some other newspaper last weekend, offered a long assessment of what is called "aliteracy": the willful refusal to read by those who are capable of doing so. His article contained many alarming moments, not least the suggestion that reading for pleasure is something often indulged in by the young but then abandoned later in life.

Now, far be it from me to impugn the time-work calculations of a busy surgeon, say, who finds himself nodding off over Vikram Seth during his handful of free hours. But beyond the sheer limitations of human endurance, the reasons offered for not reading were a mixture of perverse pride and smug domestic ideology. They were also a sharp sketch in the nature of self-cancelling privilege.

The pride is the usual thing, namely aggressive defence of what is felt, at some level, to be a failing. I have known many people who take this line, happily proclaiming themselves non-readers as if reading were for little people, people with nothing better to do. Sometimes it may even approach the level of a philosophical position. For, example, I have a British colleague, a master logician, who asserts he cannot read fiction because he knows, per intention, that all the sentences in a given book are false. Absent propositions, absent interest.

For most aliterates, it doesn't rise to such Vulcanic purity. No, it's mostly that they would rather spend time—or, more precisely, feel justified in spending time—on the endless tasks of household life. So many meals and playdates to organize, so little time. Which is fine, except when that means denigrating the rich solitude of the reader. In A. S. Byatt's novel *Babel Tower,* a young mother is brought to court by her in-laws for neglecting her baby. The main charge against her: reading silently while rocking the child, who somehow seems to have avoided permanent damage.

Not very far away from this domestic puritanism is the lifestyle pornography of the rich and mentally impoverished. Food and decorating are the least taxing of aesthetic preoccupations, vapid forms of sophistication requiring little effort and yet yielding great rewards in ostentatious superiority.

Having asked a publishing executive friend whether he would rather eat out or read, John Allemang got the following near-parody reply: "To me, that's laughable. Charlie Trotter's in Chicago, an eight-course tasting menu, Chambolle-Musigny *premier cru,* every course to die for, constant discussions about the ingredients and the reductions in each dish—there's nothing I'd rather be doing. Eating is hedonistic. Reading is ascetic and solitary."

There are so many ugly things in that snapshot of a silly life, it's hard to know where to begin. But how about just one: stop saying "to die for," you loser.

I'm tempted to be a bit pious here, if only as an antidote to the complacency of the house-and-home crowd and the insidious idea that reading is just one more form of leisure-time choice. I won't weigh in on the deep human value of literature, for that needs no defence from me; instead I'll just make a simple political point.

A few years ago I met John O'Leary, the executive director of Frontier College, the country's oldest literacy and education outreach program. In the early days of Canada, Frontier College sent young undergraduates into the bush camps and logging settlements of the north and west. There, often amid taunts and violence, they tutored the unlettered loggers in reading and writing, hoping to give them more opportunities.

Nowadays, Frontier College has shifted its notion of where the Canadian frontier lies. The new generation of instructors work at men's shelters and downtown halfway houses in Vancouver and Calgary and Toronto, giving the basic skills of post-industrial life to a diverse group of men all hanging onto the outer margins of society.

Over the past couple of years, John has asked me to come with him to Toronto's Seaton House, the largest men's shelter in Canada, and talk about philosophy, life, Plato's Cave, and whatever else we could manage to convey to the assorted small audience sitting around the bleak recreation room on the ground floor of that all too prison-like building on George Street.

It's not an easy crowd, especially when our little talk means that the television is turned off for half an hour. Explaining Plato is no picnic at the best of times, even with a dedicated and fully literate audience of smart, mostly carefree, middle class undergraduates. Here, it's all uphill. The stakes are both higher and harder to articulate. Maybe for just this reason, the resulting discussions have always been lively and passionate. Plato has been judged by these streetwise thinkers a magician of media manipulation and an obscurantist quack, which is about right.

Philosophy, the saying goes, bakes no bread; like writing more generally, it's easy for it to appear dispensable, especially when bread is what you lack—also, paradoxically, when you have too much, in the form of small-batch focaccia and flash-imported brioche. But, in this world, nobody is likely to get any kind of bread reliably if they lack the essential software of citizenship, the basic operating system of social life, literacy. It's not a luxury, it's a basic human right. To have those skills and yet disdain them isn't a laughable foible but a gross insult to yourself and others.

Mark Twain was wry on the issue: "The man who does not read good books," he said, "has no advantage over the man who cannot read them." Let's go further: the man who cannot read is unfortunate; the man who does not read is unforgivable. Here's a little writing for the happily aliterate. Instead of three hours eating eight courses of food, how about donating one hour to helping someone else acquire the skill you so arrogantly take for granted?

✦

'Tis the season to debate
24 December 2002

It's Christmas Eve, at least by some kind of reckoning, and that either means something to you or it doesn't. (In logic there are no surprises.) By now we all know about the "Happy holidays!" greeters at The Gap, the "seasonal tree" at Toronto's City Hall, and the various sentiment options employed by MPs and MPPs on their mass-mailed greeting cards. In part we know this because the *Post,* ever responsive to imagined reader interest, has run a series detailing the multicultural depredations of poor old postmodern Canada.

Does anyone really care about this? The recent debates over "seasonal inclusiveness"—stretched thin by fulminating pundits to become "anti-Christian prejudice"—have been one of the stranger developments in recent public debate. Seriously, in a year of civil-liberties erosion, illegal detention of Afghanis at Guantanamo Bay, and endless self-laceration about our so-called anti-Americanism, you'd think we would have better things to fuss about.

But no. Because this kind of stuff is easy to get steamed over, costs little or nothing in terms of real consequences, and provides lots of room for overheated rhetoric about the end of the world. The fact is, taking the Christ out of Christmas is neither inclusive nor anti-Christian, it's just what happens when you have a varied population, no state-mandated religion, and an economy powered by consumer turbines. (Also by military contracts, but that doesn't get mentioned in these arguments.) Christ went out of Christmas a long time ago, in fact, just like the holy went out of holidays. As far as sentiments go, "Season's greetings" is the only rational option left, since it has the benefit of tautological emptiness: nothing left to lose.

There is a trend here, however, which is the vocal, sometimes intemperate displeasure at perceived cultural backsliding and "menacing" innovation. It might as well be 1985 for all the furor over "political correctness" this season, like some peculiar form of cultural nostalgia.

Consider another example. Earlier this month this newspaper reported at length on the controversy over the Royal Ontario Museum changing its dating convention from the Holy Roman Empire relics of *Anno Domini* and Before Christ to the more neutral Common Era and Before Common Era. Shock! Horror!

Never mind that the C.E./B.C.E. style has been the scholarly norm for decades, or that it is perfectly comprehensible to even the meanest intelligence—much more so, probably, than the Latin for "year of our lord." Suddenly the ROM, already seduced by the crystalline imagination of architect Daniel Libeskind, was losing its grip on tradition and stability and…

Sorry, I dozed off there for a second. Who can really get worked up about this? The only good argument I have ever heard in favour of retaining A.D. was made by a semi-loony colleague of mine, who claimed that it reveals, and so makes certain we remember, the overwhelming Christian bias in the entire Western tradition of cultural dominance. Maybe we should mandate "Merry Christmas" so we're forced to see that Christ is still in the imperial position.

But here's some more distressing news for devotees of *Anno Domini*. The ROM has just unveiled a new logo for its big fundraising campaign and—wait for it—the design is no longer adorned by the traditional image of a crown! Yes, it's true: the royal designation stays but the metonymic image is gone. (The logo is also to my eye a little, um, ugly; but that's another story.)

As chair of the ROM's Institute for Contemporary Culture—the venerable museum's window on the modern world—I might be expected to applaud this move. In fact, the opposite is true. I wasn't involved in the decision, but I will miss the crown and I think losing it is a mistake, not so much out of serious monarchist sentiment as from cavalier sympathy: a matter of style, really, like preferring Lovelace to Milton even though he's the lesser poet.

One of my friends, a mother of two, told me a harrowing story last week of her elder daughter's "seasonal concert" which consisted entirely of show tunes and a squeaky off-key version of "O, What a Beautiful Morning." This is deplorable, certainly, but on aesthetic grounds, not theological ones. The traditional Yuletide hymns exert their musical power sometimes despite, and always notwithstanding, their particular theology. Replacing them with pop songs would be a crime against taste, yes, but not against Christianity.

Now I realize that the aestheticization of belief—seeing culture as largely a matter of style, not truth—will be judged just another sortie in the great war against tradition, another sign of lost substance. But the reality is that traditions always thrive on multiple, sometimes contradictory forms of devotion, and style is often a more significant arbiter of personal choice than validity. There are unbelievers in love with the smell of incense and the sound of plainchant, conservatives who like acid house and cocaine, and cultural rebels who write with quill pens and wear silk breeches.

It isn't just that traditions are always evolving, though that is certainly true. The Christmas of popular imagination is already, here in the twenty-first century C.E., a mixture of sacred and profane, nativity scenes and Charlie Brown, the archangel Gabriel in flowing robes and suave, flirty Cary Grant in *The Bishop's Wife*. More than that, our tradition in the West has always been one of challenging tradition. The tension between what's done and what's possible, between cavalier grace and roundhead judgment, is the lifeblood of our world.

Speaking of tensions, I take it back: these debates do matter after all. They are a constant, essential argument about identity. What do we believe? What matters to us? Who is "us"? Our gift to each other this season, call it what you will, should be the acknowledgment that there is no final answer to those questions—and maybe that is their genius.

✦

You can't build an empire in 18 months
8 January 2003

What could you accomplish in 18 months? Build a house? Write a book? Maybe get in shape? On the other hand: destroy a marriage; ruin a company; swindle a friend?

It's a good amount of time, 18 months, at once conceivable and ample. A lot of people tend to underestimate what can be accomplished with the time they have, for good or ill. A colleague of mine likes to say, while invigilating examinations, "Twenty minutes left. And remember, 20 minutes is time enough to go mad."

Has the Bush Administration gone mad, or were they always? The plan unveiled this week for the invasion and occupation of Iraq claims that an 18-month military presence will be sufficient for the "regime change" the president has set as his goal in the region. It also says only the most senior Iraqi officials will face trial, and—my personal favourite—secured oil fields will be used to finance the democratic reconstruction of the country.

This is a stroke of genius from a group who just announced a massive tax cut for stock-market investors even as an inherited budget surplus has dried up and the unemployment rate continues to climb. Consider:

We keep hearing that this second Gulf War is not about oil, even as ideological supporters of the first one (which wasn't about oil at the time) now admit that it actually was about oil. As with all conservative rhetoric, "the past" is here revealed as an elastic property. To wit: they called us crazy for saying the first war was about oil when they said it was really about Kuwaiti sovereignty, but now they admit it was about oil. That was then, this is now. In 10 years supporters of the current war will probably admit that this one is about oil too, but for the moment they need to win the hot-air wars, so they accuse critics of "living in the past." That was now, this is then.

We don't even have to wait for the self-serving legerdemain, however. Courtesy the White House plan, we already know the new war is indeed about oil but only as a fiscal lever. The Americans don't want the oil for themselves, just control of oil revenues to offset the costs of invasion! Critics have slammed the Bush team for opening up new fronts in a struggle whose threats are actually shadowy and unpredictable, in turn targeting Afghanistan, Iraq, and North Korea. Now we see the hidden wisdom of this, which is that *all wars shall eventually become self-financing!* At that point there is no theoretical limit to the number of conflicts you could carry on simultaneously.

In the meantime, some pretty heavy front-end expenses. More than 60,000 American troops are already within striking distance of Iraq, with about 100,000 more in readiness. Two aircraft-carrier battle groups and two amphibious assault groups will deploy to the region this month. Despite claims by Jack Straw, the British foreign secretary, that the chances of war are actually decreasing, the British will send their carrier *Ark Royal* to the Gulf this weekend.

And the Iraqis are helping things along, as only a crazy regime can do. So far weapons inspectors in Iraq have found nothing to substantiate charges that Saddam's regime has been manufacturing or stockpiling weapons of mass destruction. But instead of waiting out the inspection and working to forestall conflict, Saddam responded this week with a trademark speech full of vivid Biblical imagery and charges of Satanic corruption.

Is he just nuts or does he know something the rest of us don't? If the occupation plan is the best the White House can do, he might be saner than he looks. The Bush course veers all over the map, full of vagueness and not a little outright fantasy, inviting a disastrous outcome. In one section, the planners wonder whether U.S. troops will face a friendly or hostile reception. Were Caesar's centurions dumb enough to suppose that they would be met with smiles and hugs when they marched into Gaul or Britain?

Beyond the initial stages of military occupation, the Americans have no idea what's going to happen or who should be in charge. The Administration is even divided on the question of who should rule a democratized Iraq: pro-American exiles, who have no standing with the Iraqi people; or a cadre of dormant democrats within the country, who will suddenly emerge as compliant global partners in the wake of Saddam's collapse. This, presumably, even as some portion of the existing leadership, yet to be determined, is put on trial for war crimes.

No wonder Pentagon leaks from last year showed reluctance to attack. There is no reasonable endgame in sight, and military leaders hate that more than gays in the ranks. All the 18-month deadline really provides is an escape hatch for generals with no experience of, or desire for, political power.

Bush supporters are now adorning the president's recent moves with the honorific labels "doctrine" and "plan," as if to put this ill-conceived policy on the same plane as those framed by Monroe or Marshall. I guess a plan can be pretty much anything, and a doctrine just a plan you stick to even against mounting objection. But the real problem with the Bush invasion policy is not its shaky moral foundation or its cynical justification for seizing Iraq's oil reserves.

It is, rather, the same thing that afflicts all aspects of American foreign policy, namely, that the Americans are neither good peace-keepers nor committed conquerors. They are, instead, confused and half-assed imperialists. If you're going to build an empire, as the Roman emperors knew, you have to stay on the ground in distant countries, usually for years, sometimes for generations.

George Bush has given himself just 18 months: time enough for all of us to go mad, and for a fair number of people to die to no lasting purpose.

✦

War opposition is too big to ignore
2 January 2003

What's it like to be White House press secretary Ari Fleischer? What does he dream of when he's standing in front of the seal-embossed podium, deflecting the probes of two dozen outwardly ravening but inwardly docile reporters? Where does his mind wander?

Consider the following exchange from last Friday, pulled from the White House website but eerily reminiscent of one of those surreal plays by Will Eno where some archetypal figure of American life stands behind a microphone and tries to explain himself to a tribunal of flashbulbs and invisible spectators. (See, for example, "Behold the Coach" in the February issue of *Harper's Magazine*.)

Q: "Can I ask another Iraq-related question? This weekend, there are some more anti-war demonstrations planned in various parts of the country. Is the President troubled by these manifestations of dissent?"

Mr. Fleischer: "I think the President welcomes the fact that we are a democracy and people in the United States, unlike Iraq, are free to protest and to make their case known. And that's a time-honored part of American tradition, and the President fully understands it. It's a strength of our democracy."

Q: "Is he worried about going to war with a sizeable percentage of the population not supporting him?"

Mr. Fleischer: "I'm not sure that it's fair to say that it's sizeable. I think it is anybody's guess. But there are equal numbers of people who—larger numbers of people who, of course, are very much in support of what the President is doing. I think the fact of the matter is, most people who support what the President is doing are not going to take to the street to say disarm Saddam Hussein."

My favourite moment: the little hiccup where Mr. Fleischer instinctively realizes that he shouldn't claim that the pro-war faction is merely *equal* to the visible anti-war movement when he can just as easily claim it is *larger*. And how do we know that? We know that precisely because they do not take to the streets!

Poor old Q, whoever he is, with his timid requests to ask "another" Iraq-related question, his rather daring insistence that Mr. Bush's "welcoming" of democracy is not really the main issue, his plangent use of "sizeable." He is clearly no match for Mr. Fleischer, who doubts whether it is even "fair" to call a linked series of street-filling protests across the country—not to mention the rest of the world—sizeable. The demonstration in Washington, D.C., pulled 100,000 people onto the Mall, but presumably Mr. Fleischer didn't think it was fair to look out his window.

Here are some other relevant numbers, for those who want to look past the bizarre mind-killing theatre of the briefing room. Mr. Bush's approval rating has plummeted in recent weeks, from the heady 90 percent he enjoyed right after the September 11th terrorist attacks to a dismal 58 percent. That number comes from Gallup; *Newsweek* had him even lower, at 56 percent, and a CNN/*Time* survey put him at 53 percent.

As for war with Iraq, more than half of Americans polled—53 percent—say Mr. Bush has not outlined a clear rationale for a military ouster of Saddam Hussein. Which is reassuring, since there isn't one. That's up from 37 percent as of last September, by the way, when another Gulf War was little more than a talking point, and the Administration's peculiar axis-of-evil logic—North Korea has nukes, so let's invade Iraq—was still in a nascent stage.

A majority of Americans oppose American military action if the invasion lacks United Nations support or has only the backing of one or two allies. (That would be top-lapdog Great Britain and whoever is next in the currying-favour line, maybe Australia.) And 60 percent of respondents told *Newsweek* pollsters last week that they would prefer the Administration take more time to find a peaceful alternative to war.

I don't know what exactly constitutes a "sizeable" number—the *Oxford English Dictionary*'s "of (fairly) large size" is unhelpful—but I'm willing to bet three out of five counts. So does five out of 10, otherwise known as half.

A lot of Americans don't want this war. They are not "very much in support of what the President is doing." They're not in favour of it at all. They also, maybe more importantly, support the role of the U.N. as the only moral arbiter of international affairs. Could it be that the United States—if not its current election-stealing Administration—is finally emerging as a partner in global co-operation?

I know, I know: crazy talk. Some portion of the disapproval, perhaps even a sizeable one, is rooted in the ailing economy, plunging markets, rising unemployment, and a tax-reform package apparently aimed at making the super-rich super-richer. With the exception of the last, as Mr. Fleischer would no doubt say if asked, the Bush Administration is not directly responsible for any of that.

Still, citizens of a republic have a reasonable expectation that their governors will stimulate growth, balance payments and, at the least, punish large-scale swindlers who drain confidence as well as profits from the stock market. Mr. Bush has done none of that. He has focused on dubious foreign policy, made claims he can't now retreat from, and put the United States in the ridiculous position of trying to justify invasion on the basis of 12 empty missile canisters whose best range was 12 miles.

Meanwhile, in case it wasn't reported in your newspaper yet again today, bombs are already falling on Iraq. Military action, if not actual invasion, is under way. How many Iraqis are dead already? I don't know; neither do you. In fact, at this point it's anybody's guess.

Next question.

✦

I checkmate, therefore I am
5 February 2003

A familiar ambivalence surfaced this week as chess grandmaster Gary Kasparov attempted to face down his non-human opponent, the computer Deep Junior.

On the one hand, many of us root for Mr. Kasparov. He represents the hope that creative human intelligence is superior to the algorithm-crunching of even the biggest, fastest computer. On the other hand, some of us root for Junior. Why? Because, somewhere in there, we harbour a little fear that defeat of a supercomputer might mean—as events so often prove—all technology is fallible.

It's an old conundrum, and one on display in far more serious ways elsewhere this week. In the aftermath of the Columbia disaster, investigators gathered clues, sought reasons, reconstructed events. What went wrong? Did a system fail or malfunction? Or was there human error? A faulty decision, a moment of panic or confusion?

It used to be a truism in the aircrash investigation that in the end the answer was almost always "pilot error," a judgment that was final if harsh—and, in essence, Biblical. If you seek the roots of disaster, look no further than the imperfection of man. But that answer is too easy, since it assumes the very premise it should be questioning, namely our shaky but necessary faith in the machines we build and fly.

You see the problem. If we start distrusting machines, it's only a few short steps to the neo-Luddites and the Unabomber. Less wildly, we might start to wonder if those smart bombs and fly-by-wire F-16s are really so great after all. We assign agency (and so blame) only to Maj. Harry Schmidt, not the bomb he dropped on helpless Canadian soldiers; but surely part of that awful chain of events was the absolute accuracy of the weapon, which magnified the adrenaline-fuelled mistake of the man. Where does the line get drawn?

Distrust breeds distrust, largely because fear highlights dependence. We tend to blame ourselves rather than the machines because we must believe in them: they control so much of our lives. And when we don't blame ourselves, we most often blame that great black box, chance. In 2003, the space odyssey ended up being deadly not because a computer ran amok, just because things went wrong, the tragic accumulation of probabilities. Misfortune, not murder. But that does not solve the problem of our complex, sometimes hostile dependence on machines.

Which brings us back to Mr. Kasparov and Deep Junior. These chess matches are no longer the big news they once were, in part because Mr. Kasparov, acknowledged as the greatest player in the world, has already been defeated by a machine. In 1997, he was edged 3.5 points to 2.5 by the IBM machine Deep Blue, Deep Junior's "father," in a loss invariably referred to as "humiliating."

Nor does chess grip the popular imagination the way it did when legendary paranoiac Bobby Fischer challenged Boris Spassky in the cold war of the mind, Reykjavik 1972. I remember following that series move for move through articles in *Time* magazine—a fact that now seems not just quaint but incredible. Chess crazies still challenge passers-by in the famous southwest corner of Washington Square Park, a place where you can score coke and a rook-led victory steps from each other, but searching for Bobby Fischer is, these days, more a metaphor for nurturing your child than a celebration of chess.

The result is that this week's man-machine matches are small-time news. Facing a computer for the first time since 1997, Mr. Kasparov is playing six games against Junior, a machine built by the Israeli scientists Amir Baran and Shay Bushinsky. The two opponents are currently tied after four games, with a win each and two draws. The fifth game is today, with Mr. Kasparov playing white (and so moving first), the sixth on Friday.

The human grandmaster is employing a version of the strategy he attempted against Deep Blue, what insiders call "going off book." The computer's advantage over a human is its massive processing power, which allows it to scan millions of possible move-combinations, but also its precise knowledge of every recorded game its opponent has played. So Mr. Kasparov tried mixing it up with Deep Blue in 1997, changing his style and inventing new gambits. The program caught on and adjusted, eventually winning.

Mr. Kasparov is attempting even more radical jukes and openings against Deep Junior, hoping to throw the computer off with unorthodox combinations like quick-step deployment of a knight in front of his queen. In other words, the best strategy against a presumptively rational opponent is creative irrationality.

"I think I made a brilliant move to get Deep Junior out of the book and make it think on its own," Mr. Kasparov said of last Sunday's draw. "If you play aggressive chess and throw in a little twist you can get great positions against the strongest computer programs."

If it works, the Krazy Kasparov strategy will no doubt be chalked up as a victory of human spontaneity over machine literalness. It's the same dodge routinely used to mock Mr. Data, the stiff android on "Star Trek: The Next Generation," or the crude computers on the original "Star Trek," thick-witted logic-bashers whose circuits could be fried by the merest hint of paradox. We'll all breathe a sigh of relief and think, You can't beat a little animal creativity! Way to go, humans!

But consider the downside. Computers as powerful as Deep Junior are self-revising. They accommodate subtleties and nuances; they can modify their behaviour to meet a human's instrumental aggression. In many senses of the words, they think and create.

It follows that they can, like any human, learn to make deadly miscalculations as well as brilliant moves. When we defeat our machines, we merely bring them down to our imperfect, irrational level. We only win for losing. How very human.

✦

Cricket—a pursuit unruled by money
19 February 2003

One consequence of living in North America for too long is that you actually start to accept that everything is about money.

I can't be the only one struck by the inventiveness of contestants on the Fox Network's "Joe Millionaire" to rationalize the virtues of alleged gazillion-heir Evan Hammerhead. Instead of the obvious lunk he was, gagging on foie gras and goat's cheese, galumping along as if trying to push down a wall with his forehead, he was described as "charming," "sweet," and "a gentleman." Only a savvy New Yorker called it quits with Evan, and she is probably now, for her pains, shivering in a blizzard-chilled Brooklyn walk-up. Everyone else, including guileless Zora, the last girl standing, spoke of true love and "the fairy tale."

The fairy tale, in case you haven't been paying attention, means marrying for lots and lots of cash. Zora seemed briefly stunned by Evan's revelation that he wasn't rich after all, took a meditative walk in the woods, then let him off the hook so they could "continue their journey together," whatever that means. Ah, sweet. But, in a stroke of television genius that was massively telegraphed by Paul, the smirking Aussie butler, the happy couple were given a million dollars anyway!

Awesome. Money; not money; money! Love, money, love—who cares, what's the difference? It was great television, in itself full and complete justification for the civilization various pro-Bush hawks have insisted we must protect by invading Iraq. Forget the French: Descartes, Voltaire, Proust—sure, but what have they done for us lately? Smelly cheese and left-wing intellectuals. We have the Fox Network, pal. Get over your death wish. Ban abortion and start breeding now!

I know, I know: I exaggerate. But that's what you have to do in a market where everything is convertible into dollar value. The Bush Administration's current economic plan seems designed to undermine that market, weirdly enough, something Federal Reserve chairman Alan Greenspan recently pointed out—until it was pointed out to him that he would lose his job, and his own personal dollar value, if he continued to do so. The great lesson of the American Century: sooner or later, everyone has his price.

Which explains why the *Onion* story claiming George Steinbrenn will guarantee a New York Yankees World Series victory this year by signing every single player in Major League Baseball is only slightly funny. (The Bombers, now in spring training, have just exceeded their own record-breaking total of last season by edging the payroll close to U.S.$150-million, or about three times what Evan/Joe was supposed to be worth.) It also explains why North Americans continue to be baffled by cricket, a sport where principle has always mattered more than coin.

Consider, for a moment, the fact that two members of a small nation's cricket team can make international headlines by engaging in a political protest, cause a despotic leader to stay away from the ground, and set an example for post-colonial racial cooperation. We in Canada were briefly energized last week by the surprise victory of our XI over the Bangladeshis, a newly minted Test side, but the real story of the current World Cup is what's happening in Zimbabwe.

Two weeks ago, batsman Andy Fowler, who is white, and fast bowler Henry Olonga, who is black, issued a joint statement decrying the "death of democracy in our beloved Zimbabwe," and wore black armbands as the side faced Namibia in Harare. (The six-week World Cup series is being hosted by South Africa, currently trailing favourite Australia, but some matches are being played in Zimbabwe and Kenya.)

The two players issued the statement after deciding over some objection to the play in the Cup matches. Many "patriotic Zimbabweans" wanted them to abstain in solidarity with the "millions of our compatriots who are starving, unemployed, and oppressed," the statement said. They had decided to play, but only while publicly stating their horror that "people have been murdered, raped, beaten and had their homes destroyed."

The protest is clearly aimed at Zimbabwean president Robert Mugabe, a leftist dictator who has laid waste to much of the country's farmland and lined his own pockets while meeting all protests from white citizens with charges of racism. The voice of Mr. Olonga, Zimbabwe's first black player on the national side, blocks that move and has united the country in this high-profile protest. Mr. Mugabe, a cricket fan fond of his status as patron of the Zimbabwe Cricket Union, has been publicly humiliated.

The World Cup is a tangle of political tensions and criss-crossing loyalties. England has refused to participate, citing concerns over security; purists have objected to the presence of substandard teams such as Namibia; a Canadian player, raised in Australia, has dismissed his Canuck identity. It was ever thus: cricket has, in turn, expressed village rivalry, pitted upper-class amateurs against working-class professionals, and given voice to colonial resentment. Also, let it be said, fomented national hatreds (the bodyline controversy) and allowed free rein to religious bigotry (Pakistan v. India). It is, like soccer, far more than a game.

There is no longer a meaningful distinction between Players and Gentlemen in the sport—all participants get paid—but cricket remains a pursuit unruled by money, shot through with significance, vehicle for protest and change. Mr. Mugabe is a blight on modern Africa and Mr. Olonga and Mr. Fowler are to be congratulated for their courage in using their position to say so.

Some people like to say sports should not be political, as if to protect the imagined purity of athletic contest. But that is patent nonsense. Sports are always political—except when, like too much else in our miserable culture, they are simply, and pointlessly, about money.

✦

What distinguishes us from the Americans
5 March 2003

I recently wrote, on a commission from the *New York Times,* this column on Canada/U.S. relations. The editors sat on it for a week, then rejected it without explanation. I don't know if that means they disliked the position, or just, such is the state of continental relations, that they got bored. Probably something simpler, like Maureen Dowd hogging space again.

I thought *Post* readers might want a chance to make up their own minds. Also, in contrast to less august publications, the *Times* feels no obligation to offer a kill fee when spiking articles they have requested. Like most writers I prefer, when possible, to get paid. So here it is, the piece the *New York Times* wouldn't run!

Toronto
The trial of two Air National Guard pilots responsible for the deaths last year of four Canadian paratroopers, and wounding of eight others, has highlighted a relationship that is more dysfunctional by the week. Canadians and Americans find themselves no longer friendly.

The imminent Iraqi war, conflict within NATO, and massive border security—not to mention old disputes over softwood lumber and hydroelectricity—have all contributed to a widening gap of misunderstanding between the continental cousins. Whatever the Bush Administration might believe, the solution is not for us to fall into line but for Americans to spare a thought about why we don't want to.

It's true that this relationship has always been unequal. Most Americans think of Canadians, when they think of them at all, as inoffensive minor allies good at hockey and prone to quasi-socialist ideas like universal health care. Most Canadians, it's fair to say, think of Americans with the mixture of admiration and fear nebbishy boys reserve for their older brothers who captain the football team. With a population roughly equal to California's and a land mass exceeded only by Russia's, its cities strung out in a necklace hugging the southerly reaches, Canada is an unlikely country at the best of times. Naturally a hulking powerful neighbour makes us uneasy and, sometimes, resentful.

The unease grew after the September 11th terrorist attacks, which of course included many Canadian deaths. The failure of President George W. Bush to mention Canada in his list of thanks to foreign friends was a textbook definition of taking someone for granted. And, predictably, this resulted in paroxysms of self-hatred depressing and familiar to Canadians: one cadre of public opinion excoriated the Bush Administration for its lack of regard; another attacked the first as "anti-American," arguing that we deserved the snub because, among other things, our armed forces are so puny.

The strident pro-Bush voices in this country display a new form of inferiority complex, forever enacting a sick codependency which involves berating the Canadian government and people for lack of guts while reading every criticism of American foreign policy as lack of loyalty. They are reminiscent of colonial elites of old: more

American than the Americans, they greet a *National Review* hack-fest advocating invasion of Canada, or brain-dead "Canuckistan" jokes, with something approaching treasonous glee.

Their knee-jerk charge of anti-Americanism, meanwhile, is incoherent: how could opposition to foreign policy, illicit use of power, or even certain television shows, be equivalent to condemning an entire nation of 300 million? No, the only anti-Americans here are those supporters of the current Bush Administration who really do equate it with America, then attack critics of the first as enemies of the second.

None of this is helpful in clarifying Canada's role in the international community, or as America's geographically closest ally. This country is at a crossroads and the events of the past 18 months have shown just how much most Canadians want to distinguish themselves from their neighbours. If Canada has lost some of the soft-power status it enjoyed in the first few decades after the Second World War, when our armed forces showed themselves anything but puny, it must nevertheless maintain a position of moral independence.

This would be good for both Canadians and Americans, but it will take some doing, and we Canadians will have to be a little less polite about it. We've grown too accustomed to letting your policy drive ours simply because we don't have any aircraft-carrier battle groups.

The old cliché has it that Canadians, lacking an identity of their own, construct one out of not being American. I have never understood why this is considered inadequate or feeble. If you were the only dissenter in a room holding a dozen people, standing up and saying "I'm not the same as you" would be a clear mark of moral courage.

In any event, Canadian identity goes well beyond a game of I-know-you-are-but-what-am-I; also, let it be said, well beyond the igloo-dwelling, caribou-eating stereotypes of old. For generations, from the McGill law professor who drafted the *Universal Declaration of Human Rights,* John Humphrey, to the ranks of political theorists that include Charles Taylor and Will Kymlicka, we have been busy creating, in your shadow, a model of citizenship that is inclusive, diverse, open-ended, and transnational. It is dedicated to far-reaching social justice and the rule of international law. And we're successfully exporting it around the world not by bucking the U.N. but by seeing it for the flawed but necessary agency it is.

Listen, we know you don't know much about us, and that you don't really care that you don't. On most days, we don't care that much either. In fact, we find it funny: American ignorance is a staple of our richly ironic strain of humour, which we've managed to sell your way more than once. We like you, and respect you, and sometimes wish we had a little more of what makes you great. We even understand, most of us, that tragic accidents happen and young men get killed by their friends.

But we don't want to be you. And there are times, like right now, when we wish you had a little more of what makes us great.

◆

Happiness is an ethical state of being
19 March 2003

It's clearly a happy day if you're a fan of George W. Bush and his brand of liberation imperialism, maybe a little less so if you're the eviscerated and abandoned Tony Blair, the dispensable ally, and maybe an unhappy one if you thought human affairs would ever be ruled by reason instead of force, argument instead of invocations of God's will, diplomacy instead of war.

The question is, is your happiness really related to these large-scale external events?

Analysts and professors have been saying for some weeks that the current global situation is world-historical, on a par with August 1914, or May 1940, or maybe October 1066 for all I know—though this time the French are not among those shipping out for battle. I am prepared to believe it. And yet, I also believe that most people live their lives at anything but the world-historical level, and allow their happiness to be influenced only scantly, if at all, by the big events around them.

Two studies released this week on the nature of human happiness give the usual cold shower to the hot lathers of punditry. Not surprisingly, people mostly care about things that are right in front of their faces, like marriage and the acquisition of material goods. The studies also display the cheerful contradictions to be found in so much psychological research

Study one (reported here on Monday) found, contrary to the widespread conviction that landing "the one" will make you happy, that "most people retain a steady level of happiness in the face of life's many twists and turns," including marriage or divorce. There may be a boost in well-being right after a smooth wedding, but then most people return to whatever level of happiness they enjoyed—or didn't—before. Naturally this is very bad news for most of the current American television schedule and large chunks of this newspaper.

Study two (reported yesterday) found that "children who equate happiness with money, fame and beauty are more likely to suffer from depression than youngsters who do not place as much value on being rich and attractive." Naturally this is very bad news for most of the current American television schedule and large chunks of this newspaper.

Now, I grant you a reconciliation of these two results is logically possible. It involves unpacking the notion of "twists and turns," a concept so far lacking precise scientific definition. Psychology tells us at once that levels of happiness are steady, virtually genetic; and also that yearning after unattainable goods will plunge us into its opposite. Obviously the key point is what you "equate" happiness with, since not getting that, whatever it is, would then mean returning to your basic happiness-level, now unfortunately experienced as depression. Sad but true—and pretty much the *raison d'être* of consumer markets everywhere.

The studies were presented at a psychology conference being held this week in the English seaside town of Bournemouth, nobody's idea of a fun place in March. Just to let you know how much better we do it over in the Philosophy Department, *our* next big conference on happiness will be held in Santa Barbara in late April. And I'll be there—always assuming my Canadian passport is still honoured at "the border," otherwise known as the airport in my own city.

I got invited because I once wrote a book about happiness. It was a hoot to write, not least because I got to make fun of contradictory psychological research, newspaper visions of happiness, and the American television schedule. But at the end of the day, I kept coming back to old, old insights about happiness and world affairs, ones missed by too many psych studies and the people they poll.

Happiness, said Aristotle, is not a feeling or an experience, it is an ethical state of being. It means judging that you have made the right choices and done the right things, and enjoyed a measure of luck along the way. Where and when you are born, how the play of daily contingency affects you, do not determine your happiness, but they do constrain it. And so it often seems as though the choices of everyday life, cosmically small though they are, matter far more than events in distant capitals and war zones.

But here is the key point. You must live your entire life with honour and commitment. You must try to build something larger than yourself: a community of citizens, a community of reason, a just and peaceful world. You may be defeated, because violence, arrogance, and unreason are powerful forces in history. But that does not diminish your responsibility.

Objections to the current invasion have been ignored, as most of us suspected they would be. Popular protest and international disapproval have been unable to head off an unjust and illegal war when empire was bent on exerting its will. Rational argument was insufficient to forestall anxiety and the false connection to terror. All of these are things Aristotle would have understood perfectly well, since when it comes to imperial posturing not much has changed in the 2,500 years between him and us.

Here's a thought to remember as the new American Century dawns, in violence as so often. There are other forms of courage than physical, and other forms of happiness than what psychologists stumble around attempting to understand. There's the courage of your convictions, and the happiness of knowing you have made an effort to influence the largest events of your time.

There is also, just for the record, the cold comfort of knowing that all empires crumble when hubris and militarism alienate even their closest allies, distant wars entangle them in bloody conflicts, and popular leaders are exposed as self-serving frauds. I'm not saying this is especially good news, just that it is history's lesson.

Have a nice day.

✦

Don't blindly "support the troops"
2 April 2003

We've been told countless times over the course of the current Iraqi war, now entering its bloody middle period—the period, that is, when news coverage begins to pall even as casualties begin to mount—that we need to *support the troops*. It is a sentiment widely considered unobjectionable, imposed alike during editorial meetings, radio talk shows, and the seventh-inning stretch of baseball games. Only a callous brute would deny support for these brave young men and women.

But we should deny it, and for a very simple logical reason. If the war they are engaged in is unjust, then even the bravest and most honourable soldiers do not merit support. We must distinguish between a wish for their safe and speedy return and an endorsement of what they are doing in the deserts of Iraq. We must distinguish between their courage and the uses to which it is put.

This war is unjust by any measure considered valid in the long tradition of philosophical and legal argument that stretches from Saint Augustine, through Pufendorf and Grotius, to the Geneva Convention and the Nuremberg Trials. It is an act of aggression, not defence; it is not being waged to restore peace; it was not the last resort. Whether it is about oil, or imperial muscle-flexing, or testing client-state loyalty in the New American Century—or all of these—matters less than the fact that it lacks basic ethical justification.

You may dispute all of this, may even dispute the worth of the just war tradition. Fine. But do not suggest that opposition to the war is invalid because, now that the war is on, we must support the troops. By that reasoning, any and all war is rendered *de facto* just, since it always entails feats of courage and self-sacrifice from the admirable young. That is mere militarism, the last refuge of the argument-free. No. If the admirable young are engaged, for whatever reason, in a cause which is not just, they are doing wrong. And our blind approval of their actions is equally wrong.

This is not a popular view, especially in wartime, and it is easy to see why. The shift in media coverage since the war began is palpable. Reporters cannot hide their fascination with wartime machinery and personnel. The planes, the guns, the armoured vehicles—it's all so compelling, like a shaky-camera war movie or first-person-shooter video game. Formerly sober and balanced journalists now reveal themselves as the military equivalent of jock-sniffers, those uneasy nerd professors who pass a failing point guard so he'll be eligible for the Final Four.

The deep compulsion of war is real enough. I know: I grew up in a military family, relished the thoroughbred machines of late-century air power, came within a whisker of joining up. But the green uniforms of the unified Canadian forces put me off; I missed the belted blue tunics and jaunty style of the old RCAF, top button undone, my silver swept-wing Sword waiting on the tarmac. This stuff dies hard. When that other national paper recently ran a graphic of U.S. aircraft being deployed in Iraq, I saw immediately that some witless editor had reversed the silhouettes of the A-10 and the F-18, two warplanes that look nothing like each other. Please.

But the pull of war is more than boy's-own fetishism over hardware. All men wonder whether they would be equal to the demands of battle, the physical courage and ability to withstand pain, the need to react under extreme pressure. Could you hack it? The problem, as the shell-shocked VC-sporting officer in *Ryan's*

Daughter says, is that you just don't know. You *can't* know. And so the rest of us, the vast majority who will never experience combat, will always wonder.

Politicians and generals have always taken advantage of this, slyly mixing the virtues of the battlefield with those of the debating floor. Plato warned centuries ago that this was dangerous, since the demands of war are for glory, not justice, and the endgame of militarism is a state where only combatants enjoy the benefits of citizenship. (The film version of Robert Heinlein's *Starship Troopers* offers a vivid futuristic version of this, complete with ultraviolence, xenophobia, and Nazi-inflected uniforms.)

The current reality is less spectacular but just as sinister. The warrior's virtues are once more annexed by the non-warrior, and politicians are revealed as the ultimate jock-sniffers, rigid old men willing to send young and brave ones to their deaths. Meanwhile, they deploy selective moral arguments in astonishing acts of high-level hypocrisy.

Consider. The Bush Administration flouts the authority of the United Nations, thereby weakening its global position, then gets on a high horse about the humanitarian aid programs the U.N. has suspended because of the attacks. The United States refuses to endorse the International Criminal Court, an agency that might have brought Saddam Hussein to justice without war, yet Secretary of Defense Donald Rumsfeld angrily invokes the Geneva Convention when Iraqi television shows video of captured American prisoners. Peter Arnett is fired by NBC for saying the first American war plan has apparently failed, even as all reports indicate the first American war plan has failed.

Such artful double-standards are formidable rhetorical weapons of empire. They allow power to keep its opponents always one down while mitigating the naked application of power. Heads we win, tails you lose. Critics of this sleight of hand are then accused of "moral equivalency," as if arguing for fairness and the rule of law were a violation of some prior God-given imperative. Which, of course, in the current atmosphere of repression and aggressive patriotism, it is.

There is a word for this combination of military celebration, disdain of objection, intimidation of dissent, and abuse of sentiment. The word is fascism.

✦

I'm bailing out, Aeroplan and all
16 April 2003

Air Canada was the Bush Administration of the airline industry long before new Aeroplan fees were announced by the carrier the other day. Arrogant without reason, rich yet graceless, contemptuous of rights—it's eerie. They alienated previous supporters, changed plans without warning, and demanded bail-outs even while pursuing monopoly. See what I mean?

The comparison is unfair to the U.S. regime, really. Washington has favoured might-as-right foreign policy and insult-as-argument public relations, but it's never slapped me with a 25 buck charge to use its "free" services. So far the Americans have no tolls at the border, and their dollar is strong enough that they don't have to enforce one-way currency exchange as in the old East Germany. Those DDR marks you were handed at Berlin checkpoints, little circular bits of tinfoil, weren't good for much: gassy beer, mass transit, cheap translations of Marx. Or you could always keep them as souvenirs. What you couldn't do was change them back.

Nobody ever said travel plans were currency, debased or otherwise, but my Aeroplan points display this same irritating lack of fungibility. I have, as of this writing, *thousands and thousands* of them. I'm not sure exactly how many because I threw out the last notice from Aeroplan. I started throwing all of them out about six months ago, even though my points were growing and the packages always included various slick brochures.

For a while there, I admit, I had been childishly pleased with the growing pile of points—business trips and pleasure trips, short trips and long, I always booked Air Canada. The points racked and I entertained glowing visions of free trips and swanky hotel suites. I got a silver plastic card in the mail that branded me a "prestige" customer and I happily slipped it into my wallet.

But soon I realized that there was virtually nothing I could do with these hard-earned points, this shiny but empty prestige. I would call the plan's 800-number and ask: Could I get an upgrade to business class for a long trip? No. Could I buy an extra seat for a friend on a trip already booked? No. Could I avoid Saturday-over restrictions or bad connections by splurging points? No.

Some upgrade certificates arrived in the mail. They sit on my desk still. Every time I tried to use them I encountered some kind of obstacle previously unimagined but covered by the restrictions in agate type on the back. Wrong type of ticket. Wrong type of route. Everywhere I turned, I had to spend more money even to be eligible for the savings I was promised as a reward earned by previous spending motivated in part by those future savings. The world descended into a horrible brand-loyalty nightmare in which I would surely awake one day to find that all money had been irreversibly converted into Starbucks dollars, Gap credits, and HIV reward cards.

I broke with Aeroplan well before news of the latest service fees, which send the cost in taxes and fees for a "reward" ticket perilously close to an ordinary ticket on WestJet or one of the other no-frills carriers. "We never actually have called it free travel," an Aeroplan flack said the other day, in defence of the new charges. "We've always called it reward travel. Even before, you had to pay various taxes."

Well that's okay then. "Reward travel" is a nice round phrase. At a minimum, it covers me having to reward Air Canada for being a loyal customer by having to use their non-flexible points for non-free trips.

Aeroplan isn't the real issue, anyway; Air Canada is. The airline is in deep trouble, finally landing in bankruptcy protection last month and this past weekend laying off another two hundred flight attendants in Vancouver and Edmonton. Fuel costs and the industry-wide slump since September 11th, 2001, do not fully account for its woes. Once among the world's great airlines, Air Canada has lately become surly, bloated, unhelpful, and gouging. They remind you of the chartered Canadian banks, though minus the massive profits.

That's one reason I'm an enthusiastic convert to the WestJet, the casual-cool employee-shareholder company based in Calgary. WestJet offers low fares, single-leg bookings, and flight attendants who let you know they're single. There's no food or drink on board, which means you can pack something better. And there's no movie, which means you get to read your book without distraction from B-list Hollywood.

There are drawbacks, but only for the faint-hearted. Flight attendants crack groaner jokes and speak in funny accents. There are gate-to-gate races to see which flight can finish boarding first. Pilots come on the PA, tell you their first names, and make fun of the weather in Calgary. The whole operation seems to be run by 12-year-olds. On a recent flight I saw a couple of youngsters in brown leather bomber jackets horsing around near the gate: the crew. Who could say that these two hotshots would not, like characters out of *Catch-22,* just decide to start wheeling the plane around the sky in steep screaming banks, whooping "La Cucaracha" all the while? I pictured the one sitting up front on the left, his hands poised over the controls, saying, "Dare me, dude! Dare me! I know this baby can do an Immelman turn if we hit full power NOW!"

I would have enjoyed that, myself. But instead it was smooth all the way to Toronto, we were on time, the flight attendants flirted with me, and I got home with three days and $800 that would have been gone forever on that other carrier.

I'm out, I'm done. You can have my Aeroplan points. Well, you could, if they were transferable. But you know what I mean.

I'm keeping my East German coins, though.

✦

So, where are all those WMDs?
20 April 2003

I hate to interrupt the post-war Might-Makes-Right festivities with anything as inconvenient as facts, but it seems a good time to state the truth before Operation "Iraqi Freedom" becomes a blip in the video game of televisual history. There is, so far, no evidence whatsoever of the stated justification for invading Iraq. No weapons of mass destruction, no roving laboratories of chemical menace, no massed stockpiles of nukes or plutonium cores.

In fact, some American officials last week admitted what many of us suspected: this invasion was pursued not to root out weapons of mass destruction but as a show of U.S. power. Speaking to ABC News, the *Independent,* and the *Sydney Morning Herald,* among others, anonymous U.S. officials admitted last week that they do not expect to find the hundreds of tons of nerve gas and thousands of litres of anthrax that were the haunting spectres of the run-up to invasion.

No nuclear weapons, meanwhile, have been destroyed or moved to Syria or hidden in remote desert locations; they do not exist. The real purpose of this invasion was to show Iran, Syria, and North Korea that the U.S. is prepared to fight. Iraq presented a tasty target with a central location, soft defences, and a wacked-out dictator whose image had already been demonized in the American imagination.

Students of history—that is, anyone who remembers what happened before March—will recall that the existence of weapons of mass destruction was the hinge-point of the U.S. effort to secure United Nations sanction for its invasion. When that was too slow to come, they wrote their own sanction. Some of us thought the official reason for invasion was not the real one, but the fiction was maintained. Now that the Iraqi armed forces have folded up like a pup tent, why bother even to pretend?

It's always remarkable to find government officials telling the truth; it's almost unheard of for them to do so just weeks behind the news. It took American politicians almost 10 years to acknowledge that Operation Desert Storm was about oil rather than protecting the beleaguered Mercedes drivers of Kuwait. Here they are fessing up less than a month after that heavily stage-managed toppling of Saddam's statue. Miracle!

Of course, it would be too much to expect U.S. officials, anonymous or otherwise, to admit they were actually lying. "We were not lying," said one official. "But it was just a matter of emphasis."

Right. That is of course bureaucratic code for, "Well, sure, we were lying. But don't you follow CNN? We won! This was a swift, popular invasion with minimal loss of American life and lots of good photo ops. We even had the drama of Saving Private Jessica! Nobody really cares about the alleged weapons or, still less, violations of international law. Are you kidding? Hahahaha."

In fact, the whole notion of "a matter of emphasis" bears further study; it is a phrase worthy of Machiavellian celebration. Compact and apparently innocuous, it manages to obscure the very idea of valid-versus-invalid reasons, otherwise known as truth. Stated intentions need have no relation to actual ones. If you win the war, especially if you do so quickly, this can even be admitted. And anyone who bothers to notice can be mocked as at least a spoilsport and at most a traitor. Miracle!

Speaking personally, I'd be a little less worried about all this if the objections were coming just from my buddies on the anti-war left. Instead, it's intelligence-community insiders who are pissed off at the Bush Administration for fudging the facts.

Senator Bob Graham, that notorious radical who heads up the Senate Intelligence Committee, recently insisted that the whole of a CIA report on Iraqi chemical weapons be declassified. It included the conclusion that the chances of Iraq using chemical weapons were "very low" for the "foreseeable future." In Britain, military analysts are incensed that government ministers have been making selective use of plagiarized reports to bolster a weak case. "You cannot just cherry-pick evidence that suits your case and ignore the rest. It is a cardinal rule of intelligence," said one British intelligence officer.

Another analyst, whose work was among the selectively stolen paragraphs of Colin Powell's U.N. presentation earlier this year, pointed out that much of the information on Iraqi weapons of mass destruction had come from Ahmed Chalabi's Iraqi National Congress, which received Pentagon money for intelligence-gathering. "The INC saw the demand, and provided what was needed," he said. "The implication is that they polluted the whole US intelligence effort."

Former CIA director James Woolsey, another well-known leftist nutcake, put the whole matter succinctly. "I don't think you should go to war to set examples or send messages," Mr. Woolsey said. An aggrieved British officer added, "What we have is a few strands of highly circumstantial evidence, and to justify an attack on Iraq it is being presented as a cast-iron case. That really is not good enough." But sure it is—why not? Mr. Woolsey and his ilk obviously are clearly out of step with the times. Why wait for a good ethical reason to go to war when you can do it merely to effect policy?

This is the CIA and MI6, remember, not Hans Blix and the U.N. inspectors so reviled by the Bush hawks. Asked if the Americans would now allow Dr. Blix and other U.N. weapons inspectors back into Iraq to complete the mission they were given, a White House source said "Forget it." Which is bureaucratic code for "Forget it."

Will the American inspection teams find evidence of weapons? I wouldn't put it past them. In the meantime, there's nothing there but the bloody trail of an immoral, unnecessary invasion. Or as Dr. Blix said, "We found as little, but with less cost."

✦

A stake through my heart
14 May 2003

There's no way the writers of "Buffy the Vampire Slayer" could have known that the last episodes of their show's seven-year run would coincide with war in Iraq and its aftermath. The two nevertheless construct a weirdly apposite parallel. Yes, it's true: the chaos in Baghdad, ancient City of Peace, and the once-more erupting Hellmouth under Sunnydale, California, are oddly twinned, at least at the level of television exposure.

Consider. Both are stories of good battling evil, tinged by uncertainty and arrogance. Both show that history may repeat itself with no increase in wisdom. Both offer the spectacle of the innocent dying and the nasty winning despite exposed lies and false testimony. In a week, both will be old news as far as the TV schedule is concerned. The difference is that the fictional apocalypse will go into re-runs, while the real-world version will grind its bloody way on.

Okay, I'm half kidding. But it is worth pausing, suspended between the two-parts of "Buffy's" final episode this week and next, to celebrate what this underappreciated show taught us about life. As so often, critical acclaim went hand in hand with bad ratings. The only real surprise is that "Buffy," true TV genius, lasted this long.

Good art has the power to refract light from the larger world, to put things in perspective, and this is true in mediums both elite and mass. Over the years "Buffy" has done just that, raising the gold standard of television in an outwardly goofy form that conceals hidden depths. It's no exaggeration to say that future generations will need to understand North America's millennial culture through the lens of "Buffy" and "The Simpsons."

Through death and mayhem, cutting class and making love, slaying vampires and befriending demons, Buffy has become an irreplaceable icon, a pillar of strength and cool. Played with unvarying intensity by Sarah Michelle Gellar, she has weathered more plot twists than a Russian novel, returning from the dead, acquiring a sister and new powers with equal suddenness, saving the world countless times. She is the most compelling female character currently on television, maybe the most compelling character period.

Of course, taking that line too far is to risk the curse of all criticism in the ephemeral medium of TV, namely draining the fun from fun. The reason so many TV critics burn out so fast is that they can't navigate the linked pitfalls of excessive seriousness and simple depression. They either go academic or they go postal. I know this from experience: I was the TV critic for *Saturday Night* magazine for two years, about the allowable maximum. (This newspaper's TV critic, Scott Feschuk, is a stellar exception, a man for whom no show, not even Mr. Personality, is too brain-dead to dry up his stream of gleeful abuse.)

Fans of "Buffy" will tell you about the snappy dialogue, the sly bits of self-reference, the boffo combat scenes, with their whooshing sound effects and burst-of-dust vampire deaths. Though vastly entertaining, that is all window-dressing; it obscures the yearning and mature emotional conflict that have raised the series well above the norm. This is not really a show about good and evil; it's a show about those much deeper things, love and death.

The characters have all struggled with morality, it's true, including a disturbing recent sequence in which Willow, Buffy's best friend (Alyson Hannigan), fell headlong into a massively destructive addiction to magic. (I know it sounds silly, but trust me, it was far scarier than any AA motivational.) The real reason for her sharp decline was revenge: her girlfriend had been killed by resentful nerds in an act of random violence. The show had already treated this relationship with disarming frankness, including lesbian sex scenes that made you wonder whether the network censors were asleep at the switch, even at hipster outfits like UPN and the WB.

Buffy herself has sought, found, and lost love with heartbreaking sincerity. She's a bad picker: first a reformed vampire (now with his own spin-off show), then a genetically modified supersoldier, in between some random hapless guys. None of them has been equal to the demands of having a girlfriend with a job-description that starts and ends with "inflicting death." Gellar has made Buffy into a young woman whose tough-mindedness far outweighs her ability to deliver roundhouse kicks or stakes to the chest. She's a handful, fierce and overwhelming.

In the current endgame, her obstinacy has finally alienated everyone, including family, friends, former mentor, and small army of subaltern slayers. She was the exception who made the rules. Now she's alone as a new, darker, and more powerful force is poised to eliminate the human world altogether, aided by a creepy killer-preacher played by Canadian Nathan Filion.

Academics will no doubt debate the high points of the series. The Hallowe'en costumes come to life? The destruction of Sunnydale High? The musical episode? To my mind, the episode that stands out is one that had very little to do with Buffy's vampire-slaying skills or ongoing reluctance to accept the mantle of Chosen One, bane of all evils.

Buffy's mother, Joyce, unexpectedly dies. Buffy can do nothing to stop it. Her life, her friends, her world, spin into emotional chaos. The long scene of her younger sister, Dawn (Michelle Tractenberg), being called out of art class to hear the news, shot without sound, is a mesmerizing visual essay in grief. Anya, a demon then in love with one of the human characters, Buffy's gormless friend Xander, utters the key line. She just can't understand this "stupid human thing" where somebody is there one minute and gone the next, and never coming back, and nobody can change it or talk about it.

Yes. But sometimes we find, in unlikely places, that profound human thing, art, which allows us, for a moment, to think about it.

✦

In empire's heart of darkness
28 May 2003

Vancouver
Nobody should be surprised that post-invasion Iraq is a shambles, since that is exactly what both previous experience and logic demanded. After all, killing people is easier than ruling them. Nobody should be surprised, but still they are.

Recent cracks in the diplomatic edifice, with State Department lifers squaring off against ideologues from the White House, are just the most obvious signs of trouble. Ambassador Paul Bremer, the top civilian authority in American-controlled Iraq, was parachuted into the job after a behind-the-scenes struggle over the harsh direction of American efforts. Who needs diplomacy when you have Special Forces?

Meanwhile, there is still no evidence of weapons of mass destruction, those ostensible justifications for the illegal invasion. That means both the front and back ends of this particular business venture are currently in the tank, the sole remaining "success" a few weeks of highly visible killing. Even supporters of the president are a little worried. Pat Roberts, a Republican senator from Kansas, said he believed that weapons of mass destruction would be found, but added that "basically, you have a real credibility problem" if they are not.

You might well think so. And yet, Senator Roberts is wrong. There is no credibility problem when people don't care to evaluate leaders according to credibility. The interest level of the American people may be accurately gauged by the flurry of witless comment on the "hotness" of George W. Bush after his appearance in a flight suit, fresh from the controls of his Viking S-3B jet. Hot! (Saddam Hussein: Not!)

Back in January, the Bush Administration's 18-month post-war reconstruction plan seemed a cruel fantasy, a bad joke. Now 18 months looks positively sane. The ruling order and its memory-impaired electorate alike think regime change happens at about the pace of an "American Idol" showdown. Any problem lasting longer than a television season defies comprehension, therefore does not exist.

The trouble here, as everyone agrees, is the growing burden of empire. An anonymous state department official criticized the Administration's plan to disrupt the government of Iraq, among other things banning Baath Party members from office. She called it "fascistic." This person, whoever she is, was immediately mocked by the omelettes-mean-broken-eggs brigade for a lack of political realism, but in fact her comment was merely accurate. The American Empire is fascistic: it bypasses international law to impose its will. It uses violence to effect change. It dresses up self-interest as universal benefit.

The only difference from all previous empires, fascist and otherwise, is its degree of hypocrisy. Defeat of Iraq was not a victory for freedom or a liberation or anything else of the sort. It was a show of power in the service of self-regard and economic dominance. If you are inclined to that kind of thing, you might even say that it was a welcome surge of honesty in American foreign policy, annoyed beyond bearing by the silly restrictions of morality and law. Finally, some straightforward muscle.

Now, however, the U.S. faces the unpleasant challenge, familiar to bar-brawlers everywhere, of actually following through on bravado. The pro-Bush right-wingers are right that this cannot be done without ruthless disregard of things like individual liberties and the right to life. You have to get your hands dirty to run an empire. But the American people won't go for it—if, that is, they can be convinced to pay attention at all. Economic dominance is one thing: it doesn't look violent even when it is. Military dominance, on the other hand, means accepting overt mayhem and death.

It's been said before, but can't be said too often, that the American Empire, though a political reality, is a contradiction in terms. The country's founding myths, and sense of moral validity, all derive from anti-imperial resistance. Its culture is inward-looking, insular, indifferent to the different. Like the biggest kid on the block, it doesn't see why it should care too much about what anybody else thinks or does.

And it's hard to argue with that, especially if you don't have any aircraft carriers or supersized military budgets. But it's another thing when your own constituents begin to wonder what the hell you're up to. Without its claims to liberal justice, derived from Kant and Jefferson, the U.S. is just another bully. This isn't even a Hobbesian peace; it's might for the sake of might.

Nor will "defeated" Iraqis co-operate indefinitely. Last week, Iraqi soldiers demonstrated in Basra and demanded that their salaries be paid by the occupiers: "If they don't pay us, we'll start problems," said one. "We have guns at home. If they don't pay us, if they make our children suffer, they'll hear from us." An Arab leader added: "The Americans promised us food and medicine and freedom. But we have lost our homes, our land, our crops.... If we don't have a solution, we will fight the Americans even if they kill us. It is better than sitting here with nothing and just dying."

U.S. occupation of Iraq may someday result in something good; good things have come from unjust acts before now. But the costs of transgressing Iraq's sovereignty will be many and various, and not all of them calculable by the harsh arithmetic of realpolitik. The parallels with Vietnam are impossible to ignore, the results likely to be just as complicated and ignominious, just as tainted by the moral rot in empire's heart of darkness.

This invasion should never have happened. Now that it has, there are only two options. Either the Americans will make a muddle of it and withdraw, leaving the country more chaotic than before. Or they will sacrifice their self-regard and accept that their twenty-first-century empire is fascistic, not democratic.

Heads you lose; tails you lose your soul.

✦

Britain converts to the rat?
11 June 2003

The news comes this week that Britain is not quite ready to join the rest of the European Union in adopting the unified currency known, brilliantly, as the euro.

If you have seen these bland transnational banknotes, with their nondescript design and banal circle-of-stars EU logo, you may well believe the reluctance is purely aesthetic. This is perhaps the ugliest money ever produced by a major political association, entirely lacking in character or history.

Gone forever are those gorgeous paper-napkin French francs, sporting etchings of David or Descartes; gone the multi-hued German marks with historical figures of doubtful significance—Annette von Droste-Hülshoff (1797–1848)—gazing pensively across a lurid green expanse; lost in the pink, peach, aqua, and orange of old Czech crowns, adorned with goggle-eyed saints, long-bearded prelates, and mad-looking kings smacking of the ages, perhaps the kookiest money ever produced.

Ian Fleming's James Bond can hardly be considered a serious guide to life, but somewhere he muses that Britain's pounds, especially the old 1950s-era fiver, which had to be folded about four times to fit into the average wallet, was gorgeous, a feast for the eyes as well as the heart. The new pounds are not as impressive but Britons are rightly fond of them, especially the lovely ochre Charles Dickens tenner, which almost approaches Continental sophistication. The others, which feature Queen Elizabeth II, are less lovely but no less loved.

That's why Tony Blair's government, though officially pro-euro, realizes the time is not ripe to force the currency issue. Gordon Brown, chancellor of the exchequer, told the House of Commons on Monday that he was indefinitely delaying a promised referendum on euro-conversion. Mr. Brown promised to revisit the issue in a year but also seemed to indicate that no referendum could possibly be staged until after the next general election, not expected until 2005.

The official line for the delay is that the British economy is "out of sync" with the main economies of the 12-nation euro zone, which is a polite way of saying, *Jesus Christ, Germany and Italy are on the brink of recession.* The Brits would rather hitch their wagon to the "more congruent" United States economy, which is a polite way of saying, *Screw you, we're part of the Anglosphere.* United in unjust invasion of Iraq and foisting shoddy intelligence about imaginary weapons of mass destruction therein, why not draw the economies together too?

Which might suggest that the Brits are more likely to adopt the U.S. dollar than the euro, even though the latter is, for the moment, stronger than that most utilitarian of currencies, the undistinguished Masonic-themed greenback. As everyone knows, the only redeeming aesthetic feature of American bills is that you can refer to them as if they were people when you're trying to sound cool: *Hey bro, spot me a Jackson. Bet you a Benjamin, dude. Man, say hello to Mr. Madison.*

But I have a better idea. In fact, three of them. The British pound should be converted into neither euros nor dollars but instead the following:

(1) First, Canadian dollars. Our new designs, with their pious depictions of peace-keeping troops and rural open-air hockey games, are characteristically self-deprecating and dull. I was part of a focus group back when the new notes were being designed and regret to say that none of my suggestions were followed. I wanted Louis Riel, Mordecai Richler, Stephen Leacock, and Pierre Trudeau. Instead the nice osprey and snowy owl got bumped for scenes of our national modesty.

Now that our dollar is strong against the ailing U.S. buck, however, things look brighter. And where better to conceal the aspirations of empire than in a currency designed to look inoffensive? Also, there will be incidental benefits for Canuck backpackers in Trafalgar Square: no waiting in line at the cambio.

(2) Then, Iraqi dinars. It was reported yesterday that the American overlords in the newly liberated Iraq, where at least 29 U.S. soldiers have died violently since President Bush declared the "end" of war on May 1, have been forced to print millions of new 250-dinar notes featuring the youthful visage of Saddam Hussein. He is deposed but not forgotten. His images are defaced and statues toppled even as his fatherly face is reproduced, over and over, by "victors" struggling with a chaotic economy. As Descartes would say, *Quelle ironie, non?*

Oui, not least because the currency crisis in Iraq shows no sign of ending. Demand for the 250-dinar notes is so high because the purple-and-yellow 10,000-dinar note (worth about 10 U.S. bucks) has been fatally devalued by lost confidence. People are dumping them for 70 percent of face, speculators are scooping them up, and everyone is trying to convert them into 250-dinar notes as soon as they can. The Brits should corner this market, peg their Canuck dollars to the dinar, and convert. It would be fun, if nothing else.

(3) Finally, rats. In his recent novel, *Cosmopolis,* Don DeLillo borrows a monetary conceit from the poet Zbigniew Herbert. The protagonist of DeLillo's novel, an arrogant multibillionaire currency trader quixotically in search of a haircut one day in April 2000, dilates on the theme with one of his flunkies:

"There's a poem I read in which a rat becomes the unit of currency."

"Yes. That would be interesting," Chin said.

"Yes. That would impact the world economy."

"The name alone. Better than the dong or the kwacha."

"The name says everything."

"Yes. The rat," Chin said.

"Yes. The rat closed lower today against the euro."

"Yes. There is growing concern that the Russian rat will be devalued."

"Britain converts to the rat," Chin said.

"Yes. Joins the trend to universal currency."

"Yes. U.S. establishes rat standard."

"Yes. Every U.S. dollar redeemable for rat."

Yes. So make sure you drop your dinars before inflation gets completely out of hand …

✦

A lesson in the perils of lackeyhood
25 June 2003

London

Last Saturday's birthday-party "attack" on Prince William by a man dressed as Osama bin Laden was not terribly funny, even for aficionados of guerrilla humour, so perpetrator Aaron Barschak's self-description as a "comedy terrorist" is wide of the mark. The best thing you can say about Mr. Barschak, who donned a pink dress then scaled trees and leapt walls to make his way to William's 21st-birthday bash at Windsor Castle, is that, as a comedian, he's a good impostor.

His prank does suggest that fooling British royal security is almost as easy as getting close to Jean Chrétien, but in both cases the only reasonable response is, um, so?—except that Mr. Chrétien is more likely than the reedy Prince to visit grievous bodily harm on his attacker.

All of that is a sideshow to the real story of the week here, which is that Tony Blair is close to losing the confidence of his nation, his government slowly unravelling in a series of exposed lies and ill-judged policies that undermine the heart of Labour's social justice tradition. There is still no evidence of the weapons of mass destruction used to justify the illegal invasion of Iraq, but there is plenty of evidence that Mr. Blair is in trouble.

The Labour government's communications director, Alastair Campbell, will address a parliamentary committee today to defend the government's use of plagiarized and misquoted documents in its now discredited brief on Saddam Hussein's weapons cache. Mr. Campbell is the man who famously said that Saddam could launch a long-range weapon "in 45 minutes," a statement Mr. Blair now says was never meant to imply the possibility of an attack on Britain. This may be considered akin to Mr. Blair's claims just last week that Mr. Campbell would never appear before the parliamentary committee.

Meanwhile, the Bush Administration's latest quick-step in the WMD dance, namely that the alleged weapons are absent because they were carried off by looters, is making even committed Blairites cringe. Their grasp of logic extends beyond the usual Sunday-morning American TV panel; they realize that would make the invasion the very disease for which it proposed to be the cure. Bald circularity may slip past the jingoistic brainiacs at Fox News but it won't wash in the House of Commons. This is also a lesson in the perils of lackeyhood. Mr. Bush can get away with things at the centre of power that simply will not play at the margins, where nobody's that scared of you.

Mr. Blair's government is ailing elsewhere too. Recent hedging on a referendum over conversion to the euro has resulted in a sharp drop in support for the shared currency, a staple of Blair's platform. Backbench MPs have broken discipline over several recent Blair moves, including a constitutional rejig that resulted in abolishment of the office of Lord Chancellor, and a controversial tax plan that many traditional Labour MPs see as insufficiently graduated. On Monday, the Labour majority dropped to 74 in a vote on tuition "top-up" fees for universities. (The paper majority is 164.)

The tuition plan, which critics fear will create a two-tier system at odds with the government's stated goal of 50 percent university enrolment, prompted more than a hundred Labour MPs to abstain, meaning fewer than half of sitting members were actively in support. It's not quite a vote of non-confidence but, in parliamentary code, it's a serious warning. To paraphrase P. G. Wodehouse, if the backbenchers are not quite disgruntled, they are certainly far from gruntled.

And that goes for the country as a whole. Nobody wants a Tory government—a recent poll put Conservative leader Iain Duncan Smith still lower in the approval ratings than Mr. Blair, on the negative side even among his own voters—but Mr. Blair's brand of pro-American servitude and centrist social policy is not working. And his regular church-going, not often mentioned, is more and more a sticking point in a nation unused to the religious rhetoric so common in the United States. Mr. Blair may use the phrase "tyranny of evil" in his desperate attempts to justify the Iraqi invasion, but that language does not fetch voters here the way it does in Mr. Bush's electoral world.

Indeed, Mr. Blair must envy the kind of doublethinking voter Mr. Bush can count on come next fall's U.S. presidential election. A recent Retro Poll found that many Americans oppose actual Bush policies even while supporting the president responsible for them. "When Americans hear specific provisions of the USA Patriot act," the pollsters write of one example, "they oppose the intrusions of this law into their civil rights by a wide margin (average 77 percent). Yet when asked what impact the War on Terrorism is having upon civil rights, many of the same people say it's 'strengthening' or having 'no impact' upon their rights (57 percent)." When this contradiction is pointed out, many voters react with bafflement befitting a minor character in a Platonic dialogue. "I'm confused," one respondent said. "What is Bush for? I want to do whatever Bush wants. I want to support the President."

The term "doublethink" was invented by an English writer, and applied to what were imagined as the depredations of English socialism run amok. And yet George Orwell was wrong about Britain. Whatever may go on in America, here common sense still has a hold. You may be able to crash a royal birthday party, but you can't get away with lying forever.

Analysts do not expect a general election until 2005. That gives Mr. Blair time to rediscover his Labour roots, chart a course independent of the U.S., and maybe even bring people around to the euro. If, instead, he continues to hedge and duck and alienate his supporters, he just might find himself fighting for his political life even sooner.

✦

Technology: it googles the mind
9 June 2003

Readers of this column are naturally far too serious to spend time fooling around with Internet search engines, but on the off-chance you have a spare moment somewhere, go to google.com, type in "weapons of mass destruction," and tell the damn thing you're feeling lucky. (If you're too busy, don't worry—results below.) Even to say "go to google.com" is to employ a phrase redolent of another era, the fast-passing two years ago of cultural uncool. It's an example of what we might call pre-withered language, the sloughed-off linguistic skin of the age. In his novel *Cosmopolis,* set in the spring of 2000, Don DeLillo fingers this phenomenon with typical acuity. The book's currency-trader anti-hero muses about once-smart-sounding words and phrases now out of date but staggering on, vestigial techno-anachronisms of a wired world: phone, automated teller machine, skyscraper.

"He took out his hand organizer and poked a note to himself about the anachronistic quality of the word skyscraper. No recent structure ought to bear this word. It belonged to the olden soul of awe, to the arrowed towers that were a narrative long before he was born. The hand device itself was an object whose original culture had just about disappeared. He knew he'd have to junk it."

Take note, Palm Pilot jockeys: your days are numbered. With the growth of texting and instant images, "phone" has indeed almost disappeared—though a few years late by DeLillo standards. The preferred options now include such adjectival truncations as "cell," "mobile," "handheld," and "landline"; or, more long-standing still, "number" and "book." In fact, "phone" and "telephone" are so past-it that using them almost constitutes a form of swinging anti-cool, the way New York columnist George Clooney, in the romantic comedy *One Fine Day,* likes to begin his number with "Pennsylvania 6."

For those even younger than me, that translates as 736—a Manhattan telephone exchange. I still remember my first Winnipeg phone number—489-8651—because of its "Hudson 9" prefix, and my own Manhattan exchange used to be "Butterfield 8"—288, as in the title of a John O'Hara novel, later Elizabeth Taylor movie, about a high-class prostitute trying to go straight. "Butterfield 8, 10-50" sounds pretty good when you give it out over a martini— though unfortunately anyone young enough to give it to is probably too young to get it.

Meanwhile, people have mostly stopped saying "automatic teller," but the phrase lingers in the form of "ATM" or, redundantly, "ATM machine." In Britain you see the snappier, and more accurate, "cashpoint." Teller? Automated? Machine? These words are barely twentieth-century, let alone twenty-first; they belong to a Victorian epoch of steam-driven mechanical contrivances and piston-powered calculating devices. I'd prefer to see "cashpoint" itself give way eventually to "cashnode," or maybe just "node." And while we're at it, how about dumping "computer" (what's being computed?), "dot com" (so 1997), and "search engine" (moving parts?).

And so, back to google, the granddaddy of all search engines— or, let us rather say, *finders.* Anybody who's even semi-conscious knows that the proper usage is not "go to google," as I wrote above, but "google"—as in the imperative form of the verb "to google." Googling is good sport for idle moments, as most of us know, and checking out prospective romances or associates via google is standard practice. Knowing that she googled you after that first date is usually a good sign; if she did it beforehand, you may be in trouble. The show "Blind Date" carries on its sick hilarious course, but in fact there is no longer any such thing as a blind date. We all leave a google trail, and if we don't—well, it's probably a sign we haven't done anything much.

There are dangers lurking, to be sure, as always with the Internet. (Another obsolete word. "Net" *simpliciter* is okay, but we really need something jazzier: how about *hitspace*?) Information is partial and uncorrected, often out of date and hostile. I can't be the only writer to notice that purveyors of bad reviews seem to have a greater interest in maintaining websites than those of more sympathetic disposition. Strangeness abounds. Anyone who formed an opinion of me based solely on googling is likely to picture a semi-coherent demagogue gamely fending off armies of creepy stalkers and bitter, long-standing enemies. Hmm …

There are even ways for adept google-meisters to make your hitspace life worse. "Google-bombing" is the practice of associating a denigrating phrase—"talentless hack," say—with a certain rival so often that his name comes up whenever the insult is inserted. (No, that wasn't me.) "Google-whacking," by contrast, involves finding phrases that garner exactly one hit. My favourite is "belletristic schadenfreude," which somehow made an appearance in the transcript of a literary theory essay. Where else?

I also enjoy "google-cloning," which is finding namesake doubles in other parts of the world. There is a Mark Kingwell who is secretary of the Bath Cricket Club; also an Australian chimney and furnace repairman in Cootamundra, New South Wales. But this latter Mark has rivals: Mr. Sweep in Canberra and Mr. Stoves in Albury. I think maybe he needs a novelty name too.

My brother Sean Kingwell, meanwhile, has a doppelgänger who

got good notices as "Pierre" in the Lipson Community College production of *The Boyfriend*. Steven Kingwell, my other brother's name-clone, placed 17th in the open male category of the Brighton-Bath Aquathon, which demanded a five-kilometre swim and 10-kilometre run. Could he be related to the secretary of the Bath Cricket Club? And is he the same athletic Steven Kingwell who scored seven goals for the St. Bedes/Menthone Lions in an AFC match, whatever that is? The questions multiply ...

Speaking of questions, what *do* you get when you type "weapons of mass destruction" into your hitspace finder? The answer should be obvious: ITEM NOT FOUND.

✦

Canucks—the gays of North America
23 June 2003

Jeffrey Kofman, the ABC News reporter who quoted a member of the U.S. Third Infantry Division calling for Donald Rumsfeld's resignation, is both Canadian and gay. Reasonable people would say that neither of those descriptors is likely to affect his ability to report the news, but some Americans obviously think otherwise.

"If Donald Rumsfeld was here," the soldier told Mr. Kofman last Friday, "I'd ask him for his resignation." The Third Division is the longest-serving American unit in Iraq and has had its departure date postponed twice. Some of them, including the anti-Rumsfeld grunt, are based in Falluja, where guerrilla attacks have already killed many of their comrades. These are the guys who are dead when, nearly every morning now, the news brings reports of an RPG or small-arms attack on a convoy, road block, or supply dump.

So you wouldn't blame a hot, overdrawn infantryman for expressing a little polite anger. And indeed, conservative forces at home did not blame him (though the military certainly did). Instead, the right-wing attack press decided to go after the source. Matt Drudge, an online columnist acting on a tip he says came from within the White House, posted a story with this unforgettably adolescent headline: "ABC NEWS REPORTER WHO FILED TROOP COMPLAINTS STORY—OPENLY GAY CANADIAN." Mr. Drudge later amended the headline to omit the reference to Mr. Kofman's sexual orientation.

A few critics, notably Maureen Dowd in the *New York Times,* thought this crude slur indicated a resurgent McCarthyism, "making character assassination fashionable again on the Potomac." The Bush powers, bewitched, bothered, and bewildered by an unjustifiable invasion turning into a combined foreign-policy and public-relations disaster, are, she said, "flailing in an ever more chaotic environment." Their foolish overspending is matched only by still more foolish denunciations of criticism, especially if it comes from foreigners.

All perfectly true. But I have a simpler explanation for the Drudge Report business: American conservatives think all Canadians are gay. That's why Mr. Drudge was willing to change his headline, an act of apparent sensitivity unprecedented on his bizarre site. And since all gays are categorically unmanly, therefore un-American, therefore not to be trusted, it follows that all Canadians are not to be trusted. They may even, as with Mr. Kofman's sowing of disgruntlement among the brave troops, be working actively to undermine America. In other words, Mr. Kofman was, as an extension of a well-known stratagem of openly Canadian men, trying to make the soldiers *turn Canadian.*

Consider a few key facts. Canadians comprise roughly seven percent of the North American population. They look more or less exactly like regular North Americans, only they're funnier, more polite, thinner, and better-dressed. They are known to make and understand remarks in French, the language of effete intellectualism. They do not stare down women on the street or rely on naked aggression to pick them up in bars. Despite demonstrated prowess at violent body-contact sports like hockey, they remain courtly and deferential.

Cack-handed politicians, anxious for their friendship and market share, tell them there is no difference at all between Canadians and Americans. Visitors to their cities say the streets may be cleaner but their culture is obviously identical.

It's not all sunshine and smiles, of course. It is now acceptable for any American, even nice left-wing ones like Garrison Keillor and Jon Stewart, to make nasty jokes about Canadians. These usually turn on Canadians being touchy, vain, weak, and obsessed with being different.

Also boring. Objecting to the joke just indicates that you are Canadian, and therefore touchy, vain, weak, and obsessed with your silly little insistence on being different. Also boring.

The sole high-profile exception to this rule seems to be Michael Moore, whose film *Bowling for Columbine* contains extensive praise for friendly, relatively gun-free Canada. He is obviously a Canadian-lover, maybe even a closet Canadian. Peter Jennings, another openly Canadian employee at ABC News, was no doubt suspected of being inherently untrustworthy until he took the reassuring step of applying for American citizenship.

Mr. Jennings's move represents one option for the anxious Canadian eager for acceptance. That is, Canadians can react to their situation by trying harder to pass for American, disappearing into the general population, perhaps even seeking psychological correction for their Canadian urges. Unfortunately, this is a well-known route to self-hatred and diminishment.

They can also, as a variation on this theme, join in a sell-out game of proving their essential Americanness by indicating a distance from the rest of the vain, silly, weak group. "CANADIANS SUCK! SAYS CANADIAN." That move will get the average Canadian a column at a Canadian newspaper, but it's afflicted by a double-bind. Self-serving treachery never quite plays south of the border, since the only way to get attention there is to pass for American, and that means not paying attention to what the boring, vain, weak Canadians are doing in the first place.

These contortions will keep Canadians pointlessly occupied for some time. Isolationism, irony, and irritation—the three i's of all marginal groups—will likely remain their stock-in-trade. They will continue to turn out funny men and good music and effective newsreaders. They will amuse Americans in the same slightly appalled, come-off-it way that Christopher Street, drag queens, and the Gay Pride parade amuse New Yorkers.

There is hope, however. Mr. Kofman's vilification by the forces of right-wing ignorance might just stir the fire in the well-dressed, polite Canadian breast. Maybe this is the time Canadians decide they're tired of being denigrated and mocked and underestimated. Maybe this is the moment that a new era of Canadian pride takes hold, when Canadians object to vile foreign policy without embarrassment, trumpet achievements without shrillness, and maintain worldliness and independence without fear.

Come on, say it with me to the folks down south. Say it loud, and say it proud: *You're stuck, we're Canuck, get used to it.*

✦

Sydney could use some rude waiters
6 August 2003

Sydney

I got into the most exclusive restaurant in Australia last night and almost didn't notice. Now, I grant you this is precisely the sort of thing my pals over in the Style section of that other national newspaper are always telling you, not what you expect to read in the august precincts of the Comment page. But bear with me, there is a point.

Just to be clear, then, I was at the most exclusive restaurant in Australia entirely by mistake and the only reason I know it is the most e. restaurant in A. is because the front page of the *Sydney Morning Herald* said so. Even to say I got in is to say something more like my girlfriend walked through the open door when the gorgeous tan surfer boi in designer clothes standing outside suggested it. He may even have worked there. She was well inside before I could say, "You know, I'd really rather go for sushi."

That's what we did. But not before noticing the clean minimalist lines of the banquettes, the jewel-box bar, and the usual cast of slinky-girl and bulky-biceps waitstaff festooned here and there. A good-looking place full of good-looking people. And when I say full I really mean—oh, what do I really mean? I really mean empty. The sidewalks before it unthronged, the street free of limo, cab, and paparazzo. In fact, Jimmy Liks, the most exclusive restaurant in Australia, was so empty they were cadging customers off the street.

But still, straight from the pages of *Wallpaper* magazine, the sort of place post-millennial Sydney is more and more becoming known for, a sleek twenty-first-century playground for the lifestyle-porn crowd. Visiting this city is a vertiginous exercise in cultural time-travel, as long as your destination is, as in all hip design magazines, the very near future. In their plus-14 hours ahead of Eastern Time, the Aussies have invented, among other things, chlorine-free ozone-purified public swimming pools, an architectural style that mixes Asian futurism, British colonial grace, New Orleans sultriness, and Art Deco curves, and currency notes made out of see-through wafer-thin acetate sheets that can't tear or rip. (Alas, this also means they don't fold very well, or lend themselves to old Abbott and Costello gags hinging on the torn sawbuck.)

Famously, there is no tipping here, which is a boon to tourists but removes the enlivening element of risk found elsewhere. In New York, for example, less than 15 percent is liable to bring your waiter sprinting down the street after you so he can practise scenes from *Who's Afraid of Virginia Woolf?* or *All About Eve* in a loud voice. In London every service-industry exchange, from ordering a pint to getting in a cab, is an argument waiting to happen. Even in Toronto, allegedly so reserved, an undertipped waiter is likely at least to sneer or sniff or roll his eyes, maybe mumble something unintelligible *(Fuck you very much!)* or make an unmentionable addition to your coffee.

But here, nothing: mateyness, cheerful change, smiles, and waves. Nor is there much sign of panhandlers or unemployed people or street-borne sirens. Don't get me wrong, I love it here. It's just that, as a Torontonian, I find it a little strange to be heaping on another city all the condescending praise we used to get from visiting New Yorkers. So clean! So quiet! So well-designed! So little crime!

And that's when I saw the deeper issue. The story about the popular restaurant wasn't just about it being popular. It was about it being so popular that people were being turned away, and so it became unpopular. Customers were made to wait an hour or more for a table. Some believed this was because they were not pretty or glamorous enough. If they did get in, the service was sometimes rude and self-serving. I read all that and thought, well that's what you need, isn't it, if your city is really going to make the big leagues? Not democracy, but elitism.

"Eighty percent of the time, the customer isn't right," owner Joe Elcham said, reversing a more genteel retail adage. An "older woman" had complained recently, he said, of a 90-minute wait. "Perhaps I am not beautiful enough?" she said angrily. Never let it be said that Mr. Elcham is not equal to a debating challenge on the threshold of his establishment. "I'm not here for you to dump your insecurities," he told her. "Maybe this isn't the restaurant for you."

I love the fact that this is front-page news in no-nonsense no-worries Australia. Mr. Elcham, a routine trash-talker anywhere else, has become a national villain here. In Canada this sort of thing would be confined to yet another cranky Joanne Kates column wondering if she is, in fact, too old to dine out on College Street. To which the only answer is, where is Mr. Elcham when we need him?

This beautiful city, poised on the edge of the wide Pacific, is on the edge of a bigger future too. But a cruel tension lurks as Sydney hits the hipness big time. To get there it's going to have to lose some niceness and gain more edge—including, yes, more rude waiters. Have faith, Sydneyites. As Paris and London and New York all prove, the paradox of rude waiters is that they produce, in the end, cooler and more interesting cities. It's not nice but it's true, one of those mysteries of the transition from regional phenom to global contender.

I should know. I'm from Toronto, where we're trying to make the same move. Unfortunately, we seem to have received your share of rude waiters while you got our allotment of good architecture ...

✦

U.S. negligence is killing journalists
20 August 2003

American soldiers are killing journalists in Iraq now, which is either a bold escalation of the Bush Administration's War on Criticism or a result of frustration and fatigue, I can't decide which. Lucky for me I'm writing this from the comfort and safety of my Toronto office-bunker, so not at great risk of not-so-friendly fire from trigger-happy troops.

I admit the attacks took me by surprise. After all, the journalists covering the war have done their level best to pose no threat to anyone or anything, let alone the truth. Never before have reporters been so docile, so (to infringe Fox's trademark) "fair and balanced," in their coverage of an unpopular war, rallying and cheering and bending their necks to the stroke of Ari Fleischer's verbal lash. Embedded newsies succumbed to severe attacks of gear-envy, jock-sniffing, and manhood-diminution. The main injuries they suffered were bruises from the scramble to abase themselves in front of real men, the ones with guns.

You'd think even a flailing Administration, baffled by growing opposition and plummeting approval ratings, would be happy with such uncritical coverage. But clearly it was not enough. Bad news is a constant danger, like sunburn and insect bites. And of course, Reuters is an independent agency and might have some "anti-American" agenda, like accurately reporting the news. Something had to give.

Oh, I'm kidding. I know the soldiers didn't kill the journalist deliberately. Or rather, they *did* kill him deliberately, but not because he was a threat. Or rather, he *was* a threat in their minds, but not just because he briefly appeared to be. Or rather, it *was* just because he briefly appeared to be, but not because they *were* wrong about that. Or rather, they were wrong about that, but sometimes a videocamera does look like a lethal weapon, doesn't it? Or rather, it *doesn't* look like a lethal weapon, but it just might be one and who says shoot first and ask questions later doesn't make sense?

Mazen Dana, a 43-year-old cameraman with the Reuters news agency, was shot and killed Sunday as he was videotaping near a U.S.-run prison on the outskirts of Baghdad. The soldiers, firing from two patrolling tanks, say they mistook his camera for a rocket-propelled grenade launcher, which is also a piece of metal equipment sometimes carried on the shoulder. The press advocacy groups Reporters Without Borders, based in France, and the Committee to Protect Journalists, based in the U.S., have demanded a full investigation. This is the second death of a Reuters journalist in less than a week, which might have an effect on future recruitment efforts.

Now let's be clear—as clear as we were urged to be when some adrenalized U.S. Air National Guard fighter jocks dropped a 500-pound bomb on some Princess Pats in Afghanistan last year, killing four and seriously injuring eight others. Yes, there is such a thing as the fog of war. And yes, accidents happen. And yes yes, all people, combatant or not, who voluntarily enter a war zone are implicitly accepting its dangers.

All true. And yet, and yet.

The press groups are charging the American soldiers with "negligence," and there is certainly a case to be made for that. Unlike the Afghanistan incident, this error occurred in broad daylight. Fellow journalists say the military personnel on site were aware of their presence. "We had been there for half an hour" when Mr. Dana was targeted and shot, said one. A videocamera is a about the size and shape of a briefcase, whereas an RPG is launched with a narrow tube about four feet long. *The Oxford English Dictionary* defines negligence as lack of attention or care. Mr. Dana was probably wishing for either less attention or more care when the soldiers opened up on him, but yes, negligence, I think so.

The problem, however, as with the disgruntled grunt from the Third Infantry Division who called for Donald Rumsfeld's resignation a few weeks back, is that the individuals will be punished and the situation left untouched. We all know that the cracks in the U.S.-led invasion of Iraq have been showing for weeks, that this latest death is not just another casualty of war but a clear warning things are likely to get much, much worse. Britain rages in a controversy over the puffed-up arguments for this illegal war, with Prime Minister Tony Blair's closest aides now admitting liberties were taken in presenting information to Parliament. And still—I know, you're tired of hearing it, but still—no weapons of mass destruction have been found.

Meanwhile, the situation on the ground grows bloodier by the day. Resistance within Iraq is stiffening, now attacking civilian targets as well as coalition troops. In the past week, saboteurs blew up a large oil pipeline to Turkey three days after it reopened, a water main was bombed in Baghdad, and a sewage plant set on fire. The police chief of Mosul was shot and two other officers were killed in an ambush; a Danish soldier died in a bomb blast; some American soldiers were shot as they left a restaurant. An attack on the United Nations headquarters in Baghdad left 15 dead, including the U.N.'s top official there. "Every American needs to believe this," said General Ricardo Sanchez, the head of U.S. forces in Iraq, "that if we fail here in this environment, the next battlefield will be the streets of America."

That's nonsense but it contains a hint of truth. The death of Mazen Dana is a small but sure sign that the Americans are already failing in that "environment." The real question now is not whether they can succeed—they can't—but whether they can even withdraw without a lot more deadly "negligence."

No matter what they do, or when, it's too late for Mazen Dana.

✦

Are profs at their best when faking it?
3 September 2003

If you've read these pages during the past week, you've heard the seasonal chorus of woe: Canada's universities are in dire straits.

There are more students and less money, longer lines and fewer places. Ontario's double-cohort has jammed classrooms and residences; debt and construction costs show no sign of receding; campuses are a-swarm with a rabble of irritated and ill-served young people.

The results of a statistically nonsensical but headline-worthy American survey ranked my own school, Toronto, well down in the categories of boredom, confusion, and long lines. It made U of T sound like a version of the monstro-mart grocery stores mocked in an old "Simpsons" episode, "where shopping is a baffling ordeal."

Another survey, meanwhile, showed that wily students have developed an array of diversionary tactics to avoid being called on in class. A recent survey found that 70 percent of boys and 82 percent of girls have used such tricks as pretend writing, pen-dropping, eye-contact evasion, and my favourite, pre-emptive question-asking. ("Hey, professor. What's your new book about, anyway?")

My colleague Clifford Orwin, saying what many think but won't say, lamented the other day that most of our students are "post-literate."

Let me be clear: I don't quarrel with the basic message. The Canadian university system is indeed oversubscribed and under-funded. I'm not surprised to hear that students at my institution and elsewhere find the crowds frustrating and sad. And I can't deny that most of those who actually make their way to the classroom have difficulty reading, interpreting, and writing about the classics.

Alas! What of cloistered retreat and quiet contemplation? Whither the tradition and rigours of scholarship, the chance to study the best that has been thought and written? You might hope students are at least drinking beer and having (safe) sex, but even that seems doubtful when they're spending so much time waiting in line and working to cover tuition.

Where to from here? There are, it seems to me, four main routes leading away from the annual bad-news festival:

(1) *Tinkering*. Most sociological studies and newspaper essays on the subject would have us "solve" the "problem" of higher education with some combination of increased funding, decreased expenses, fewer students, more teaching, more professors, more buildings, and

more accountability (whatever that means). There is much internal disagreement here, with people often confused or inconsistent about what will work. They all share the same premise, however, which is that the university system, while in need of repair, is minimally sound.

The problem here: nothing much ever changes.

(2) *Choosing.* Thinking about (1) leads us to see that our universities are actually an untenable combination of scholarly enclave and vast socialization machine for future job-seekers. They can't be both. We should either make them genuine academic institutions, with corresponding deep cuts in admission and charges of elitism; or embrace their mass-culture role as holding tanks for emerging adults and stop trying to teach anything in particular, except maybe how to fashion a resume.

The problem here: nobody is willing to bite this bullet.

(3) *Deploring.* As a result of combining (1) with (2), people both inside and outside universities become disillusioned. Students, even some professors, wonder what the hell they're up to. Parents and columnists resort to anti-intellectualism when confronted by any form of thought not directly translatable into money.

The problem here: nobody wins, except the columnists, who get to congratulate themselves on being smarter than anyone else.

(4) *Pandering.* As a result of combining (1), (2), and (3), it can seem as though the answer is making education more entertaining, courting the seven-minute attention spans of our bored, irritated, impoverished, disaffected, jobless, and yet highly accessorized students.

The problem here: this never works. Reducing higher education to television might enjoy short-term success, but in the end it does a disservice to student and subject both. I probably throw around as many pop-culture references as the next guy, but if I don't manage to say something about Plato's relevance to everyday life, I haven't done my job.

Is there anything else left? Let me suggest, half seriously, the following:

(5) *Faking it.* The thought came to me recently when I was contacted—this is true—by the producers of the television show "Faking It." The conceit of this show, speaking of pop-culture references, is that a person skilled in one profession, cookery or law or cowpunching, is abruptly tossed into a new profession, architecture or surf instruction or furnace repair. The subject then must rely on wit, brains, and resourcefulness to fake an absent expertise. The results are often hilarious, sometimes moving.

The producers were looking for a "male professor/librarian/graduate teaching assistant" who might be willing to give up a month of his life pretending to be something else. Since the subject had to be under 31 as well as in "GREAT physical condition," I was disqualified on age alone, never mind my straight-up, with-a-twist liver; but I spared a moment to wonder what they had in mind for the presumptive dweeb: SWAT recruit? Astronaut? Pro wrestler?

The philosopher F. C. Coppleston said, years ago, that he never quite got over a bad case of impostor syndrome as a professor, even after he had written many books and a multi-volume history of his subject. He was a gifted and inspiring teacher, and this sounded crazy to me. Now I see that his insight goes well beyond any personal performance anxiety.

When it comes to higher education, nobody really knows what works and what doesn't. We're all feeling our way, balancing goods, testing hypotheses, above all trusting our passion. We do best when we are absolute beginners, uncertain and inexpert, relying on wit, meagre brains, and resourcefulness—when, in a word, we're faking it.

As so often with philosophy, this won't solve our problems; but it just might help us find the wisdom to see them clearly. And I bet it'll be often hilarious and sometimes moving.